# Love in a Time of Broken Heart

Also by **Benig Mauger**

*Songs From The Womb: Healing The Wounded Mother*
Published in the USA as *Reclaiming the Spirituality of Birth*

*Reclaiming Father: The Search For Wholeness in Men,
Women and Children*

# LOVE IN A TIME
# OF BROKEN HEART

## HEALING FROM WITHIN

### BENIG MAUGER

*Soul*
*Connections*

Published by Soul Connections, 9 Leinster Park,
Harolds Cross, Dublin 6W, Ireland
www.soul-connections.com

2008 Benig Mauger

Printed in Ireland by Colour Books Ltd.

Jacket design and typesetting by Paul McDaid.

Permissions

The author thanks the following publishers for permission to reprint material copyrighted or controlled by them:

W.W. Norton & Co. for permission to quote from *Letters to a Young Poet* by Rainer Maria Rilke, translated by M.D. Herter Norton. Copyright 1934, 195 published by W.W.Norton & Company, Inc., renewed © 1962, 1982 by M.D. Herter Norton. Used by permission of W.W. Norton & Company, Inc.

Ferrar, Straus and Giroux, LLC for permission to quote 'Love after Love' from *Collected Poems 1948-1984* by Derek Walcott. Copyright © 1986 by Derek Walcott. Reprinted by permission of Ferrar, Strauss and Giroux, L.L.C and Faber and Faber Ltd., London.

ISBN 978-0-9547012-1-5

## Dedication

To all the broken hearted in the world, and
in memory of my dear friend, Suzi Gold,
all my love

# Contents

# Acknowledgments

Bringing this book to birth would not have been possible without the support of many people whose help I am truly grateful for. I want to thank the following in particular:

First of all, to my clients and all the men and women who have shared with me the joys and pains of loving and living, thank you. I continue to feel privileged to be part of, and to witness, the struggles of all my fellow travellers on this journey that is life.

To the people at Rex Ranch in the desert of Southern Arizona, USA, where my journey began. To my friends in the US, especially Bruce DiGiovanni, Mary Flanagan, Giselle Whitwell, Rupert Encinas, Winona Hubrecht and Gerry Breen, who were there at the beginning.

To the mountains of the Sierra Nevada in Spain, whose majesty and beauty cradled me as I wrote, and to John and Julia Yates and their dogs who housed me in their beautiful home as I wrote my first draft.

To my gifted and brilliant graphic designer Paul McDaid, yet again, for his wonderful work in providing the book with its cover, and to John Long who designed and kept my website in order, giving the book its public face.

To my brilliant editor, Maria O'Donovan, who came on board in the nick of time and whose endless, gentle patience and efficient skill I appreciate more than she will ever know.

To my friend John Dunne whose brainstorming on a beach in Connemara gave the book its subtitle.

Special thanks to Bruce DiGiovanni for his love and enduring friendship, and for first drawing my attention to the fable of the Little Tin Soldier and the Ballerina.

To my agent Nigel Norwerth, whose enthusiasm for my work spurred me on, and who continues to act as my ambassador, bringing my work around the world. To Brenda

O'Hanlon and to Leslie Gardner who read some of the text in the early days and set the book on course, and to fellow writer Donald McKinney for his advice and suggestions.

To my friends and colleagues here in Ireland whose encouragement and understanding helped keep me on course as I was writing. A particular thank you to John Waters for the endless days and evenings of discussion, tea and sympathy, as well as solid friendship. To my dear friend Karen Ebbs, for her gentleness, wisdom and enduring friendship, and her particular understanding of an artist's heart.

To John Harrington, the most gifted and wise healer I know, for listening patiently to an enquiring soul whilst reviving an at times weary body and even more weary heart. I am truly grateful for your presence in my life.

To Noeleen Murray whose vitality and generosity revived a flagging spirit, encouraging me when I got tired, and to my friend Elizabeth Walsh for her friendship and encouragement, for reading and re-reading parts of the text and her perceptive suggestions.

To various 'angels' and, most particularly, Patricia Masters, whose gift of insight held the book in spirit whilst it grew in me, and whose wisdom and guidance was invaluable. Patricia passed into the angelic realm this year as did my dearest friend and soul sister Suzi Gold, whose joy and loving spirit I dearly miss. You are in my heart now and always.

To my friends and soul mates who helped in various ways, especially Kathy Westwood, David Berk, Lilla Bek, Chris Kemple, John Terry, Michael Cooney, Robin Buick, Alan Gold, Mary Edwards, Sharon Mason and Maria Garcia. To my tango buddies, who share my passion for the perfect dance of love: the tango!

To my former life partners – my soul mates – who walked with me on my journey thus far, and to my family, extended and 'adopted', who kept the home fires burning so I would

## Acknowledgements

not get lost. Particular thanks to my three children Benjamin, Annig and Jamie – my angels here on earth. To the spirit of my beloved dog Miro, whose sudden death pulled me in to experience heartbreak yet again, and from whom I learned about unconditional love.

And finally, to my birth place and soul home Connemara, where part of the book was written, and which continues to inspire me and sustain me.

Benig Mauger,
Dublin,
December 2007

# Introduction

For one human being to love another:
that is perhaps the most difficult of all our tasks,
The ultimate, the last test and proof, the work for which
all other work is but a preparation.

*Letters to a Young Poet:* Rilke

Several years ago I suffered a relationship break up that shook
me to my roots. A woman twice divorced, I had certainly
experienced a broken heart before, but this experience was
different. When my former partner and I broke up, I felt I
had jumped from the highest cliff down into the depths of the
sea. I floundered in these depths and did not know whether I
would come out of them or not. Loving and losing the man I
believed I was destined to be with for the rest of my life, and
who was my soul mate, propelled me into a deep and profound soul journey. Devastated after the break up, I entered
the darkness of my soul and, in time, discovered a world more
beautiful than I ever imagined possible.

How can heartbreak and soul pain be beautiful? I hear
you asking. This book will answer this question and many
others. With our hurried and increasingly fragmented lifestyle, it can be difficult to connect with our inner selves; and
the tendency to project love, as well as happiness, outside ourselves makes it hard for us to find this happiness–and this
love. If there is a message in this book it is that we can find
happiness and love if we go within and follow the path that
heartbreak opens up for us.

Suffering a love wound can lead us straight into a confrontation with the deepest part of our natures. In embracing the darkness in our lives and our emotional wounds, we encounter our darkness and, paradoxically, our light. Embracing the darker aspect of our souls restores us to a wholeness we long for but rarely have the courage to seek out without being led there through illness, bereavement, divorce or other life-changing events.

Life-changing experiences are just that – events that propel us into the dark night of our souls to encounter an unknown, and sometimes threatening, inner landscape, and these encounters change us. Though we long for inner wholeness, most of us do not consciously seek out the shadow – we are afraid of it. The message of many mystics and poets, however, is that we are rewarded when we embrace the not-so-beautiful in our lives and hearts. Our reward comes to us in a stronger self, founded on what we find on a journey on the road less travelled.

Relationship break up and heartbreak are common, but it is less commonly understood that this break or fracture brings us to a new wholeness. When your heart breaks it is broken wide open, and this opening brings us to divine or unconditional love. Entering the dark night of the soul, which is how many mystics and St John of the Cross, in particular, refer to spiritual alienation, pulls you into the inner terrain of your soul to encounter the divine within. This encounter can change your world and set up resonances in your soul that can permeate and, I believe, enhance the rest of your life.

As a major life-changing event, heartbreak can take us straight to the divine. It was love and most particularly losing love that took me there. I found that writing this book led me on a spiritual journey I had not anticipated. I had known emotional suffering before, of course, but somehow this heart-opening seemed to touch me in a more profound place. Despite my intense suffering, I found I grew. I questioned all aspects of my life, not just my heartbreak. On the journey to heal my heart of this love wound, I learned many things. I learned that suffering and endurance builds soul stamina and develops our spiritual muscles. Inner questioning and self examination led me to encounter aspects of my essential nature. Like many people, vulnerability was not something I liked to think about too much, and I certainly did not want to appear vulnerable. With this experience, however, I had no choice. I was thrown into the pit and had to confront my own demons.

In times of profound vulnerability a deeper intelligence comes through. This is one of the most valuable essential truths I discovered on my journey.

With a heart broken open, the divine enters – and we can but follow where it takes us. The intensity of experiencing such pain throws us into such a spiritual crisis that we have the opportunity to set off on a journey one seldom, if ever, returns from unchanged.

Writing this book has been a spiritual journey for me, one that I have loved. When I started writing, I had one particular thought: to write about heartbreak and, as a natural progression from my earlier books, to explore and explain the forces that psychologically form us in our later relationships and also inform our choice of partners. Understanding that our early lives and experiences shape us, I wanted to map our journey as lovers. From such a psychological base, my aim was help people understand their emotional and relationship patterns so that, armed with this self-knowledge, they could make empowering choices in their relationships and lives. Since I also knew that most, if not all of us, experience heartbreak, I also wanted to chart our journey to healing after love dies.

In my earlier work, *Songs from the Womb - Healing the Wounded Mother*, I wrote about the formative impact of prenatal life and birth on our lives. Addressing the loss of soul that often results as a consequence of the over medicalisation of childbirth, I outlined ways of healing birth wounds, and sent out a call for an understanding of the psychological and sacred dimension of both the experience of giving birth and of being born. I know that at that time the focus of my attention had been drawn there for a purpose: to help create more soulful birthing conditions for mothers and babies, by highlighting the sacred and spiritual dimensions of childbirth. From a psychological perspective, highlighting the formative nature of our earliest experiences simply added a dimension to what was already known about the human psyche and our propensity to live out the emotional patterns formed in our childhood.

Some time later, acutely aware of the generally neglected role of the father in the process of child rearing, I wrote *Reclaiming Father–The Search for Wholeness in Men, Women and Children*. In this book I examined the seminal role played by fathers in the psychological lives of their children and addressed, furthermore, the growing father hunger present in our society, where an increasing number of children grow up without the active presence of fathers. In this context I looked at the effects of absent fathering on men and women and how that affects our intimate relationships. Since, as a complement to our mothers, our fathers are responsible for activating our masculine energies, absent fathering contributes to a frail masculine image in both men and women and *Reclaiming Father* exposed, through its exploration of the inner dynamics of love relationships, the need to reclaim father in order to recover a sense of inner wholeness.

In this book, *Love in a Time of Broken Heart*, I have gone one step further. I have brought together mother and father to explore both our inner and outer marriage and explain how our earliest experiences of being mothered and fathered influence how we relate in intimate relationships. The inner marriage, our sense of wholeness, is based on our early life experience. Soul and family patterns are transmitted to us in the womb and in early life. Father is the complement to the mother and activates in us masculine energies which, together with the feminine, fuels our search for inner wholeness and outer union. Outlining the impact of early life, as well as archetypal and family heritage, this book also offers a framework for understanding patterns and stories we may be living out in our relationships.

As a Jungian psychotherapist, I understand the central importance of the inner marriage–the spiritual union of the masculine and the feminine within. I know that this union is essential to the spiritual well being of every individual. I also know that, for some of us, this path to inner wholeness is given expression in our love relationships and, more specifically, our search for love and our soul mate.

*Love in a Time of Broken Heart–Healing from Within* is about just that. It is about the universal search for love and how we go about achieving this inner wholeness. It is also about the difficulties of loving and maintaining an open heart in the face of a growing trend of relationship break up. In a time of increasing emotional isolation and fractured relationships, the search for love is universal. Our fragmented lifestyle has made the search for wholeness all the more urgent; the huge growth in mind/body/spirit and alternative healing consciousness is witness to this. Additionally, when we experience the death of love in heartbreak, we have a need for healing.

We all seek wholeness to ease our sense of spiritual loss. Our feeling of separation or spiritual alienation pushes us to find ways to heal this loss–to find love. In our soul hungry world, however, love is often misunderstood as being external to us, making it difficult to not only find this love but to heal painful experiences. Our fragmented lifestyle has permeated our love lives in that, generally, we think of love as outside of us. Despite being told that love is to be found within, we still seek it outside. We often form relationships out of need and, when that need fails to be met or the relationship breaks up, we are devastated. We imagine then that love is not something we can ever count on and often close the door of our hearts, vowing never to love again; or we may move on and continue our search for love in a new relationship. However, whilst we remain disconnected from our inner lives and place love outside of ourselves, we are likely to remain disappointed and still wounded.

How can we heal our hearts then? By healing from within – and this book is a guide to doing this. In the later chapters, you will learn ways to begin and engage with the soul work necessary to heal your heart. Using the specially-designed workbook to begin your healing journey, this book will guide you through the essential inner landscape of healing. By reconnecting with and embracing your vulnerability and early wounding, you will recover your spirit and your sense of spiritual purpose, as well as heal your heart. By reclaiming your inner masculine and feminine you will balance these energies within you so that you can recover the sense of wholeness we all seek. And finally, by uncovering your emotional patterns and the belief systems or story that underpins your emotional life and your relationships, you will be able to free yourself from destructive patterns and soul bonds that may be holding you back.

As the core of our lives, relationships are the best place for soul growth. If we are willing to meet the challenges involved, they are an aid to self-discovery. All the characters in this book are involved in the search for love. On their journey, they discover something of who they are. Additionally, since the book addresses the emotional turmoil resulting from relationship breakdown and outlines ways of healing love wounds, there are stories of heartbreak and of struggling with the loss of love. Most of us have been there, and if you find yourself resonating with some or many of the characters in the book, the chances are that you will be inspired to further your inner journey to healing.

A word about the structure of the book: since I have a tendency to tell or write stories, or more specifically to use stories to explain psychological and spiritual truths, I found the use of myths and fairy tales, as well as personal stories, became a central part of the book. As a Jungian, the use of myths and fairy tales to amplify the human journey and illustrate psychological truths is a given. As a writer and poet, this propensity was further amplified so that in actual fact, when I originally had the idea for the book, I thought of writing a novel. I wrote many of the stories first, and then gradually the rest of the book took shape around them to give the book its present form. I have included several short story pieces carefully interspersed throughout the chapters. Though they stand alone, their added purpose is to give life to universal human and psychological truths; and to help you identify with each character's journey to find love and healing.

There are many books about relationships today–how to find them, stay in them and relate with ease and harmony. Dare I say that this book is different? Yes. Apart from a workbook on *Healing from Within*, it is not a 'how to' book; it will not tell you how to conduct emotionally healthy relationships but it will, through the characters in my stories, bring you to find yourself or parts of yourself in the characters engaged in relating, loving and healing.

When I set out to write the book, I endeavoured to offer a framework through which to see our patterns in relating, and to offer a way of healing love wounds. However, as I wrote, my focus changed. I found I was taken on a spiritual journey to chart the course of the human heart and how we seek and encounter the divine in our lives through our relationships. To this end, I have divided the book into several parts, each outlining different aspects of our journey.

To write this book, I mainly followed my own heart. Though backed by a firm grounding in both traditional and

Jungian depth psychology, pre- and perinatal research and my practice as a psychotherapist, the spiritual insights that informed me as I proceeded to write this book came from a different source. I found that, as I entered the terrain of the heart and allowed myself to be directed by an inner voice I felt to be spiritual guidance, more profound truths emerged.

Having taken time off from my practice to write the book, I headed to a mountain retreat where I could be alone. I took many books with me, fully expecting to find the answers to heartbreak and to relationship difficulties in a deeper exploration of the psychological ground I am already familiar with. But I was mistaken. It was in the poetry and writings of the mystics and the work of great poets such as Rilke and Rumi that I found the fertile ground I was seeking. It was also in the daily spiritual practice I had initiated before I began writing that I found the discipline I needed; and it was in the beauty and majesty of nature that I found the essential nurturing to give birth to this book.

Perhaps in a subtle way, this book is about mending splits or separations in many different areas, not simply heartbreak. Writing this book helped me to bridge another important division that affects my professional life and those of others in the same profession. As a traditional practicing psychotherapist interested, and increasingly drawn to, more spiritual and alternative approaches to health and healing, I have been conscious of a potential divide between the two approaches to healing. I am aware that in the main, those in the psychotherapeutic camp sometimes lack the trust necessary to believe in the power of the transcendent or the divine in our lives, and those in the 'spiritual' or healing camp can be ignorant or dismissive of the importance of the psychological aspects of our lives. Spiritual and alternative healers sometimes dismiss the suffering necessary for true change and the necessity of embracing the shadow or wounded aspects of our lives. Psychologists, with a tendency to concretising human life, can be in danger of remaining stuck in the wounds of early life.

There is a middle ground. I saw it then and felt that my work henceforth would be about somehow bringing these two disciplines together. This book, or rather the shape this book has taken, is the result. There is always the potential for healing and for wholeness, no matter how wounded one is.

The marriage of psychology and spirituality is one of my main foci now, because the time has come when our evolution demands it. No longer satisfied with a purely concrete, causal or literal approach to psychological problems, people are being driven to seek healing within, through deep inner soul work. An understanding of the transcendent and mystical, that is deeply grounded in the psychological, is necessary if we are not to get either bogged down in the narcissism of 'woundology', or swept away by an ungrounded mysticism that promises healing without struggle.

Through deep psychological and spiritual explorations of the inner and outer dynamics of adult love relationships, this book outlines what it means to be human and to seek love. The final chapters chart the inner journey to healing and wholeness after heartbreak. Incorporating fresh insights drawn from the weaving of psychological and spiritual truths and using the power of myth to amplify our human journey, *Love in a Time of Broken Heart–Healing From Within*, offers I believe, a fresh and unique perspective on love, relationships and the healing of love wounds.

Although this book is a personal statement based on many years of experience as a psychotherapist, wife, lover and mother, I want to thank all the men and women that have worked with me. Though by far my most personal book, the stories of those that have shared with me the joys and pains of loving and living are woven into the pages of this book, along with my own.

Thank you. All the characters in the book are fictitious and are generally composites, and any personal stories have been disguised to protect the identity of those involved.

Most of all, I thank you the reader for having chosen, by reading this book, to courageously enter the landscape of your soul and follow the journey to inner healing after your heartbreak. Know that I am with you on your journey. More than a book, I hope *Love in a Time Of Broken Heart–Healing From Within* will be your guide in difficult times, when you need to find healing and inner wholeness. And when you need to find love again.

## A Conflict of the Heart

Isabel arrived early to her appointment and decided to walk around the small plot of green at the end of the street rather than wait in her car. Her heart was bursting: tangled and bruised feelings collided with desperate questions and uneasy answers. Just as well this new therapist lived at the edge of town because if needed, before or after her sessions, Isabel could walk. She loved walking in nature; it calmed her and restored something essential to her well being, something that got lost in the storms created in loving and living.

It had been almost a year—she should have been over it by now. She had managed to before; this relationship was shorter than others but she had been touched in a deep place. This was a deep soul relationship and, as such, it pulled at the unfinished tapestry of her life and destiny. She knew she loved him still and this knowledge yanked at her periodically, though she tried hard to deny this fact. Seeking out a therapist she had been told specialised in relationships and bereavement, Isabel hoped to put an end to this madness. What kind of a fool still dreams of union, reunion with a lost love? What dreamer still longs to give birth to dreams that have already been shattered by reality? Isabel had no answer to these questions; they lay inside her like a mass of tangled wires leading nowhere, like open-ended question marks.

She reached the small park and, since thankfully it was a dry day, decided to sit on the small wooden bench half hidden under some low pines. It was late morning and, apart from a few lone shoppers heading for the supermarket behind the square, not many were about. Sighing, she sat down heavily and, forcing herself to survey the scene in front of her, began observing a woman hurrying along the path towards her. Isabel's attention was caught for a moment by her demeanour; young, maybe in her mid-thirties, this woman looked already aged and worn. Clutching several shopping bags, she seemed harrassed and preoccupied.

As she passed, Isabel had a chance to see her face and saw that, behind this veneer of age and weariness, the woman was pretty, even beautiful. What had happened to mar such youth and beauty? Allowing herself the luxury of fantasy, she wondered if the woman had suffered a love wound? Had she been left for someone else or perhaps her husband walked out on her, leaving her with small children, or maybe she had done the leaving?

Isabel's thoughts turned inwards again and, irritating herself, she wondered for the umpteenth time whether he, her old love, felt like this; whether he too suffered or whether he had already forgotten, placing her and his heart neatly in a locked cupboard. She wondered if he had kept the key or had discarded it and moved on. She wondered had she and their time together now become a distant memory? Did he miss her, or ever think of her now? Was he with someone else; was he happy? Isabel knew nothing, only that she suffered.

*My heart has become a battlefield. Longings mingle with the pain of loss, dreams are splintered and dragged into corners where sunlight for a moment brings them alive and, around corners, the ever-encroaching crash of mangled feelings advance with a deadly, dark calm. I am afraid to stop thinking, afraid to forget the beauty and exquisite joy of love glimpsed in the moments of tenderness that passed between us, like stars plucked from heaven and offered to us, eternal lovers – I do not want to forget.*

*Just now, the sun I felt at the back of my head when we first met four and a half years ago – that feeling came again, but not for long. Then, in that time of sunshine, everything slotted into place, a puzzle completed, the last central pieces clicking into wholeness, my twin soul, my heart, my love.*

*How quickly it all changed, so that darkness and bitter*

*pain twisted the lines between us that had previously run smoothly, like a neatly ploughed field. How soon we began to miss the essential in each other, so that meeting meant clashing. How soon we turned our joyful union into the law court of love. When did you begin to feel the dismantlement of what we had created together? When did sensing each other, as we regularly did, become burdensome? When did our love become blotched with dark, tangled feelings and when did my love become for you not joyful but a source of guilt and pain? I wonder why we had to turn love into a battleground and why you became so disempowered and, being so, began to turn your self-hatred onto me.*

*What kind of a fool am I to still hold out for the pearl of true love, and imagine that I have lost it without you? Why does my heart pull me to you so much still? Why are you in my heart, my soul, my head? Is it because we have not yet completed our journey together? Like an unopened suitcase of clothes from a past holiday, our relationship remains shut and unsorted until someone who has a key comes upon it again.*

Isabel's love for James and her longing for the closeness, the physicality of him, filled the great emptiness that opened up inside her when she thought of him. Instead of diminishing with time, her longing and her love grew with her, shaping her, changing and strenghtening her self-understanding. Now he was no longer there, she recognised the feelings as her own–she wondered how she could ever have doubted it, the pure strength and clarity of her love for James. Nothing and no one touched it or came near to touching the infinite beauty of that love.

She wondered again, for the hundreth time, if he felt it too – how could he fail to, such was the purity of it? She knew a long time ago that they both had dreamed the same dream of love. His soul and hers had held hands over the dense blanket of their lives. Life and love was simple then.

No matter where she went–taking every detour by way of driving out the memory–it followed her; it was part of her and her longing for him hung about him like an aura. She wondered if there was something radically wrong with her, that instead of fading with time her love for James and her longing for him became stronger and rose as sharply and as clearly as the first frost in winter. At times she glimpsed the division; she became aware that her pain was hers, that she created it. No matter what he did or did not do, she was free. More than this she realised that it was she that kept herself trapped and, in that knowing, she set herself free to love. Her love gave her wings to feel, to feel the beauty of their soul connection. She knew that no matter what, she would never lose it.

However, her flight of love did not last, as every now and again she would be dragged down, as a bird in flight, by the changing wind, by fear, anxieties and insecurities. The thought of him in the arms of another woman would cut her like a knife; even worse the thought that maybe he preferred this fictional woman and had found happiness with her doubled Isabel up in pain. Her heart screamed in agony and she wrenched herself away from these thoughts, knowing that though she had created them they could become real.

Again and again, Isabel's spirit would rise in her to show her the futility of such thoughts. When she loved, her soul soared and answered her questions, and she knew with a fierce certainly that she and James would be together. They were together. She was not ready to leave him yet, though she knew she must if she was to set herself free,

Sometimes, when she recalled their last few weeks together and the great and very real difficulties of their relationship, she savoured her freedom and knew in her heart that she was happier without it. She knew too that she had passed well beyond him, and that she was still leaving. She had left the life that was his far behind and now she was without the baggage she had been forced to carry when she had been with James. She relished that lightness. Her energy had freed itself. In a strange and paradoxical way, Isabel was now free to love.

After a dream, which indicated she could now bridge the gap between them by their abrupt and violent cessation of communication, she resolved to send him a very short note. This would be done in freedom, a light touch, to say goodbye and hello, nothing more. Inside, she allowed herself to dream; set free by her love, she allowed herself to imagine, to fantasise. She gave her wildest dreams wings so that she imagined James seeking her out–changed, serious, open and vulnerable, his realisation like an open book for her to read. He would come for her: he loved her and they would be together again because when something is meant to be, everything in the world conspires to make it so. She remembered that it was little more than a year ago that she had bought and given him Paulo Coelho's *The Alchemist*. Inside the front cover she had written the words, *To James, to help you believe in your dreams again, from your soul mate and lover, Isabel*. She knew her dream would become reality. How could it not?

Isabel's flight of love ended as she approached the front door of Kitty Keeble's house. After a few moments, her knock was opened by an older woman with beautiful dark eyes. Isabel liked her immediately but, more than that, she felt she knew her. Some vague, distant memory stirred in the furthest recesses of her sharp and crowded mind. The other woman felt it too, a shadow seemed to pass over them both, momentarily and, as lightly as a bird in flight, it lifted and was gone.

PART ONE

# THE BRAVE HEART

# Chapter 1

## Love in a Time of Broken Heart

Desperado, why don't you come to your senses
You've been out riding fences for so long now
Oh you're a hard one
And I know you've got your reasons
These things that are pleasing you
Can hurt you somehow.

*Desperado:* The Eagles

Most of us are devastated by heartbreak. When a major love relationship fails, our life as we have known it is shattered, changed beyond recognition and maybe repair. We wonder how we will manage without our partner, our wife, our husband. If it was a long relationship, where we depended on each other, we might feel totally lost, at sea, abandoned on the wide ocean without a boat. We might only feel half of a whole.

When your heart has been broken, it is not easy to love again. Many people with heartache shut the door of their hearts, batten down the hatches and only venture out when they think it is safe. Sometimes a person with a love wound will become psychologically or physically ill, or both, and when the pain gets too bad they may go for therapy.

It takes time to heal a love wound and a great deal of patience, endurance, suffering and inner work to unravel the great conflict that opens up in the heart after love fails. One thing is clear, however; healing always comes from within.

In today's world, where up to 50 per cent of marriages end in divorce, there are a great many broken hearts. Aside from marriages, long-term relationships are increasingly fragmented so that most of us will at some stage in our lives experience heartbreak. Heartbreak is essentially a universal phenomenon but how it is experienced and how it is handled is very individual.

Many people can identify with the sentiments immortalised in the words of the song *Desperado*. After heartbreak it is common to close down as a protection from hurt. We are afraid to love and yet a part of us is still drawn to love because it is in our nature to do so. For a while we may ride fences, preferring to cruise along the river rather than get into the ocean. Beyond the fence the gate stays firmly shut; though occasional excursions off the fence and towards the gate may happen, the whiff of love sends a scared heart hurrying back to the safety of the fence.

Nonetheless, for the majority of us, being alone is not what we want. Most of what ails the people who come to see me for therapy is a sense of loss and a desire to feel love and to relate. Humans are social beings at heart, and unhappy relationships and loneliness always affect us. We do all seek to love and be loved. And after a while, riding fences does not work. As the song goes, you lose 'all your highs and lows, and your 'feeling goes away'. You live in a sanitised bubble, emotionally cut off from others. Mistaking love and emotional commitment for loss of freedom, you end up in a prison of your own making.

**Ice in the World Heart**
Since there is always a collective level to our personal experience, our emotional loneliness is mirrored back to us in the world. The world today can be a lonely place. We live in an age of disconnection where, ironically, communication has never been easier. With our advanced technology, we have transgressed physical and geographical boundaries previously not thought possible, and yet we have never been so lonely. If the increase

in mental illness and an escalating suicide rate is anything to go by, profound emotional alienation and high stress levels are part of modern life. At the time of writing, world events have shattered the heart of man so that, I believe, we are living in a time of broken heart. Nations are traumatised and shocked into a place of fear. Individuals are searching for deeper meaning in lives that have become increasingly disconnected from soul.

The loneliness of man is nothing new. The Swiss psychologist Carl Jung wrote about it in the early and middle part of the last century: 'Through scientific understanding, our world has become dehumanised. Man feels himself isolated in the cosmos'.[1] Concerned with the way in which people felt internally ill at ease led Jung to postulate that modern man was in search of his soul. He felt that with evolution and the necessary development of consciousness, something vital to man had been lost. Loss of soul has been the price demanded by our economic prosperity and modern way of life.

Jung's work and writings demonstrate to us how deep our alienation is from our spiritual natures. Jung discovered through his work that many, if not most, people were actually suffering from a malaise of the soul which expressed itself often as a sense of lack and which was the result of a disconnection from their inner lives.

Spiritual in this sense has little to do with religion and all to do with a sense of connection to our souls, to our essential selves. Now, more than half a century later, this loss of soul has, if anything, increased and explains why in an age of material plenty so many are seeking help in counselling, therapy, new age healing and spirituality.

Our economic prosperity and technological advances have been made at a cost. Modern life offers us practically everything we desire materially but it does not fulfil our deepest desires: those of the human heart. The huge growth of self-help and positive-living consciousness is witness to this. Starved of soul food, we rush to our nearest mind/body/spirit bookstore, alternative practitioner or spiritual healer to be healed from soul wounds we cannot identify but know only as a gnawing sense of lack.

I believe this general sense of soul loss has impacted on our already emotionally stretched love lives. In our present climate, many people find intimate relationships difficult to handle and maintain. The increasing number of relationships and marriages that fail seems to indicate that we have lost the art of truly relating to one another. Our ability to be truly intimate with one another is part of the lost vocabulary of the soul that we are now seeking to rediscover; or perhaps it is simply that the stresses of modern life have taken its toll on our inner lives so that the qualities of patience, trust and endurance necessary to maintain intimate relationships have become lost in the scramble to succeed externally.

Most people are confused about relationships and wonder what intimacy really means. We have a sense that relationships, particularly intimate relationships, are hard work. Staying present to ourselves and at the same time to our lover, when our hearts are engaged and pulled this way and that, is not easy. Furthermore, there is no model we can follow that works in today's world. We are taught that we should curb our neediness and be self-sufficient, and yet be prepared to share everything with our partner. In a curious paradox, we are encouraged to be emotionally open and vulnerable but not to be dependent on others to fulfil our emotional needs. We have yet to create a model of healthy intimacy that is empowered but still vulnerable so that emotional dependency and independence can live together.

For those who have experienced a relationship break up, the task of relating is even harder. A man I knew who had split up from his girlfriend of many years told me he could only feel whole again and enjoy a degree of peace in his life if he was alone. Relating, loving was too demanding for his poor heart, he said, which had already taken many knocks. Loving again and having the courage to begin a relationship after heartbreak demands that we take a leap of faith–and it is this leap of faith that most people find difficult. Being whole within oneself and relating intimately takes work, and endless patience, trust and love.

From a collective societal loss of soul to individual broken hearts, it is easy to sense a general coldness in our emotional climate. And love in a cold climate does not flow easily. True emotional and physical intimacy involves trust and the ability to open up to the other. So many of us, who have had our trust betrayed in the past, find it hard to relate on this level and so we remain isolated in a protective shell. In the grip of fear, we assume all sorts of veneers and behavioural patterns, which are designed to protect us but which in reality actually isolate us, not only from others but also from ourselves. Emotional and sexual celibacy can be positive life choices for those who make them, but very often they are imposed on us because of our own fears of relating to other human beings. Too many of us are cut off from our true feelings and from the voices of our souls; and so we find ourselves living in an emotional wasteland.

This emotional wasteland appears to be part of many aspects of modern life. In *Songs from the Womb* and *Reclaiming Father*, I wrote about the emotional wasteland into which babies are born when modern medical birthing practice interferes in the natural process and results in a loss of soul in mothers. When technology replaces nature, it is usually at a cost. Though such technology can be life saving and, at times, necessary it needs to be combined with respect for the human soul. However, in the same way that we have to create a model of intimacy based on empowerment through vulnerability, we have yet to establish a birthing system that combines technology with heart.

Additionally, our present climate of 'quick fix' and speedy resolution consciousness does not encourage us to love in an open, soulful and true way. The ease with which we can move from one relationship to the next is just one expression of a 'cup-a-soup' society, reared on instant gratification. But like fast foods, this does not do it for us. We are still lonely and we still seek love.

Experiencing love is an intrinsic part of our soul's journey and our search for inner wholeness is reflected in our desire for outer union. Love is both a human and divine passion that we are all destined to experience. However, if the cultural and emotional climate into which we are born is not conducive to opening up and flowing with our divine natures then we become disillusioned, gradually closing down our heart centres. Hurt and emotional pain makes us pull back from our interior lives and protect ourselves; we close our hearts more and more. By doing so, we encounter a great many difficulties because, in effect, we are blocking our life force, our true essence.

## Confusion Around What Love Means

Despite being told that love lies within, we still locate it outside of ourselves in another person or material possession. We are very confused about what love means. Disconnected from our inner voice, we imagine that love is 'out there in someone else' and if we are lucky enough to find that someone, we will have found love. Despite being told that love is to be found within, we still seek it outside ourselves and so place a great burden on our relationships.

Love is an ideal to which all human beings aspire, nonetheless. In our soul-hungry world, however, love is often elusive and it is frequently equated with pain, suffering and even the loss of freedom. We often form relationships out of need and when that need fails to be met, or when the relationship breaks up, we are devastated. At that point we may imagine that love is not something we can ever count on; moreover, since we are out of touch with our inner lover, we often close the door of our hearts with a sigh, vowing never to love again; we may build a wall around our hearts as a protection; we may join the 'no commitment' brigade, careful not to become too emotionally involved in any relationship.

When we form relationships with our heart centres closed, we are operating from lower energy centres and our relationships will be based less on a love ideal and more on such things as sex, money, emotional and material security or power. These relationships may be functional but, ultimately, they will not make us happy and, as a result, they will often fail.

As previously said, many people are afraid to love because of the suffering that can accompany having an open heart. Short-term 'light' relationships that do not carry any great degree of emotional burden are becoming increasingly common in Western society. Such relationships are symptomatic of people's emotional reticence in a time of broken heart.

Our emotional detachment from one another, as well as our disconnection from our inner selves, is part of modern culture's fragmented lifestyle. We have a fear of loving, a fear of truly opening our hearts to life and to another human being. As a result, we may prefer to 'cruise' through life, 'riding fences', not getting too involved.

Are we broken hearted? Certainly our difficulties with loving and our culture of fractured relationships indicate that many people today find intimate relationships difficult to handle. Intimacy is not a given and, as I mentioned earlier, we have not yet created a model of healthy intimacy based on combined vulnerability and strength. There are many reasons for this. Perhaps the emphasis in the last decades on the recovery and healing of emotional wounds has created an imbalance in our psyches so that the ability to be truly intimate is part of the lost vocabulary of the soul that we are now seeking to rediscover. Relationships, particularly intimate relationships, demand courage, patience, the willingness to endure and live with conflict, unconditional love and compassion, qualities perhaps lost to us in today's society reared on immediate gratification.

It is not easy to heal the heart and learn to trust. A leap of faith is required-a leap that many people are not prepared to take. The spirituality enshrined in the 'new age' consciousness of the last decades has opened society to many spiritual traditions and alternative healing methods, but it has tended to focus on personal healing and entitlement. This has given a certain narcissistic quality to contemporary spirituality and eroded in many individuals the qualities necessary to build soul stamina. And soul stamina is what you need to be able to use your heartbreak and other painful life experiences to deepen your connection to yourself, God and others.

Love in a time of broken heart is fraught with difficulties. It is not an easy task to delve deeply into your soul and uncover your shadow- it takes courage. Yet healing your heart and learning to trust again is as vital to your soul as food is to your body. Love and a sense of inner wholeness is vital to our spiritual well being. Love is a sacred gift. And, in effect, when we cease to love, we cease to live, because love is part of our souls. Additionally, we have known for some time that the loss of soul that Carl Jung noted over 50 years ago now is still with us and perhaps increasing.

Love and a sense of soul are connected. And since we are suffering from soul loss, I believe that restoring our ability to love is the key to healing the soul wounds that so many of us suffer from. Despite our economic prosperity and technological expertise, we are hungry. People are searching for deeper meaning in their lives and to connect with their inner essential selves. I believe that our greatest challenge today is to open our hearts and learn to give and receive love.

## Healing the Heart: Healing from Within

Loving and being loved are ideals that all human beings aspire to. To love and seek love are archetypal forces. They are one of the strongest, if not the strongest, motivators of human existence. It is vital that we strive to heal our heart wounds and, by doing so, reconnect with life. Our hearts represent our life force and our connection with our spirit. It is in the heart that our human and divine natures meet. Our hearts are the messengers of our spirits, so that listening to the heart connects us with our soul and our life's purpose.

When writing about healing, it helps to remember that the human heart is very resilient and, rather like the liver, is capable of regenerating itself. This means that at some level, having our hearts broken is necessary in order to open us to the sacred and to a more profound experience of ourselves. Love will always renew itself so that it is true to say 'the heart that loves is always young'.

Many spiritual traditions and eastern religions in particular consider that the path to enlightenment is through the heart. As a consequence, having a broken heart can be a necessary sacred initiation into divine or unconditional love. There is a saying among Sufis asking God to break one's heart: 'Shatter my heart so a new room can be created for a limitless love.' A love wound can thus become an 'opening' to unconditional love and the transformation of consciousness.

All growth demands a sacrifice. Suffering the pain of heartbreak can open our hearts and take us deeper into our souls. It is through life crises and traumatic experiences that many of us are called to listen to our souls and to find the deeper meaning of our lives. When we accept the spiritual lessons involved in our life tasks and personal struggles, it both heals and frees us. And this allows us to transcend our wounds rather than to remain stuck in them.

Healing love wounds involves a journey into the terrain of our souls–it involves a process of deep self-examination. Part of this journey entails uncovering and understanding our life and relationship patterns which will have originated in our archetypal soul contract and the imprint of our early lives.

Our soul contracts and archetypal imprints consist of agreements we made in spirit before we were born, together with our familial and cultural psychic inheritance. We are all born for a purpose. Furthermore, our births and early life experiences form patterns we carry with us into future life. We will return to these points later in the book.

Jungian psychology frequently uses myths and fairy stories to illustrate the soul's human journey. Jung believed that there exists a collective unconscious which contains the histories of all peoples and the universal currents of life, and that we are individually influenced by this collective unconscious. Great myths and stories contain archetypal patterns we can relate to. As well as uncovering our individual life story and soul purpose, we can use the lessons from myths and stories to help us understand how life's challenges are spiritual tasks of empowerment, meant to help us grow. The Greek myth of Eros and Psyche, for example, is perhaps the best-known love story used to explain aspects of feminine psychology, as well as the psychology of love. It is about love lost and found, and reading it can help us work with our heartache.

However, there is no short cut to healing. Fear, emotional and spiritual pain, and all the conflicted and confused feelings that surface during such an upheaval in our lives as heartbreak simply have to be endured. We have to allow and accept–that is the lesson of life's difficulties because most challenges are opportunities for growth and ultimately spiritual tasks of empowerment. This means that, difficult as it may be, we have to 'live the questions', stay with what is and be in the moment. The journey to healing involves enduring the battlegrounds of the heart. It means 'being' rather than 'doing'. That being said, there are many things we can do to help our journey through the dark night of the soul. The first key to healing is understanding that it lies within you. Healing always come from within so that healing the heart always involves an inner journey. Basic to this inner journey is acceptance, learning to be with what is, and enduring the battlegrounds of the heart.

Chapter 2

# Battlegrounds of the Heart

I want to beg you, as much as I can, to be patient
toward all that is unsolved in your heart and to try and
love the questions themselves like locked doors and
like books that are written in a very foreign tongue.
Do not seek their answers, which cannot be given you
because you would not be able to live them. And the
point is, to live everything. Live the questions now.
Perhaps you will then gradually, without noticing it,
live along some distant day into the answer.[2]

*Letters to a Young Poet:* Rilke

It can be difficult to stay with what is, particularly at times
when we question, when our hearts are in conflict and we seek
resolution to ease the burden we feel. As a habitual 'seeker', I
am always asking questions, much to the irritation of some of
those closest to me. It has taken me a long time and a great deal
of inner work to allow myself simply 'to be', and I still catch
myself looking for answers to everything. My father recounts
how, as a little girl, I was always asking questions, most often
whenever we went on journeys. Rather than being excited about
going up in a plane as other children might be, for instance, I
used to ask him repeatedly whether the plane would crash and
whether we would reach the top of the sky! Missing some inner
security, I rarely if ever imagined that life would be fine without
my having to put in a great deal of effort.

After gestating this book for over three years, I made a decision to take the summer off and retreat to the mountains of the Sierra Nevada in Spain to fully engage myself with the work. While I was there, a period of five weeks or so, I found I lived the book, lived the feelings, and lived the conflict of the heart. I would wake up in the morning and enthusiastically get to work, eager to put form to the myriad of ideas, thoughts and feelings that had filled my mind and were now pushing for space in my heart. I wrote and allowed what was there to tumble out onto the pages.

Later I would survey what I had written and frequently became critical, finding fault. I can't write that–where does this fit in to the overall structure of this book?; what am I really saying?; why am I writing about this?; this isn't what I planned and so on. All these questions and thoughts tumbled around in my heart and often I was left worse off than when I had started so I would delete most or all of what I had written.

I learned that there are days to write and days to hold back from writing because the words do not come when they are not ready. True creation happens naturally, it cannot be forced. I learned that those were the times that my heart needed to simply live and that it was still living whatever it was I wanted to write about–old loves, for instance. After writing all day about love and relationships, I would put my computer away and retreat to bed with a novel, thinking that is that for now. A work well done! Then my psyche would loosen itself at night and I would have long complicated dreams about former lovers and partners. I would find myself having to engage in revisiting parts of my heart I thought I had put to bed and left a long time ago. Old relationships came and inhabited my space and would not go away until, grudgingly, I gave in and gave them time, more time. I knew that nothing would be written until I lived what was there in my heart clamouring for attention.

One night I had a dream in which I was clearly told 'write

about the battlegrounds of the heart'; the words were clear but the rest of the dream vague. The next morning I sat at my computer, waiting. When nothing much happened I tried continuing a chapter I had already planned and started but I felt bored, unmotivated, tired. A phrase kept coming into my head: 'a conflict of the heart'. Finally, I put away my Saturnian need for structure and certainty, and indulged myself in something I find difficult, just letting go and letting be.

After a while a great knot, that had been stretched taut across my heart, began to slowly unravel itself. Conflict of the heart; I knew all about it and began to write.

I wrote about love and how often we live in a conflicted state because it is part of nature to feel conflict. I wrote about my own heart and its loves and hates, and how often I am in conflict with it. It has taken me a long while and a great deal of endurance to like and appreciate my own heart, with its depth and its contrasting territories. The human heart is beautiful as it is, with all its complications, its highways and byways and its tearing contradictions. I asked again and again, how is it that one can love a man that is totally unsuited to one, that one can fall in love and yet 'kill the thing we love'? How is it that we can feel such conflicting emotions at the same time? And surely the human heart cannot bear such a heavy burden as a million and one feelings, all jostling for attention?

The words came slowly. I had to endure, I had to let whatever was in my heart live and be. I found that I was often in conflict with myself during this time. I had gone away to be alone, and apart from the everyday demands of my usual routine-filled life. I needed to be alone, with no commitments other than writing the book. Surrounded by exquisite mountain nature, I could just be and enjoy what came.

After the initial novelty of settling into my retreat had worn off I found that, though I craved solitude, I also felt the need to engage. After working all day I would walk to the nearby mountain village and sit at a bar, hoping to draw someone into conversation. I frequently hung around the *Ayuntamiento* (town hall) to see if there was any news of upcoming fiestas or dances. I wanted to meet, dance with and enjoy male company in particular. Keenly aware of my then single state, I felt a huge conflict between engagement and solitude. Alone, loneliness gnawed at my heart like an annoying wound that would not quite heal and kept flaring up. I am not cut out for this, I would say to myself, and yet next morning would have me peacefully and happily pottering around, getting ready for the day; my day, when I had no one to bother me and could just do what I wanted without considering anybody else.

I learned about the conflict between the need to engage and be in relationship, and the need to be alone. It seems to be that at a fundamental level the experience of aloneness is necessary to fully appreciate relationship. I believe this is the experience of every human being and that this conflict is an innate part of our nature. During this retreat I also learned about my own heart and its conflicted nature, and after I had stopped resisting and trying to put it into some kind of order, I learned that this is the way it should be. By living the conflict in my heart I was truly being there and that, curiously, living this conflict would enable me to write about it.

I read books, psychology books and soon put them down. It was poetry and love poetry, in particular, of Rilke, Neruda and in the sacred writings of Rumi, St John of the Cross and others that I found what I was looking for so that, when I returned to my desk and wrote about love, the words lay down in a quiet and calm way. I knew that every love story contains this conflict, and more importantly, that the future of any individual love story lay in whether the challenge to endure this conflict was met or not.

Rilke wrote that 'All emotions are pure which gather you and lift you up; that emotion is impure which seizes only one side of your being and so distort you'.[2] This calmed my troubled soul so that I was able to let my heart rest a while and know that what I would write would come from my heart. And frequently at night I would take out my paints and paint what was in my heart, there, under the Spanish stars. I gained great solace from painting.

Some six months previously I had fallen in love with the tango and my need to dance seemed to reflect a restlessness I felt, as well as a joy. It also offered me a way of expression and communication. To dance the tango in close embrace with a friend, a lover or a stranger seemed to offer everything I needed at the time and in the lack of that contact in my mountain retreat, when I had finished writing for the day, I listened to tango music and painted.

Something settled in my heart as though the music and the painting restored some kind of order to conflicting feelings. Later I read that dance, and I have always been a dancer, is a more primitive form of expression, one which the soul needs when it is healing certain very deep wounds, particularly to one's femininity and sexuality; love wounds. I linked this to the Little Mermaid tale I have always loved, and came to see that dancing the tango was, for me, very spiritually healing because it is also, of course, about the inner marriage: the perfect union of male and female. It is about love.

## Living the Conflict of the Heart

I seemed to have been destined to experience and write about love and the conflict of the heart. At the tender age of seventeen I found myself loving two boyfriends at the same time and wondering how it was that I was able to do this. Mindful of their feelings and given an ultimatum, I eventually chose one, the one who would eventually become my husband. However, the process was very painful for me and I can still recall the pain that my young heart had to go through. I remember that

I cried solidly for three days. Perhaps this was the beginning, in me, of really experiencing loss which making a choice always demands. Every decision and choice necessitates a letting go and the ability to bear the consequences of that decision.

To be human is to be full of the contradictions of life. The need to love is basic to human nature but there is always at base some conflict between loving ourselves and loving others. It is the ego that engages in conflict. To engage in a relationship means having to be aware of the other person's needs and desires, and reconciling these with one's own needs is not always easy. Nor is it meant to be. I know many people, myself included, that have run away from relationships because of a fear of having to face this conflict or a fear somewhere that one could not handle the everyday compromises involved. Sometimes the conflict of the heart is such that a resting place is necessary before a regrouping can happen. But most of all, I have learned that one must face the conflict head on for it to pass and resolve itself in a meaningful way.

Nature can be very restorative. When I am living a particularly turbulent time, I retreat to my soul home in Connemara, in the west of Ireland. There, the constancy of nature, the mountains I can see from my windows and the voice of the sea restore me gently to some place of peace and wholeness. It is as though, reconnecting with the rhythms of nature, I return to myself. Sharing myself with nature, becoming part of the heartbeat of the world, reminds me I am here and it is OK. I can lie back and let the sea hold me and allow the spirit of the earth to cradle me.

Rilke speaks of this too when he tells the young poet that the sea 'cleanses me with its noise and lays a rhythm upon everything in me that is disturbed and confused'.[3]

My life has taught me there are a great many flavours and colours to love, and that one does not need to be actively engaged in a relationship to feel love. As a woman who loves very deeply and feels passionately, I have grown used to the largeness of my heart, and I know at a deep instinctual level that enduring the conflicts of the heart is part of my soul journey. Destined to struggle with and endure the battlegrounds of the heart, my soul contract involves teaching others about love. Heartache is familiar to me and various painful experiences have prepared me for my task. My life experiences so far have taken me deeply into the terrain of the human heart.

## Holding the Tension: the Still Point

How do we endure the conflicts of the heart? Enduring conflict calls on us to stay with the tension in any situation rather than to seek to get out of it. Many Jungian writers have written about the need to hold the tension of opposites within. Holding the tension means enduring the suffering and conflict we feel and not seeking to run away and distract ourselves, because ultimately, it will still be there when we come home at night. Holding the tension releases something new, in time. Staying with and enduring conflict builds soul stamina. However, staying in the place of 'not knowing' is very difficult indeed. It involves a great deal of trust, something in short supply in many of us.

How often do we busy ourselves with seeking answers to our problems outside, thereby missing what is there, in our own hearts? Holding the tension and staying in the moment, we live the paradox. We live the questions. And it is in that time that we enter the still point. This is the still point of the soul when something greater is allowed in.

Rilke, in his '*letters to a Young Poet*', writes about the need to go inside oneself; 'to go into yourself and test the deeps in which your life takes rise; at its source you will find the answer to the question whether you must create. Accept it, just as it sounds, without enquiring into it'.[4]

In this space, the past is dismantled and ego desire makes

way for the soul. Often such a sacrifice is demanded of us when we endure the heartache and the battlegrounds of our hearts. Letting go of what we think we want and simply being and accepting what is means something new can arrive.

Sometimes we have to get out of our own way.

In the same way, staying with conflict and differences in a relationship, and living the questions rather than always seeking answers, releases something new into the relationship, freeing it to be what it is meant to be at that moment in time. When there is serious and continual conflict it is because something needs to be addressed, something needs to change. Sometimes this change is an inner change in one or both partners and sometimes it is the relationship itself that needs to move along to a different tune.

I remember one occasion when my former partner and I were going through a particularly painful patch in our relationship. I had gone to have dinner with him and we were both painfully and, uselessly as it turned out, trying to work it out and restore order to our partnership. Talking, hurting, trying to solve the conflict, suddenly I let go. I stopped talking and after a moment so did he. A quiet moment passed between us. We looked at each other and I knew then that it was useless to go on. I believed we had entered the still point somehow and within that pregnant moment lay the seeds of our future.

Our relationship was hurtling, inevitably, towards its end. As I drove home that night, sad and lonely, T.S. Eliot's words kept coming into my head.

> I said to my soul be still, and wait without hope,
> For hope would be hope for the wrong thing,
> wait without love
> For love would be love for the wrong thing:
> yet there is faith
> But the faith and the love and the hope are all
> in the waiting.[5]

Sometimes we just have to wait. And waiting in this sort of situation is very painful. I did not want our relationship to end. I was very much in love with this man. However, continuing together at this time was impossible and would have been inappropriate, as it turned out. I see now that resisting the change or the end was merely prolonging the agony of what had become inevitable. The continual conflict between us had become unbearable to both of us.

Love always drags up the unconscious and has the potential of adding extra dimensions to the soul. Increasingly unhappy in this relationship with a man I loved but who could not give me what I wanted, a committed partnership, I needed to move away. My soul was demanding more of me in relationship and I needed to free myself up so that I could eventually move on.

But it can be very hard to go. My ego was telling me no, I want to stay, I want the relationship to be this way and that, I want him to be different, I want him to offer me a commitment, and if only he would change it would be all fine, and so on.

As Jungian author Clarissa Pinkola Estes writes, the desire to force love to live on in its most positive form only is what causes it to die. Sometimes, simply staying with what is, acceptance of what is, and being there can elicit a change. Allowing what wants to emerge means not only dismantling the past but also putting aside ego desires so that the soul can come in.

Something new always materialises from what T.S. Eliot calls the still point. The still point is a place of soul; it is a place of healing: 'Except for the point, the still point, there would be no dance, and there is only the dance'.[6]

## Coming Home

Enduring such a conflict of the heart, and living the tension, in essence brings us back to ourselves. We are always seeking to reconcile opposing forces within us. Suffering the battlegrounds of the heart in a relationship represents each individual's struggle with their own natures, both human and divine. There is always a pull between our higher selves, our soul, and our ego-driven, lower selves. We are always seeking to reconcile the two and to live more fully in tune with our essential natures. We know that it is only by balancing the opposing energies within ourselves that we can grow to wholeness and live more in tune with our souls.

Most of us know that economic prosperity and material wealth, for example, do not guarantee happiness and do not feed our souls in the way that gazing at a beautiful sunset or walking by the sea can. And most of us would rather have someone to share the beauties of the world and our lives with. Most of us want to love another soul. However, as human beings we are on a journey and our spiritual path may go through very different and contrasting terrains. For some of us, love affairs and the challenges of loving another person represent a large part of that journey.

Our hearts are strange creatures of passion, bravery and also wisdom. However, the wisdom of the heart is only now beginning to be recognised as valid in a world dominated by logos and the rational function. Rational linear thinking has been elevated at the expense of the heart and the feeling function. And yet it is only by combining the two that we reach union and wholeness.

I read somewhere that being fearless means acting from the heart and enlisting the mind. However, since we are essentially divided between our hearts and our minds, we are unsure how to balance the two. Being thus divided fragments our power and our ability to make conscious and empowering choices. It means that we have a tendency to be either overly rational or overly emotional. So we can easily dismiss what is coming from our hearts because we are lost in our emotions. However, it is only by entering the battlegrounds of the heart and engaging and enduring the conflict within that one can live a full and embodied life–and that one can love.

Ultimately, in a way that I have come to know well, we need to be comfortable alone and whole in our aloneness in order to live in healthy relationships. We cannot expect others to fulfil our needs or fill our inner emptiness. The more we feel complete, the easier it is to be with a partner and allow them to be themselves. Loving the other and remaining true to ourselves is the challenge we have to meet in relationship.

Sometimes a period living alone is a necessity before re-engagement can happen. Commonly, the break up of an important love relationship propels people into a time of reflection, pain, even depression. This is the time to pull in, to sail home and drop anchor in a safe place away from the storm.

When there is a storm and a shipwreck, we pick up the pieces, limp home and batten down the hatches.

In this alone time, in the fresh rawness of your heartache, you draw yourself in and lick your wounds. When, with time and tide, the rawness has eased, you begin to pick and sort through your tangled feelings and start the work of healing. The work of weaving together disparate fragments of your heart and your life will one day mean that 'Perhaps you will then gradually, without noticing it, live along some distant day into the answer'.[7]

## A Conflict of the Heart 2

Kitty had told Isabel she must keep a journal. To find release she must find a way to express the complicated bundle of her hurt and conflicted feelings. Writing, she would gradually unpack the crowded and untidy suitcase in which she had placed her lost relationship. It was only by opening out each feeling, each thought, like a wrinkled garment, that Isabel and she would be able to piece things together thereby restoring Isabel's soul to a place of wholeness. Remembering and sorting–like Psyche who, in order to be reunited with her lost love, Eros, had to sort through seeds and complete various near-impossible tasks–Isabel had to sit and sort. Gradually, over time, this process would bring results, Kitty had said. Picking and sorting sound more like a witch doctor sorting through bones, thought Isabel. But then again, perhaps therapy was just that, some form of witch doctoring. Sighing again, she let her memory take her back to when it had gone really wrong with James.

Isabel had spent the new year alone. She had expected to spend it with James, and when he had failed to come disappointment, as well as anger, mingled with her sense of loss. She was not so surprised by his sudden change of plan, for she had grown used to his casual ways. However, part of her knew she had had enough of them. The feeling of being let down yet again led her to wondering what it was that had compelled her to love a man who was, it seemed, destined to fail her.

The first morning of the new year found her frantically writing in her journal. Isabel's new year resolutions were important to her. The phone had rung mid morning: it was James wishing her a happy new year. Later, when she returned to her task, she came at it with her heart churning confused thoughts and colours onto the pages. James, James, it was always James. To ease her mixed up thoughts and feelings she wrote them, as though by giving them form on the pages they would magically coalesce into a picture she would recognise and know. Afterwards, she peered at the pages of writing. Angry dark letters mingled with softer loving ones and all were placed there like desperate orphans, tumbled out of a bus awaiting homes.

She suffered.

*A new year, a new life, a new me? My promises to myself involve finding the courage to cut the ties with the past and to let go of what is no longer good for me and holding me back. After the trauma of the letdown by J, I feel betrayed. I am exhausted by the conflict of my heart. A line has been crossed now, I feel. He has let me down once too often and I have let myself down by allowing him that power. He has hurt me yet again. My heart is in conflict because it pulls me in two ways. My inner king lies shattered and perhaps mortally wounded on the battlefields of love. He has deserted me. My knight in shining armour has betrayed me too. He has become instead his majesty, the baby! And yet my soul pulls me back to my knight, the knight of my dreams, my James, the honourable, steady soldier who never gives in. Can I have been mistaken? Is he not my soul mate, my twin soul?*

*I read back over the three and a half years of writing about a love that was so strong it transcended the boundaries of time and space. I had finally met my life partner, my soul mate, my lover and eternal friend. I embarked on a journey with him, first to find him, and then finding him slower than I, my task became to pull him in. In periods of rest, he came and stood quietly by my side, afraid to take the lead, afraid to offer me his hand. Occasionally though, he would take and hold my outstretched one.*

*What happened? Why did you become an angry resentful child – a man who would not commit to me?*

*The man takes his woman out into the world because he loves her. You have been holding me back from the world while you stay busy with your toys. You keep me in the nursery with you. I have become caught in your struggle to emerge from childhood.*

Isabel struggled to keep abreast of the endless questions that pushed, as always, for answers.

*Did you ever love me? My soul says yes but my heart is conflicted. If I have to leave you now in order to honour myself, I ask for the courage to do so. If this is the right thing for me then why does it hurt so much? Have I really been loving a man who is incapable of love and who moreover does not love me? If after three and a half years I have to let you go and sever all links with you then what have these years meant and will I ever find you again? Was I so mistaken? What has happened to you my James? You were my sun, my moon and my stars, you made my heart sing-you still do – but I must pull away.*

With her heart a battleground once more, Isabel put her journal away and went for a walk.

PART TWO

# THE WISE HEART

# Chapter 3

## Love and the Soul

Love bade me welcome; yet my soul drew back
Guilty of dust and sin
But quick-eyed Love, observing me go slack
From my first entrance in,
Drew nearer to be sweetly questioning
If I lacked anything.
'A guest,' I answered, 'worthy to be here.'

*'Love':* George Herbert

Love is the nature of the soul. Mystics and poets alike have written about it since the beginning of time. Love is primeval and archetypal, and part of our make up. We are all lovers at heart. And, since love has a transcendent aspect, one does not need to have a human partner in order to experience great passion. Celibate mystics like John of the Cross wrote some of the greatest and most inspiring love poetry. Many others – the poet Emily Dickenson, for example – felt the fires of love without entering into a physical relationship. Love is a powerful emotion. It is an ideal to which all human beings aspire. Most people fall in love at some point in their lives and many of the challenges of everyday living have to do with giving and receiving love. Love inspires us, challenges us and moves us.

Over the last few years I have noted, both in my practice and my life, that the search for love is complicated by a difficulty in receiving or accepting it. I believe that understanding this point was, at some level, a motivation for writing this book.

Although we continually seek it, surprisingly, we do not find it easy to truly receive love when it comes our way. We are usually unaware of this, but at some level a part of us feels unworthy to receive love; an inner sense of unworthiness, which makes it hard to receive love, is usually the reason that love fails.

Although the search for love is universal, we often draw back from love when it comes to us. Why do we do this? To be comfortable with love requires the ability to live with an open heart, something most human beings find very difficult. Just as meeting the challenge to love unconditionally is hard, so is maintaining an open heart. And although the wisdom of the heart is something we have long known about, we often ignore it because the human condition and our life experience make it difficult for us to trust. When we do not trust it is because we are fearful, and this blocks our ability to love and be loved. This is one of the paradoxes of human life; to seek love and yet fear it.

As two of life's most overwhelming emotions, love and fear are intertwined. To truly love requires surrendering control, and this frightens us. When we are fearful, we do not love. Filled with apprehension, we cease to trust. As a result we may shut down a part of ourselves; or we may remain conflicted between the surges of our heart and the commands of our mind, so that we are immobilized.

When we make life choices that are motivated by fear, it is because we have lost touch with our essence, with our divine natures. At such times, our light and our ability to love and trust become opaque and we forget our divine natures. For example, if we have had life and love experiences that have hurt us, we may shut down our emotions and refuse to open our hearts to loving again; as a therapist I know this is the surest way to suffer soul loss.

In reality, the 'ailment' that afflicts most people who come to me for therapy is not being able to either give or receive love.

## Love is a Passion both Human and Divine

The search for love is archetypal, ageless and universal. There have been many famous lovers in history, and our myths and fairy tales are full of lovers and seekers of love. The heroes and heroines that people our dreams and psychic imagery are always on a quest that involves defeating the enemy, union with a beloved and a return to wholeness. This hero's journey is intrinsically imprinted in each of us and forms part of our spiritual journey. A hero or heroine is one such because they have passion and conviction, and the courage to follow their path despite great difficulties. They inspire us because they show us the finer side of human nature, and a part of us seeks to emulate them.

We all have an inner hero or heroine, and part of us is always engaged in the hero's journey to arrive at spiritual fulfilment and inner wholeness. There is a divine aspect to love, which is reflected in human love; and the search for love, for a perfect partner, is universal. I read recently that falling in love is one of the great adventures promised to the soul in return for its agreeing to be born on this planet. This moved me greatly and I believe it is indeed so. Love, and the search for it, are how we touch the divine within ourselves.

Although love is a human and divine passion that we are all compelled by our natures to seek, we have tended to separate the two aspects in ourselves, thereby inhibiting our ability to receive love. When we are separated internally, we suffer soul loss, and this is most often expressed as a loss of faith in ourselves. This separation, between human and divine love, is false, and responsible for many of our difficulties with love. Indeed, it is our general sense of fragmentation that produces both our search for love and simultaneously, our inability to receive it.

Over the centuries, wonderful writings and sacred poetry from the mystics have attempted to address the misconception that divine love is separate from human love. Even celibate Christian saints and mystics (whenever they wished to describe the heights of mystical union with God) used images and symbols drawn from human love and marriage. In his writings, St John of the Cross, one of the greatest spiritual love poets of all time, said that a few bars of a Spanish-Arab love song that he heard one night wafting through his prison window inspired his best work. In his poem, 'Dark Night',[8] he writes:

> In the delicious night,
> In privacy, where no one saw me,
> Nor did I see one thing,
> I had no light or guide
> But the fire that burned inside my chest...
> Oh night, sweet guider,
> Oh night more marvellous than the dawn!
> Oh night which joins
> The lover and the beloved
> So that the lover and the beloved
> change bodies!

St John of the Cross had the soul of a lover. His longing is directed at God; it is not directed at a human partner. However, this does not diminish either the great fire of love that burned in his chest or the ferociousness of his passion. Many people can identify with the fire and passion of love, and the need to express it in poetry or music. This is the divine side of love and it is present in all of us. Our task as human souls is to marry conditional human love with unconditional, divine love.

Love can take us straight to the divine. And it is sometimes through loving (and perhaps losing) another person that we are thrust into a spiritual search so that our love relationships become an intimate part of our spiritual journey to reach the inner depths of our own souls.

## Love as a Spiritual Search

We are all born with the capacity to love and be loved. Love is the nature of the soul; essentially it is both a divine and fiercely human passion which all of us are compelled to experience. Looked at from a spiritual perspective, all of us are souls clothed in human form, and our essence is divine. So also (in a way that I have come to know intimately) is our search for love. Just as we are both human and divine, there is a human and a spiritual dimension to love. This means that our search is spiritual, given expression in human form. We want to express our love by loving another person.

Love and the search for it underpin our existence. As babies we continually seek love to help us thrive and grow. It is hard for us to find our way in the world without love and a secure sense of being protected and nurtured. A feeling of being loved is part of a spiritual ease essential to our well being. Recently, I have begun to realise that our search for love is, at its most fundamental, a search for God or a search for another spiritual source. The more I travel into my own interior landscape, the more I feel this.

I also believe that the search for divine or infinite love is reflected in our love relationships, which are themselves mirrors of our souls. In short, as we search outwards for the person we believe will 'complete' us, we are simultaneously searching inwards for a sense of wholeness. In this sense, our love experiences become challenges of a sort. All initiations are spiritual tasks of empowerment that we can choose to either engage with or not.

Through writing this book I believe I have finally understood the reason why one has to experience love and loss, having grappled for some time with these issues in my own life. I believe that loving and enduring the pain and suffering of love in our lives teaches us how to open ourselves up to our spiritual source. Such suffering opens the heart chakra–each time we suffer in love we open the heart a little more thereby opening ourselves up to unconditional, divine or infinite love.

An older woman friend and spiritual teacher once told me how, when she asked why it was that people had to suffer so in love, received the following reply: we learn to love God through loving another person; loving is part of our spiritual journey–a journey which, like all spiritual journeys, leads us through dark and painful periods of suffering.

## Yearning for a Lost Wholeness

Why do we search for love? In some deep part of our soul we all have a sense of love, as well as a memory of wholeness, and of belonging. We also have a sense of having lost this wholeness, and this sense further fuels our search. Psychologists would tell us that what we are searching for is to return to the nirvana of our mother's wombs. My own belief is that while the birth experience is most definitely a 'trauma', as well as being our first great experience of physical separation, it is merely a reminder of an earlier separation, one that tears at our soul and causes us to search endlessly for the person who will give us the desired sense of completion.

Our soul holds a distant memory of love; of being part of a great force–a oneness and part of love. We also hold a sense of having lost this and our soul yearns for reunion with a beloved, twin soul. Often this is a nameless yearning we feel in our hearts, and we imagine it will be healed through meeting the perfect partner, our soul mate.

Our innate sense of belonging and of loss is archetypal and primeval. The fundamental nature of our great myths is the struggle to return to a state of oneness. Whether this longing is expressed through various world religions or spiritual traditions, or simply in everyday life, they all lead us to the same place, a desire to return home. Jungian author and poet, Robert Bly, suggests that many parables represent in essence, our fall as human beings and our return. It takes endless trials and labour to get back to the divine, to God or to infinite love. There we know we are safe; we are cradled and loved. We have returned home.

We are increasingly fractured and our lives are increasingly fragmented, making the search for wholeness all the more urgent. In earlier times, the sense of oneness was taken for granted; in the modern world, this sense has been lost. We tend to think in parts, thus fragmenting our lives and making it difficult for us to appreciate the wisdom that comes through our hearts and the essential mystery of our soul, which always seeks wholeness. Love mends the separated part of man and is intimately connected with our inner lives, and with having a sense of trust in the bounty of the universe.

In his book *The Mystery of Human Relationship*, Jungian author Nathan Swartz- Salant writes about the principles of Alchemy: 'The enduring strength of alchemy in ancient and medieval times, and its innate weakness in the modern age, is its tendency to relate all human activity to an awareness of the essence or oneness of all creation. This belief is based on the notion of an 'essence' which pervades all creation and which connects qualities as opposites'. Swartz-Salant continues: 'Alchemy lasted 2,000 years because it addressed such issues as a person's relationship with the oneness that every soul deeply knows and easily forgets'.[9]

In the writings of Carotenuto we see yet again the theme of knowing and then forgetting, the idea of loss, of what was known and is still felt somewhere deeply in the soul. The wisdom of the heart, and a sense of connection, were commonly felt in earlier times, whereas today many people have lost this connection, and a desire to find it underpins their spiritual or psychological search.

## A Sense of Separation

I remember one evening some years back, I was working with a spiritual teacher who asked us while we were meditating if we could try to experience once again a sense of oneness with the spirit world. After perhaps ten minutes, I began to feel myself drifting into a state that I can only describe as bliss, followed by a sense of serenity and utter peace. I felt loved and held in a way that defies description. It was perhaps just a brief moment of ecstasy; whatever it was, it left me feeling completely bereft when our teacher gently asked us to leave our spirit guides and return to earth and outer reality. I cried bitterly at the feeling of loss I experienced at having to return to reality, and abandon the sense of feeling completely loved and embraced. Abandoning that love and the sense of having to endure utter emptiness afterwards is something that I will never forget. Yet, as my spiritual teacher gently reminded me afterwards, this type of experience is the very challenge of human existence – the challenge of suffering loss, combined with the knowledge that we will never be truly alone if we manage to connect with our spiritual nature.

We continually seek wholeness. Since all of us are a combination of spirit and matter, we are constantly seeking to balance the two elements. We are also a combination of animal and divine, both human and god-like. We retain both spiritual and physical characteristics, as well as longings and aspirations. While one aspect of our quest for wholeness is about reconciling these opposites within us, at the very core of our essence the opposites are not in opposition. But we have become separated. We are constantly seeking wholeness, constantly searching for love, as a way of making ourselves feel whole again.

It is probably also another indication of our fallen or separated state that we tend to think of human love, with all its romance and sexuality, as the area that is furthest removed from our spiritual lives. In fact, the opposite is the case. Great spiritual teachers have endeavored to teach us that God is within as well as without, and that the adventure and mystery of loving each another was designed to be the way in which we were to come to understand that our relationship with the divine was one not simply of creature and creator, or servant and master, but of beloved and lover.

The confusion in many between the love of God and the love of another human being has arisen as part of the body/mind split that has occurred in the modern psyche. Though our evolution demanded more consciousness, many feel it has taken us away from our hearts and from a sense of inner wholeness and wisdom. As other authors have contested, a split between nature and spirit, and body and soul, to a degree needed to happen in order for us to become conscious, but this split now needs to be healed for it has gone too far. Jungian analyst and author Schwartz-Salant writes in *The Mystery of Human Relationships:*

> Today we must recognise the shadow side of the great development of ego consciousness, namely the creation of defences that allow too much separation of the ego from the unconscious and from the emotions of the body.[10]

A body and soul split affects us most particularly when it comes to our hearts and to love.

## Love Mends the Split

Love mends the split within us and heals a sense of division and separation, because it is in the heart that our dual nature meets. All of us are a unique combination of spirit and matter, body and soul, human and divine. I believe that these energies meet in the heart.

I like to use the image of the cross, an ancient symbol, to remind us of the union of earth/body and spirit/mind. The vertical line depicts unearthed spirituality, and the horizontal line depicts de-spirited earth. They come together in the middle, i.e. the heart, and it is here that man connects with both spirit and matter. The wisdom of the heart is where the soul resides, and connecting with it is vital to heal our emotional wounds.

In my last book I write about how difficult it is sometimes to avoid being split when we are relating. In *Songs from the Womb* I discussed the body/mind split as it relates to embodiment and being there for one's partner in pregnancy and birth.[11] To be fully incarnated involves both body and mind. Loss of soul happens when there is a division between body and mind. The soul is what unites the two aspects of our human nature so that we are, therefore, complete and whole.

Just as it is in the heart that the split can be healed, it is also there that division and the sense of separation takes place. Jung and Jungian authors have written about the split. Swartz Salant, discussing the unifying qualities of alchemy and other transformational processes, suggests:

> Spirit and matter are two sides of the same coin. The one is felt through the mental-spiritual realm, the other through embodied life and the somatic unconscious, the subtle body. But these experiences are split at the level of the heart chakra, as in the Tantric thought which influenced the great alchemical text, the *Rosarium*.[12]

In other words, the body and soul split happens in the heart because it is here that both sides of us meet. When we are cut off from our feelings, our hearts, then we are certainly split. As an alchemical text, the *Rosarium* proposes a healing of the split by uniting the opposites, the sun and moon, king and queen, and so on.

Healing the body/soul split is essential, because the split has undoubtedly affected our ability to love, and is responsible for the sense of loss we feel in our souls. How do we do this? Healing our sense of separation involves the willingness to engage with our souls and undertake an inner journey. Healing means reconciling the opposites within, as symbolised by the principles of alchemy and outlined in the *Rosarium*. If we are to live soulfully, we must look into our hearts, for it is there, as I said earlier, that wisdom and understanding reside.

Healing the split can only be done through the heart, yet many of us have a distinct reluctance to admit to our deepest feelings. A part of us is afraid of its great depths. It is acceptable to be in the lofty realms of spirit and to be in the body and purely physical experience, but to include one's feelings, many of which are not pleasant, is a much harder task. Carotenudo writes:

> It is as if we are all ashamed to admit that our souls are subject to burning with passion or breaking in anguish.[13]

It is essential to heal the split between mind and body, or spirit and earth, especially if we want to love. It is vital to our spiritual well being that we mend this split so we can be restored to wholeness.

## The Wisdom of the Heart: Self Knowledge

Not only do we deepen our spiritual knowing through loving another soul, we also learn about ourselves through falling in love and experiencing love relationships. Therein lies the wisdom of the heart; it leads us to a deep, inner creative place. When we feel deeply we enter into our vulnerability and a deeper intelligence comes through us.

This is something I have experienced myself and I know that loving and experiencing the loss of love have helped me to grow. Both in the process of loving and in all the pathos associated with love, I have learned about my heart, about its yearning and its passion, and about my own nature. It is as if each love experience has led me deeper into my own inner landscape. Each love that I lost and each relationship that failed, for whatever reason, opened my heart more, due to the depth of feeling and suffering I endured.

I learned that I am a creature of passion, and I also learned that I have a large capacity for love; that when I am in touch with my heart and listen to it, I am reaching into the depths of my creativity. The suffering I have endured has revealed myself to myself more than any analysis could ever do, and my love experiences have added a great many layers to my soul.

When we love we are immediately in the realm of the soul. Love reveals us to ourselves in a way no other experience has the power to do. Carotenuto writes: 'the intensity and exclusiveness of the love relationship transform and enliven the way we interpret both external and internal reality. It is as if a multitude of images and emotions filled up our sensory channels, opening a new dimension to the soul. The beloved becomes a driving force towards the search for one's own truth, a window onto both the outer world and our own soul.'[14]

When we fall in love we lose all reason. In a sense, when we are in love we enter a different consciousness, one where enchantment plays a part because we are no longer in control. In that respect, love has a transcendent power which lowers our consciousness – we let go somehow and that in itself enables something which pulses in us to come through without having to battle against the usual barriers of rationale and inhibition.

In this way, love liberates us. Suddenly, the whole world opens itself up to us, along with endless possibilities that had never seemed available before. When we are in love, we are close to the divine because we are outside time, and the normal restraints of causality and linear time.

Love therefore awakens and strengthens creativity. A man who is in love will imagine that he can do the noblest of deeds and be inspired to do so to please his beloved. A woman who is in love becomes a goddess possessed of great beauty, her capacity for nurturing and seduction greatly heightened.

Love brings us back to ourselves and reveals extra dimensions to our soul. We learn so much from our hearts.

## Love is the nature of the soul.

Isabel, a woman whose story is revealed to you gradually throughout this book, was a woman who loved a man passionately and who suffered deeply when their relationship ended. Her writings bear testimony to how her love affair and her suffering revealed the most profound depths of her soul and then helped her to grow. After the relationship break up, Isabel travelled widely and spent many months alone. She struggled for a long time with her deep feelings of pain and anguish, her loneliness, her intense love and her loss. When her suffering became too great she wrote:

> *I will not pretend anymore. This is no ordinary feeling, no ordinary love. I miss you like I miss the sound of the endless rhythm of the waves. A fundamental, timeless, ageless essence has been lost to me. A part of me is floating, elusive, and I cannot catch it. I am dying without it. I am in the desert and I've lost you, my deepest love, the light of my soul, my soul mate, lover and eternal friend. Perhaps you were right; I love what I see or what I glimpsed in you – a possibility that never fully manifested itself. I miss the everyday smell and feel of you – the intimacy we so easily and effortlessly shared when you stood aside and let yourself be known. I miss the you that knew me – the real me. I always knew you knew the true me underneath the layers. You knew me*

*without words. Perhaps we tried too hard to mould ourselves to each other's vision, or perhaps it was the unfinished tapestry of our unlived lives that pulled us finally apart. Whatever it was, it stretched the fabric of our relationship to breaking point and beyond. Will anyone ever know me like that again?*

Isabel grew; her suffering honed her so that gradually, over time, she gained new depth as her love wound healed. In the space left by her lost lover, she returned to herself and learned how deep her heart really was, and what capacity it had to love and be loved.

Chapter 4

# Relationships and the Search for Wholeness

My bounty is as boundless as the sea,
My love as deep. The more I give to thee
The more I have, for both are infinite
*Romeo and Juliet:* Shakespeare

Love can take us to a very deep place within us and the experience of love (and loss) can connect us directly to the divine and to our spiritual path. For many of us, as we have seen, being in a relationship represents part of our soul's journey and our search for wholeness.

It is through relationships that most of the challenges of human life are expressed and exposed. And it is through relationships that we learn many of the lessons we need to learn as part of our spiritual evolution. Love and loving, within a relationship, helps us understand ourselves and become conscious. It is through relationships that we learn about our natures, our hearts, our connection with other people, and all of humanity. Additionally, if we allow ourselves to become vulnerable in relationships, then we have a chance to grow.

There is a deeper side to human life than the external and practical, and love can take us there. As already discussed, love is the nature of the soul so that, like the soul, it is boundless and mysterious. Love calls on us to surrender to a force that is greater than ourselves. Love always calls us to something greater, and, if we do not resist, sooner or later we will enter the same fire that all lovers at some stage have to walk through.

## Descent into The Fire: Love as Initiation

Falling in love, and the experience of love, can be seen as an initiation. The metaphor of fire here is apt, for whether we feel love as a great fire in the chest or as though we are burning with passion, love takes us into the fire, so that we are changed by the encounter with the other. Fire is symbolic of transformation. And all true lovers walk through fire. As already said, love takes us into an extra dimension of our souls so that our current reality is changed.

What love gives us is hope for psychological totality. Being in love reveals our neediness and our vulnerability; when you fall in love you fall into the unknown. The whole idea of 'falling' indicates a descent into a dark place. And 'every dark thing one falls into can be called an initiation'.[15] 'The descent' is a mythological term for the period during and after a powerful event in which one is overwhelmed by a wave from the unconscious.[16] When we fall in love, we fall into something. We do not see things the way we used to. In the tradition of the Romantics, we may pine for our loved one, we may not eat and our sleep is disturbed with dreams of our lover. We feel different, softer, more open and therefore vulnerable.

The notion of a descent forms part of any psychotherapeutic or other process of change. In psychotherapy, for example, symbolic death and rebirth is essential to any process of inner change. To be reborn we have to descend back into the womb of the Great Mother. The goal of the descent is to find a new connection between earth and spirit. Psychologically speaking, it means that new consciousness can only happen after a death or a 'letting go' of the consciousness of the past.

This descent happens also when we fall in love. We lose ourselves as we were and we look to find what we have lost into our lover. We project parts of ourselves we are unaware of into the partner and a process begins. Our normal psychological boundaries are loosened so that we have the opportunity to change and grow, but also become more vulnerable.

Transformation always requires a sacrifice. It requires letting go of who we are, our current reality. We have to drop our defences, and what we currently know, before we walk into the fire. We descend into the dark night of the soul and the unconscious forces containing our own particular complexes are suddenly exposed. In this state, our inner story is activated and we begin to live out of it. We suddenly discover we are needy; or we become aware of a sense of abandonment that has lain asleep within us and is now alive again, which frightens us. We wonder what we will do if our lover ever leaves us. If abandonment is part of our soul story then we carry it in our cells and it makes us cling to matter, to the person, as though our life depends on it.

If the relationship does break up we may imagine we will die, that a part of us will die. Through being at one with our beloved we perceive our isolation in their absence. 'I cannot live without you' become more than words but a living reality to our hearts that fear nothing more than the loss of our loved one.

It is one of the great paradoxes of love and the human condition that the experience of union goes hand in hand with separation. Emily Dickinson writes of the great descent into the fires of love:

> He touched me, so I live to know
> That such a day, permitted so,
> I groped upon his breast –
> It was a boundless place to me
> And silenced, as the awful sea
> Puts minor streams to rest.
> And now I'm different from before
> As if I breathed superior air –

Or brushed a royal gown –
My feet, too, that had wandered so –
My gypsy face–transfigured now –
To tenderer renown.[17]

## Into the Depth: Opening to Love

Being in love and suffering the loss of love, throws us into a deep place. Our hearts are touched and we open ourselves to depths of pain and joy, to profound feeling perhaps never experienced before. Though we are all destined at some stage to have our hearts broken, it is less often understood that this 'break' enables us to 'open' our hearts more. And that this opening is to the divine, to infinite love. In profound vulnerability, a deeper intelligence comes through; we do not generally know about that vulnerability which comes to us, unbidden, in the darkest night of the soul.

I have felt this depth many times. I have welcomed this stranger, usually when I am suffering the most and have stayed with the suffering rather than distracted myself out of it. I have learned that suffering is sometimes so great that it is indeed as though the heart actually breaks. When this happens, in time something new seems to emerge from the depth of our souls, a deeper intelligence that can hold and sustain us if we are willing to trust it and go where it brings us. Something profound happens when we reach this depth; a subtle change and shift in awareness which begins to open up new possibilities, new life.

Experiencing this descent has given me depths and allowed me to learn about compassion. In actual fact, we cannot learn compassion: it is there, to be discovered, like a jewel buried deep in the stone layer of our heart, which has to be cracked open to reveal its treasure. And compassion is where our heart pain is meant to lead us. It is only by having our hearts broken that we die and are reborn into new life. Each time we suffer a death of the heart we have the opportunity to know love, to open our heart chakra even further and to know compassion.

I have above my bed in my soul home by the sea a beautiful bronze plaque bearing the words, 'The heart that loves is always young'. It was given to me by a dear friend after I had suffered a death of the heart when the man I loved and I split up. Desolate and broken hearted, I had spent a few days with this friend at his country retreat and shed many tears, vowing I would now close down and never allow myself to love again. Before I left he took me to his pottery studio and chose this plaque which he placed in my bag as a gift. I have it above my bed as a reminder to myself to keep my heart open.

## The Empowered Heart: Compassion

Maintaining compassion and an open heart is not easy. We learn about compassion through our various religions and through charity, as well as by observing great humanitarians like Ghandi, Mother Theresa and others. But to actually experience it is another thing. And, once experienced, to keep our hearts open and act with compassion in a consistent manner is a very difficult to do.

I had an opening experience when I travelled to Israel some years ago. I was wandering around Jerusalem and had come to the Mount of Olives, a hill on the outskirts of old Jerusalem. Nestled there is a small garden, the garden of Gethsemane where Jesus was said to have endured his 'agony in the garden'. It is a small enclosure, dotted with beautiful old olive trees, knotted and gnarled with age. On the spot where reputedly Jesus wept, a small church has been built with the altar shaped as a tear. As soon as I entered this place I felt something special. I could feel a pain in my heart which I can only describe as a kind of opening to all the suffering of the world. I waited in this little church while a bus load of tourists came and went. I wanted to be alone and when the church door shut I knelt and wept, there alone in the church.

I felt deep love and I felt pain. I felt, it seemed, the suffering of Jesus as he spent his last night in torment, enduring the greatest conflict a human heart is capable of. The next day, as we know, began his Passion culminating in his crucifixion and death. Whether one believes in the existence of Jesus as saviour or not, his myth is symbolic of the inner journey of death and resurrection we all need to go through in order to individuate, to become whole. His story is the story of endurance, love and compassion.

I have never forgotten this experience and I wonder was this when I first became aware of my true soul task. Was it a kind of calling? It was certainly an opening of my heart to compassion and love in the deepest sense, which I have encountered many times since. I have always had a tender heart and felt heart pain and compassion very readily before I ever heard of the heart chakra. As a little girl who would cry easily, particularly at any cruelty inflicted on or pain I perceived in helpless animals, this experience was just a further opening along the way.

Perhaps it was love that took me there. I was then in my early forties and very much in love with the man I considered my longed-for soul mate and life partner. Although this relationship ended some years later, I know without a doubt that this love, and the suffering I endured particularly when we parted, brought me to a deep heart place, deeper than I had ever been before. And though one has a tendency to close down after a love wound, I did not. I could not, because my heart had been opened and, once opened, as long as we remain conscious and are willing to endure or suffer, it can never close again.

## Answering the Call: Taking the Vow

The call to unconditional love is an integral part of an evolving collective consciousness whose time has come. Answering the call, however, demands we embrace our humanity, our emotional wounds and our vulnerability. It also demands that we surrender to the 'other'. In outer weddings, ordinations and other ceremonies, the taking of vows is a symbolic act which transcends the individual. The vow is a vow to the *other*, to God, to another person, to one's work.

The taking of vows is an essential part of individuation. Jung writes of the necessity of this vow as a step to inner wholeness: 'The unrelated human being lacks wholeness, for he cannot achieve wholeness only through the soul, and the soul cannot exist without its other side, which is always found in a "You".' Wholeness is a combination of I and You, and these show themselves to be parts of a transcendent unity, whose nature can only be grasped symbolically, as in the symbols of the *Rotundum*, the rose, the wheel or the *conjunctio solis et lunae* (the mystic marriage of the sun and moon).[18]

A vow to the other is an essential part of our soul's journey to wholeness. Sometimes the vow is to the creative muse, as with some of the great poets and artists like Rilke, whose wedding was an inner marriage to the divine within. It can also be to God as with the great mystics, and it can be to one's calling in life. For others, this call to the divine, to wholeness, is through a lover and soul mate. But ultimately, the vow represents in all human beings a longing for transcendence, for wholeness and it is an affirmation of relationship.

A vow to the other always brings with it fears and anxieties, since we do not know where commitment to this mysterious other might bring us. I still remember that moment when, as a fresh young woman of barely twenty, I walked down the aisle with my father to the man I was to marry. I remember that, as we neared the altar, I had a moment of panic, suddenly terrified of the commitment I was making. I know that I was trembling a little as we reached the end of the aisle.

In a way, the taking of vows is a kind of initiation into the world and represents a commitment to knowing the other, to transcend our individual egos and work towards wholeness and communion. The gradual erosion of rituals in our lives has meant that this taking of vows is less prevalent. We need to value the symbolic aspect of vow taking as a commitment to relationship, in the world, within, and with the other.

## The Inner Marriage

The teachings of spirituality and some elements of Jungian psychology are similar and complementary. Increasingly I have found that a weaving together of elements and teachings from both have informed my life and my work.

In Jungian psychology, the term used to describe the balance of the masculine and the feminine within each individual is 'inner marriage'. The idea of the inner marriage is akin to the inner search for wholeness that is part of every individual's spiritual journey. In a psychological sense, 'inner marriage' means progressing towards individuation in order to become whole within oneself. This is a subject that I will deal with in more detail later in the book, since it involves becoming aware within relationships of one's unconscious processes and projections onto one's partner.

Some people make a distinction between the search for outer love with a partner and the inner marriage. This is a mistake. Many people, furthermore, entertain the idea that in order to pursue a spiritual path it is necessary to be without a partner; that being involved in a relationship is a distraction from pursuing one's inner journey. However, I believe the opposite is true and that it is through relationships that many of us grow closer to our spiritual source, and learn more about ourselves.

Connecting with other people is an essential aspect of how we live our lives. Being engaged in an intimate relationship offers us the opportunity to enter into the depths of our soul, but only if we engage with it consciously. If we do not engage with it consciously, and if we project everything onto our partner, expecting them to fulfil our needs, it may indeed serve to become a distraction from our own inner journey.

In Jungian psychology this searching for and return to wholeness is termed individuation. Jung suggested that this drive to wholeness is inherent to the psyche and is a process of gradual lifetime unfolding. Individuation is a natural process – an inner union that, in essence, is essential to the spiritual well being of every individual. This inner marriage is about the balancing of the masculine and feminine within oneself. Jung also believed that every human being has contra-sexual components; in other words, all of us have masculine and feminine energies, and what every individual seeks (either consciously or unconsciously) is a balance between these two energies, in order to feel complete. Men, for example, have an anima or feminine component, and that impacts on their ability to relate. Women, on the other hand, have an animus or masculine component; this impacts on their creativity.

In addition, both men and women are greatly influenced by parental imagery. For all of us, our first relationships create the template for later relationships – particularly relationships involving love and intimacy. Also, since our mothers and fathers are generally the first male and female in our lives, they make up our inner images of male and female, and so influence our choice of partners later in life.

Outer union with a partner is merely a reflection of our need for inner union. Or, to put it another way, the drive to relate in love is merely the outer manifestation of the universal drive for wholeness and union within. That is the reason why, for so many of us, the urge to love another soul and have a partner is so strong.

From a psychological perspective, moreover, the quality of an outer marriage is dependent on the inner marriage of the two individuals concerned. Relationships are affected by both partners' inner worlds and how they negotiate that world. Inner malaise is projected outwardly into most relationships, thereby complicating them. Many of my clients come to therapy because they are experiencing relationship difficulties. Though all are involved in a process of seeking inner wholeness and harmony, they seek help from me because they believe that if they can get their partner to change then the relationship difficulties will be resolved. Others believe that if they were to meet the right person then the enormous void that they feel within would be filled.

Very early on in the therapy they learn that both the work that needs to be done and the answers to their questions lie within themselves; that there is no point in projecting one's needs and problems onto one's partner and expecting them to change. One must always look within oneself; all change must first take place internally and progress externally.

## Into the Unknown: Love and the Shadow

The journey to wholeness and union through love is also a journey to our interior and, as we saw in the last chapter, to self-knowledge. When we enter this interior we find many things we were not previously aware of; we find the shadow. The shadow is a term used in Jungian psychology to describe all that we repress from consciousness and more. Our shadows not only comprise what we would perceive as our negative aspects, but also our potentialities; what we could be, or could become – qualities that we have not as yet activated.

We generally project shadow parts of ourselves onto our partners and people in our lives. In the positive, this might mean seeing in our partners qualities we would like and have not activated in ourselves, such as joy or optimism. In the negative, we see parts of ourselves we would rather not see, such as selfishness or greed, for example. Recovering the shadow is not always either easy or pleasant. It involves the willingness to dig deep, be honest and suffer. It involves accepting the darker or less pleasant side of our personality.

We all have shadows. As Solzhenitsyn wrote: 'the line dividing good and evil cuts through the heart of every human being. And who is willing to destroy a piece of his own heart?'

The shadow lives in the unconscious. Love loosens the boundaries of the soul so that aspects of our unconscious can be revealed to us. In this sense, love can be understood as an emotional storm that overrides the ego, since we are no longer in charge. This loss of control can present problems in a relationship unless both partners make a concerted effort to remain as conscious of their issues as possible.

Loving opens our vulnerability and throws us into a condition of need. Loving our partner means that we need him or her and are suddenly open to all sorts of vulnerabilities. Supposing he meets someone else? Or suppose he does not love me as much as I love him? What if she grows tired of me? What if he does not call and make another date? What if he gets to know how deeply I feel, will he then leave me? Will the intensity of my need frighten him away? The abandoned child in us will ask all these questions and more.

Lovers are often thrown into a turmoil of conflicting emotions. A million questions will swirl around their hearts and remain unanswered, like love letters left unopened. Lovers can be miserable and uncertain just as they can also be enchanted, happy and full of optimism about the world.

The process of loving causes a rupture of our usual narcissistic defences. We find it hard to maintain our usual reticence and control over our emotions. We are defenceless against the feelings that have erupted from our heart, feelings that seem to have joined with our souls somewhere. Thus, dark and tangled feelings like jealousy and insecurity, that we would rather keep hidden, suddenly emerge out of nowhere. We are appalled at the way our heart behaves in our lover's presence, throwing us into such an emotional turmoil that we may talk too much, act nervously, or say daft things. Or we may be driven to silence as we struggle to find the words that will not come.

Love takes us to an indefinite place where we will encounter the unknown. And being in the unknown strikes fear in our hearts. We do not know what is going to happen next. We are out of control. We are frightened. We present a million questions to the wind and none of them are answered. Does my lover feel the same? Am I good enough for her? Am I what he wants?

And then there is hate and fear. Can we both love and hate someone? The answer is yes. In a curious paradox, whenever a particular emotion is present, so also is its opposite number. Carotenuto suggests that 'the conflict between love and hate is always present in all passionate relationships, even if it remains unconscious. The interaction between these opposites may torment us, but it also constitutes the secret energy source of life.'[19]

Fear and being in love almost always go together and it can be hard to live with both. That being said, love can give meaning to an entire lifetime because it sets up resonances in the deepest abysses of our being. And sometimes it only takes one very deep experience of love to feel this and to be changed forever. In a way, love is eternal and it exists outside of time so that it is like being propelled into the world's soul and invited to take part in the universal currents of life.

## Conflict Between Heart and Soul

The soul loves relationships; they form the basis of its life and how it learns its lessons. However, the heart often has a hard time since it represents what is essentially human about us, and it can be hard to always be on the soul level of things. Most challenges we meet will engage our hearts and our nature at the level of the ego. We will be conflicted, pulled this way and that, and we will sometimes have to endure a great deal of suffering. I have found in love relationships, particularly between soul mates that feel a deep connection, that this discrepancy between soul needs and the human heart is very apparent.

When we meet someone with whom we have a deep connection, who feels like a soul mate, we can experience intense love yet sometimes conflicting emotions. Many soul mates feel that they have somehow 'known' each other before – in another life maybe. They feel a sense of familiarity with that person – a recognition. In the context of the soul's journey, we are destined at some point in time to meet our soul mates in order to fulfil our soul's contract (we will discuss soul contracts in the next chapters). When we meet a soul mate, we can experience *soul* love, a very powerful unconditional kind of love and, on the other hand, be struggling with this love in a real sense. This soul love is often filled with a sense we cannot explain – a sense of old and perhaps unfinished lifetimes together, that we are compelled to complete and live out. Soul love is very powerful and when a love relationship has this 'unfinished' quality it makes for intense relating.

When we are deeply in love with someone we project the beauty of the soul onto them, and may find it hard to see them as they really are. He or she represents at that time everything our soul desires. But there is usually a great division between the soul of a person and their personality. Unless someone is very highly evolved, they will be living out of their personalities. When we seek to become conscious, and to live more genuine and truthful lives, we are working towards living more in tune with our souls. For most of us, this is a constant struggle. Our ego desires tend to want to run the show. Falling in love opens up the chasm and actually offers us the opportunity to live more in tune with our essential selves.

There is a scene in the film *A Room with a View* which addresses this very well. Lucy has just spoken to Cecil and ended their engagement. 'But I love you', replies a despondent Cecil. 'No, you don't, you love me as a possession, like a beautiful painting. You don't love me for who I am, and I want to be myself", responds Lucy, who has sensed that the love the other wild, young man has for her, is real, and true.

This is the beauty and the gift of soul love. It means that one loves the person for who, they really are, in their essence. However, the difficulty comes when we project soul qualities in our lover that they cannot live up to. Then it ceases to be love, but rather a burden we are asking our partners to carry. To feel soul love is to see that person for what their potential is rather than for whom they really are. A person can feel a deep and powerful love for someone who cannot carry the projection and who is, at a personality level, quite far away from it; someone whose human personality does not ride very close to his or her soul potential and who may be unsuitable.

When this happens, we are blinded by the power of whatever soul connection we feel so strongly, making it impossible to see clearly. We will love at a soul level and often be disappointed when our lover does not meet our expectations. Then, such a lover becomes flawed and falls from the pedestal on which he or she has been put. We dress our lovers in the robes of a king and then wonder why he doesn't fit them. Our king falls and fails us, and we hurl our disappointment at him. Our queen, our goddess becomes a normal, mortal woman complete with human flaws and frailties, and we blame her for shattering our image.

And we miss the elevated feelings of loving a king or a goddess.

Conversely, for the partner, such a strong soul projection can be very hard to bear. Sometimes, indeed often, it breaks the fabric of the relationship altogether. This happened with Isabel and James. And for Isabel, it caused an almost constant conflict of the heart.

## Soul Connections

Why are certain people brought together to experience love?

Why do we choose certain partners to accompany us on the love journey but not others? Later in the book I will deal with relationships in much more detail. Here I thought it best to outline the spiritual dimension, and therefore include what reasons the soul might have for joining certain people together.

First, let us remember that the self and the soul embrace not only oneself but also all humanity. The self in the Jungian sense is a psychological entity that encompasses our ego and our sense of higher self. Both are part of the soul. The self embraces an ethic of being socially useful. This means that when we are connected to soul, we transcend ordinary ego consciousness and our own desires; as a result we find it easier to consider others before we consider ourselves. We are motivated to achieve a higher good for all and to give love unconditionally.

In my book, *Reclaiming Father*, I wrote about soul connections, looking at how partners come together from the perspective of the soul and the lessons the soul still needs to learn.[20] From both a Jungian and a spiritual perspective, the soul's journey does not end in one lifetime. Life is a continuum, and our soul's existence may span many embodiments. We choose our embodiments in line with our spiritual challenges. This means that a soul wishing to incarnate will seek out the particular parents and circumstances that will offer it the greatest opportunities for growth.

The soul incarnates into several human lifetimes in order to learn the lessons it needs so that it can grow. We may have chosen to come into this embodiment to deal with such things as loss and separation, for example, or to experience the great pull between freedom and belonging, which complicates our lives when we are in a relationship. Our lives are so arranged that such experiences are presented to us as challenges. We will draw into our lives certain people and experiences so that our souls can learn the lessons they have agreed to learn. We do this quite unconsciously because our soul needs are not always apparent to us. At a personality level we flee from pain and so we may find it hard to face the challenges which, at a soul level, we have agreed to take on.

We enter relationships because, either consciously or unconsciously, we want to grow. This is a natural part of our evolution. Our soul will guide us there if there is a particular experience that we need to learn from. It often takes great courage to accept the challenges that the soul sets up for us. If a man has a secret heart wound, for example, and he is challenged strongly enough to heal it, then usually he will meet and be drawn to a woman with a similar wound. In each other they see mirrored what most needs healing in themselves.

A man's heart may be protecting a great fear of abandonment, something he may have experienced as a child. The woman may also have experienced abandonment. These two souls will come together so as to learn to deal with loss and abandonment. How they relate together will be woven into the unfinished tapestry of their lives. What happens in the relationship and whether each individual soul heals their original wound is left up to them and how willing they are to free their souls and grow.

We think we marry through conscious choice but in reality the ego has little choice when it comes to love. We are drawn to certain people because of our soul needs – and these are usually not apparent to us. Life is so arranged that the unconscious tends to pair partners who share wounds that complement each other and at the same time carry possible healing. Each love affair carries with it the potential for healing wounds that the couple usually mirrors in each other because the psyche always moves towards wholeness.

At the core of falling in love is a vision of wholeness.

## Soul Love and Conflicts of the Heart

Love affairs are never simple and love between two people

can be complex in the extreme. When you are in love, you can find it difficult to hold a perspective. Your lover is everything to you. That this lover might be totally unworthy of you or have severe personality defects simply floats by you. Your friends are careful and treading a fine line between telling you what you want to hear, because they are happy you are happy and truthfulness; they cross their fingers and hope for the best. Everyone is in awe of love. It is something special that occurs spontaneously and occasionally and, like a rainbow, pours forth a special energy that feels like magic. In some ways you could say that falling in love is like being part of an outpouring of divine love. It is sacred and special, and people observing lovers sigh and nod knowingly, maybe remembering a time they felt like that. When love arrives and strikes, reality generally goes out the window!

However, all lovers experience a conflict of the heart at some stage in their relationship. There is always a subtle conflict between oneself and the other. When the novelty and the initial magic wear off, critical eyes replace the rose-tinted spectacles, and negotiation begins. At some level we are disappointed that our lover is not the king or goddess we had believed in. We wonder if we were mistaken and are appalled that at some level he is not 'good enough' and we even hate ourselves for being thus disappointed, and not being able to love him for who he really is. In very intense soul mate relationships, where idealization is great, the soul and the heart with its needs and desires begin to pull apart, revealing gaps and flaws that confuse and dismay us. As previously said, often a person will embody all that their lover's soul wants and yet at a personality level they fail.

The feeling of falling in love at base has nothing to do with literal, causal reality; it has to do with another reality; that of the soul. We fall in love with qualities that person embodies which we have not yet activated in ourselves. To go further, we fall in love with a part of ourselves split off and lodged in the other. When, as is inevitable, the glow of being in love fades and that person is revealed for the human being they are, with all their faults and frailties, we begin to experience the conflict. Our lovers have let us down, they are hole-in-the heart lovers and deserve to be at best changed, or at worst, discarded.

When someone loves intensely, there is a tendency to idealisation. There is great pressure on the lover to be perfect, and when one or other of the lovers idealises, then the other partner feels the strain of this. The more idealisation, the larger the fall; the brighter the persona, the darker the shadow.

When someone is in the grip of soul love, the personality of the lover with all its flaws is not seen and, more importantly, not dealt with. The unfinished story that had magnetised these two souls, so that they may complete a soul contract, is too strong to deny. When this happens, and the pull of the soul is very strong, the relationship is often conflicted and intense, since at a personality level this love is hard to live up to.

We are, as human beings, challenged to love unconditionally, but this we find very difficult because we only know how to love conditionally; we strive to learn though, and loving another person is a vehicle for this. One partner may be much more aware of the soul level of the love affair than the other. Then there is tremendous pain and suffering, as we saw with Isabel, who had placed James in her soul love, but could not reconcile the two parts of her and the split she saw in him.

Sometimes, when a person is spiritually evolved to a degree and has worked on themselves, then their personality may not be far from their souls. They are integrated. Other times, more usually, the personality lags far behind the soul and the lover, tied up with the soul projection, cannot embody it. He or she topples from the pedestal they have been on, or ceases to fit the godly robes they have been dressed in, and falls to earth with a bang.

## Soul Mates

Love between soul mates or twin souls often has an all or nothing characteristic, a 'we can survive anything quality', which means it has the power to transcend boundaries and take you further than you have ever been before – but it can also lead to destruction and intense suffering because most relationships cannot survive the great demands placed on it.

When this sort of energy takes a grip of the relationship usually one of the lovers will feel the burden of the other's projection as too much to carry.

James often said to Isabel that he felt she deserved so much better; that he felt he could not live up to what she had placed in him. 'You love who you want me to be,' he used to say. It used to upset her when he said this.

However, he was right. Most relationships cannot sustain such an intense energetic charge which usually comes from unresolved patterns from past lives lived together and no doubt a sturdy soul contract.

Such a situation lends an intensity and fluctuating quality to the relationship which can make it difficult to endure on a long-term basis. In such a case, a polarisation between the ego and the soul starts to happen. Whilst one partner remains firmly rooted in reality, the other vacillates between heaven and earth or between idealisation and denigration. When in heaven, the lover is wonderful, a cherished soul mate and loved so much; yet when on earth, this same lover is useless, has too many faults, does not meet their needs and so on. It can be very confusing and sets the heart on a swing, oscillating between joy and pain, love and hate, anger and happiness. A soul-mate relationship of this sort often does not survive because the intensity of the emotion fuelled by the soul is too much to bear.

In the following chapters I will deal more with soul connections and soul mates, but in the context of this chapter it is important to understand that all our love affairs and relationships have a meaning for our soul's journey.

\*\*\*

Isabel was totally torn in two. A part of her knew she should expect more from James, and was aware she was being disregarded and occasionally mistreated. She deserved better. But the soul side of her flew with her passion, and she saw James through rose-tinted glasses, excusing his faults on his emotionally barren childhood, his lost father or other cause. He was her soul mate, her lover and eternal friend. In the grip of this soul love, she imagined that her love would cure him, save him, and together they would ride into the sunset.

Isabel herself was dimly aware of this tearing conflict in her heart and towards the end of their relationship wrote:

## The Jewel in The Stone: A Point of No Return

*How can I really explain how I see, shining through the armour and veneer of worldly ties and mistakes – a clear pure soul – so clear, so unattached, a pure soul – I feel you. That is what makes it so hard for me to part from you.*

*I feel you – I know you – you bring me wisdom – but I do not think I can take up the challenge you seem to offer me – which is to detach from you so much.*

*I am so confused at some level deeper that I can't understand, but feel.*

*I want to trust and love but every now and again I fall prey to fears of infidelity and lapsing attention. I fear that you are beginning to pull away and stretch from me in your disillusionment. I fear you may lose yourself in outer activities, perhaps another person; a woman? Idle fears probably but you seem to be at a point of no return.*

> *I feel that we are at a time of change: either you move forward with me–us together – or you will leave me or try and force me to leave the relationship. I do not wish to – I still very firmly believe we can live together in perfect harmony and our relationship has not yet achieved its full potential. Will you let us live? Will you keep us? I love you, my James, my lover, my soul mate. Will you come through the mist, the darkness that surrounds you and us – follow the star, my love – follow the light of the sun that always shines for lovers and shines for us.*

Isabel's pain and confusion almost fragmented her totally. Pulled this way and that, and torn by the intense feelings of love and impending loss, Isabel suffered. Sometimes she feared for her sanity because this kind of situation can make a person feel they are going mad. Isabel frequently felt this as she endured the vacillations of her heart. She wanted to stay with James. She wanted, beyond all else, to make this relationship work. But then, how could she continue in a situation where she was being almost constantly disregarded and intimidated by James' unreasonable and tyrannical behaviour?

Isabel was inclined to sell herself short in intimate relationships. Her tendency to imagine she could heal or save her lovers, would ultimately mean that she would place herself in compromising situations. These were not the compromises and adjustments one makes in relationships to accommodate each partner, but trying to hold the soul connection and love often meant bartering her own integrity. Her wounded Inner Child, perhaps with a fear of abandonment and a great need for love and security, would propel her into trying to placate her lover to stop him from leaving.

She sold her soul for love.

## The Wise Woman and the Little Girl

It was a sunny Saturday morning in early autumn and the streets of central London were already crowded. Shoppers mingled with tourists and since this was the museum area harassed parents with half reluctant children all spilled out of the subway. Rosie consulted her A to Z. It should be here somewhere she thought and headed down a side street, thankfully away from the crowd.

It's strange the things you notice when something important is about to happen. And Rosie was to think back on this afterwards and remark on how she had noticed that the streets were stained in bird shit. A lot of it. Was this an omen? She wondered. Turning left, she consulted the map again and then peered at the piece of paper on which she had written the address the woman had given her when she had phoned last week. It must be down here. As she drew closer, Rosie's courage began to fail her and panicking, wondered should she turn back. She slowed her pace. What on earth was she doing going to talk to a stranger, and a woman at that?

Rosie was twenty-nine and had this year embarked on a psychology course. Though it had not been a requirement, she had volunteered to start Jungian analysis. She was interested in what had come up in the short time she had attended the course and thought of this as a journey. Attractive and feminine in appearance, Rosie was wiry and strong and gave the impression of always being on the go. Small and compact, her restless spirit did not allow her to inhabit her body or stay anywhere for very long. Capable and resourceful, Rosie knew somehow that she was missing something; and that this something was vital to her soul. Though her marriage was reasonably happy and she and her husband shared a conventional middle class life, she was not entirely happy. There had to be more, she thought.

Rosie buttoned her jacket against the chill in the air and lifting her head, a habit she had which indicated determination, she set forth. Within a few minutes she had reached the woman's door. She knocked and found her hand trembled a little.

When I first saw Rosie, I was surprised. From her voice I had thought her taller, bigger maybe. Though articulate and self possessed, the little girl in her was very apparent to me. When she sat down and began to talk this little abandoned child spoke easily. An attractive girl with a tumble of blonde hair and brown eyes in a face that seemed too small to house them, she peered out at me expectantly. With her eyes she asked a thousand questions. Though neat and contained, her small body housed a restless and lost soul. Did I have the answers? Of course not but there was something in the starkness of her vulnerability that made me want to hold her.

I have been seeing my wise-woman (I call her that) for almost three years now. Our journey has taken us closer and closer to each other and to part of myself. I write to ease the pain and the sorrow uncovered by our meetings. I have grown to love this woman fifteen years older than I who seems to see into my soul. Sometimes when the path becomes too painful and full of thorns and obstacles I feel I cannot overcome, she comes and sits by me. She holds me in her heart and waits all the while telling me she is there with me. I write, I read to her, she listens and something precious passes between us. I learn many things.

I learned that I had a hole somewhere in my heart which nothing or no one seemed to fill. I learned I was always searching and that I would continue to search because I did not know what it was I was looking for. I learned that in loving I lose myself and that a long time ago, I suffered greatly at the emptiness I encountered when I expected love. I learned that though I sought it everywhere, I was not skilled in the vocabulary of love so that I would search for it in the wrong places. I learned-too that though strong, I held a very small abandoned little girl inside. Once, my wise-woman told me that I was like an empty ocean and that no matter what she or others gave me it would never fill the great emptiness inside.

Sometimes I would tell her my dreams and with her skill and my help we would unravel them. They were treasures of the soul, she told me and we must always listen to our dreams. I kept a journal and when we did not meet, I would write in it instead. Somehow then, in the emptiness I felt without her, I kept her with me. I would write as though speaking to her. This way, over many, many hours, I talked, she listened and I suffered. I cried a lot and sometimes she too cried especially when we reached places we both knew.

We sailed on wide and sometimes stormy seas and laughed when the boat we were on bought us not to where we had expected it to but to quite a different destination. We opened doors and went down dark corridors following always where my heart led us. Sometimes nothing much seemed to happen but she taught me to follow the ebb and flow of life and explained that there was no map to the soul and that no matter how many roads you travelled you would never arrive at the end. So deep is the mystery of the soul that you cannot ever hope to reach it or understand it. Though it took time, I learned to value this and was glad to be able to live the mystery, no matter where it led me.

And so we went along.

Rosie and I worked together for three years. We worked well, and when I found that for various reasons I had to return to my native country, I was filled with trepidation. How would I break the news to Rosie? Despite her strong self-contained exterior, I knew she had become dependent on me and our work together had long ago entered a deep place. It had crept up on her, this dependency, during the course of our journey together.

I felt pain because I also knew that I loved her and a rupture now would be hard for both of us.

People think that therapists, by virtue of their profession, do not feel, or rather that we are immune from the ravages of our client's pain because we need to keep a distance. But that is not true. Keeping just enough of a distance to be helpful and observing, we, if we allow it are pulled deep into the underworld with our analysands. This must happen if we are to be able to properly empathise. Jung talked a lot about the alchemical process as symbolism for the individuation process that is embarked on in analysis. Both are changed in the encounter. And Rosie had changed me just as I had changed her.

In the three years not only had Rosie grown psychologically, she had also given birth to another baby. And this child's birth had, as in common in childbirth, opened up many new doors and uncovered new, deeper wounds. The birth of her son had catapulted her into a time of pain where she revisited her earliest years, even months. Aware of Rosie's early history, I knew this premature ending with me would take her back to at time when she was prematurely taken from her mother. Maybe like her mother, I suffered greatly at this abandonment I was unwittingly visiting on her. But, trusting in the unconscious and the wisdom of the soul and its journey for both of us, I resolved to tell her as soon as possible. We would have some time to work together on it. At least that was one consolation. And who knows, perhaps this situation had been unconsciously bought about to help Rosie's journey along the way. And who was I to imagine I had the power to alter her destiny or her path.

Three years on and my wise woman is leaving. Like the first day when I noticed the bird shit on the streets, I will always remember the morning she told me. I remember the pattern on the carpet, a navy border with small brown and tan swirls, the shouts of passing children and most of all how it seemed suddenly very cold in the room. I must have gone pale because she asked me if I was all right. I don't remember what I said but she did switch on the electric heater. I remember watching her as she crossed the room and thinking, she's leaving, this can't be true and remember a sinking feeling. She's leaving; it's unthinkable.

She asked me to tell how I felt, that it was really important that I tell her. That when, many years ago her own therapist had left, she, my wise woman had felt as though she had been taken to a cliff and asked to jump. I felt nothing. Try as I might and try as she did over the next few months (three actually) to get it out of me, I felt nothing. I was numb, too numb to feel. But she had long gone before I ever realised that. I don't know if she ever did.

*Dear W, Its Rosie here. Remember Rosie of the poetry and brown eyes! I know it's been some time but I wanted to tell you that I left my husband. It's been a year now and he is getting married to someone else. I'm pleased about this because he needs to be with someone. I'm not so sure about me. I have met a man that I like but I have no interest in marriage. I feel trapped. I realise that any kind of institution or situation brings this up in me.*

*Actually, if the truth were told I'm kind of numb in the love stakes and don't really want a man but again, I feel trapped. Trapped by my situation with my two small children. The baby is going on for three and Jack is nine. They see their father of course but I can't manage alone. And Ed is generous and kind and seems to love the children. As well as this he has money and so I know I'll be all right.*

*Dear Rosie, Of course I remember you, and with great affection!*

*I'm sorry about your divorce but you sound O.K. about it. What puzzles me is your situation with Ed. Do you love him? Or is he merely filling a gap? Are you afraid of the alternative? That is, you alone with the children? Is he convenient at the moment when you are afraid of being alone, or do you really love him as you say you do? Things sound hard for you at the moment so take it easy, one step at a time and try and stay centred.*

*Dear W, Ed and I were married last month. I am very happy. He seems mad about me and has moved in here with me. We are looking around for a new house. He is very good with the children and things are fine except for his family. His mother is being very difficult. She hates me because I took her only son away. Ed was already thirty-five and not married so I guess she thought he's stay with her always. And I've found out that his mother keeps him. What I mean is that Ed gets money from her probably in return for some sort of emotional currency, I don't know. I only know it's not a very healthy situation and Ed doesn't seem to be able to stand up to her.*

*You asked me if I loved him and I can say now that I do. In fact, I'm beginning to realise that if he left or anything happened, I would be totally devastated. We have a lot of laughs together; he shares my sense of humour and can always be relied upon to make us laugh.*

Rosie thought about what W had said and wasn't entirely happy with her letter. Do I love him? What is love anyway she wondered. Is it a feeling, a thought, both? All she knew was that she needed him and could not at this stage envisage a life without him. She knew she needed help with two young children and a life alone was not something she ever wanted. He helped her, was there to pay the bills, moan to in the evenings, help with the children and was a companion. But was he a lover? If she was honest, not really. Ed didn't seem too interested in love making and had a strange relationship with his mother.

In the beginning, when they met, he had seemed infatuated with her and worked hard to gain her love. Born of a rich family he had lived an indulged easy life. But he was a troubled soul and suffered from a kind of existentialist anxiety. Burdened with an overactive and inquisitive mind, he lived almost entirely in his head. Material and physical things both bored and overwhelmed him. It was as though he lived on another planet. He told me once that when he was younger, a therapist had told him he was mad but that he lived in a cell padded by money. In other words, money kept him from feeling his madness.

I guess, really what has happened is that I have taken on almost the entire emotional life of the relationship. In fact, thinking about it, I think I represent his feelings, his heart. He doesn't know his feelings or indeed if he has any, though he tells me he loves me. Not as frequently as he used to. In fact not much at all now.

And lately he has been staying out a lot.

Rosie pressed her lips together and sat down to write. After W left, her journal had become a godsend. Into it she poured her heartache, her confusion and her hopes. She wrote about the loneliness and pain she felt when her wise woman was gone and the trouble she had moving to another therapist. She wrote about the great empty ocean that was her soul and the ache in her heart that nothing or no one, even her children, ever seemed to fill. She wrote about this strange place that she now found herself in; married to a man who couldn't ever give her what she needed because he was the sort who could never be intimate with anyone.

Rosie never tired of writing. She had a whole shelf full of journals and dream books. She kept them all. Sometimes when her heart ached particularly badly, she would review them and scan the most recent of her dreams to see if she could find relief. Writing calmed her, as did nature. It was as though forming the words quietened the feelings or at least made them bearable. It was strange to see the words lie down in an orderly and calm fashion and know that they had come from such a mangled place.

PART THREE

# THE LEARNING HEART

## Chapter 5

# From Spirit to Child: Birth into Being

Our birth is but a sleep and a forgetting,
The soul that rises with us, our life's star
Hath had elsewhere its setting
And cometh from afar
Not in entire forgetfulness,
But training clouds of glory do we come
From God, who is our home.
*Intimations of Immortality:* William Wordsworth

Our inner journey to healing involves going way back into our histories. How we come into being greatly influences how we live our lives and how we are in relationships. Our earliest period functions as a school where we learn how to love and relate to others and ourselves. The journey from spirit to child holds within it the key to understanding the origins of an individual's psychological, as well as spiritual, evolution.

If we want to understand ourselves in relationship and the patterns that underpin the way we relate, we have to be prepared to look within and review our formative years and our earliest experiences. As babies and small children we are closest to our spirit and our essential selves. Our first relationships teach us about life – and about love. It is during our formative years, when we are coming into being, that we lay down the foundations of our later relationships.

Working with pregnancy, childbirth and babies has taken

me to a new level of understanding about the soul, and has greatly enhanced my work with my adult clients. I have always felt privileged to be witness to a new baby's entry into the world. Each birth was a sacred moment that I still treasure. The wisdom and purity of soul is very present at birth, since the newborn has not long left the spirit world and it still carries the divine as a recent memory. You can see this in a newborn baby's eyes.

I have written extensively on the birth experience and more particularly on the formative impact of prenatal life and birth on our lives.[21] Birth and life in the womb are soul experiences that create patterns we carry with us into future life. However, the more I work in this area, the more I believe that, in line with our spiritual challenges, some of these energetic patterns are pre-existing in the unborn child. The incoming soul brings archetypal patterns and potential with him or her, and these are dependent on what it has chosen to learn in this embodiment. Human life offers a soul the greatest chance for growth, as the opportunities to learn are great. The human journey is a difficult one, with many challenges together with many joys.

Each person has a sacred soul contract, which represents an agreement each soul makes before being born. Caroline Myss, author of *Sacred Contracts* writes: 'A sacred contract is an agreement your soul makes before you are born. You promise to do certain things for yourself, for others and for divine purposes. Part of the contract requires that you discover what it is that you are meant to do the divine, in turn, promises to give you the guidance you need through your intuition, dreams, hunches, coincidences, and other indicators.'[22]

As already said, the soul's journey does not end in one lifetime. Life is a continuum, and our soul's existence may span many embodiments. We choose our embodiments in line with our spiritual challenges. This means that a soul wish-

ing to incarnate will seek out the particular parents and circumstances that will offer it the greatest opportunities to fulfil
its soul contract. I will return to look at this more fully later
in this chapter.

### Love and Babies: 'Our Birth is but a Sleep ...'

My work with pregnancy and birth was a spiritual opening
for me in that it revealed and confirmed the ever presence of
the divine in our lives. Unborn souls are close to the divine.
It is possible that they are also closer to knowing their soul's
purpose. There is a story told that on the night before birth
the little unborn soul is carried all over heaven and earth by
an angel of God. It learns all there is to know. The light of
knowing burns brightly in its face. Just before it is put back
into its mother's womb, the light is extinguished, thus the tiny
depression at the base of the infant's nose and peak of its lips.
From birth on, one searches for this feeling of knowing God,
of completion and divine love.[23]

Love is not a problem for babies since we are all born
with the capacity to love. The memory of being part of a great
oneness and love are all close to the child since he or she is still
largely unconscious of the sense of ego awareness. The 'forgetting' that happens to a soul once it incarnates and begins its
human journey is muted in the baby. The memory of infinite
love and oneness gradually fades as the child begins the process of differentiation out of the maternal matrix and forms its
own separate ego and personality. The following story illustrates this very well.

A little girl awaited with great eagerness the birth of her
sibling. Her mother went into hospital to have the baby and
at last the great day came when her little baby brother was
brought home. The little girl, keen to be alone with her new
brother, kept insisting that her parents leave them in a room
together. Her parents, concerned about the possibility that

sibling rivalry might get out of hand, reluctantly agreed but not before they had hooked up the baby intercom so they could hear what was going on, in case of a problem. The little girl thanked them and gravely shut the door. She approached her little brother's cradle and bending low, she said 'Little baby, remind me what God looks like, I'm beginning to forget!'

The divine knowing is there in all of us, however.

## The Myth of ER

Our origins in the divine, our fall, and our endless search to return to something we feel but cannot remember, seem to be part of us. In Plato's *Republic*, there is a detailed description of the stages a soul must go through before incarnating on earth. In the story of ER, a soldier who returns to consciousness after being left for dead on a battlefield, ER finds himself suspended in a state between life and death. Tibetan Buddhists call it a 'bardo' state meaning an in-between place, between heaven and earth. He found himself in a kind of station where souls were passing from one plane to another. Souls that were preparing to incarnate on earth went before three fates: Clotho, who spins the thread of life; Lachesis, who determines its length; and Athropos, who cuts it off. Many lives are then set out before the souls waiting to incarnate and they are advised to choose. There were all sorts of lives of every type. Plato makes it clear that some souls were new but others had lived before and their choices were influenced by their previous lives. After the souls have chosen they are led before the three fates, and their choices and destiny are sealed. Then before entering life on the earth plain they are marched to the Plain of Forgetfulness and required to drink from the River of Un-mindfulness. As they drink, they forget everything that has just transpired.[24]

It makes complete sense that if we knew what was to happen in our lives, we may never make any choices. If you knew, for example, that you had contracted with your soul mate that in order for you to learn the lessons involved in being abandoned, he would leave you after ten years of marriage, then you would never bring yourself to start this relationship! Similarly, would you choose to become involved with someone if you knew beforehand he would cheat and rob you? Or how could you bear to give birth to a child if you knew that some years later she would be killed in a brutal manner?

Since through our sacred contract we are seeking to achieve our divine potential as the fullest expression of our spirit, we are propelled to live and reflect life in particular ways according to our soul's choices. These choices are not usually apparent to us because we are not generally conscious of our soul's sacred contract. Over time, our lives, relationships and experiences may gradually reveal our contract; nonetheless, we do unconsciously carry memories of our soul's code. It becomes easier for us to become conscious of our spiritual tasks when we pay attention to our dreams, our intuition and our inner voice.

Our soul only gradually awakens us to our relationship with the divine. We go through life experiences to become spiritually mature. We have to earn spiritual qualities; they are not handed to us on a plate. To develop the capacity to love unconditionally, for example, we have to raise our consciousness to a level beyond our own basic needs. Like heroes in a mythical journey, we have to struggle to make the right choices and achieve spiritual qualities. We must be initiated, and life offers us many initiations that we are challenged to endure and overcome. Perhaps it is for this reason we need to forget our origins in the divine. If we thought we knew it all there would be no need to struggle, to strive.

We learn lessons by meeting and overcoming life's challenges. Learning forgiveness, for example, is a spiritual quality we need to develop. If we have been let down or abandoned by a lover, learning to forgive him or her will constitute a challenge we will sooner or later have to face.

It took me a long time to reach the stage where I could forgive my former partners for the pain I felt they caused me. When I understood that our life partners tend to be our soul mates, I found it easier to forgive them and I realised that, rather than harbouring resentment, I should be grateful to them for having the courage to fulfil our agreement, our soul's contract, and for helping me meet some of my challenges.

With one man in particular, whom I loved very much, this was the case. I believe we came together so that I could learn to deal with abandonment, principally, and develop the capacity for unconditional love. Our relationship did not work out but loving him and suffering his loss when we broke up opened my heart in a special and very deep way. Now I can look back and thank him and still love him, knowing that something was completed. This does not, of course, diminish the sense of deep hurt I felt at the time. But I believe I would not be writing this book if I had not been driven into exploring the deepest terrain of my own heart.

We are meant to forget our divine origins, and the agreements we made before birth, so that we can live fully and fulfil our soul's contract to the best of our ability. By enduring and overcoming life's obstacles and challenges, we grow. Our initiations are our spiritual tasks of empowerment. If we can manage to think this way about our lives and to believe, furthermore, that we are provided with everything we need to help us fulfil our soul tasks, I believe we can live with less fear, knowing that everything that is meant to come to us will come, and that divine guidance is always present. Taking this attitude helps us to trust that all is in divine order.

**Roots of the Soul**
How far back do we need to go to find the patterns that un-

derpin our lives and determine our relationships? Where do the roots of the soul lie? When I wrote *Songs from the Womb*, it was to highlight the formative impact of our prenatal lives and the birth experience, and to draw attention to the loss of soul many encounter due in large part to the over-medicalisation of modern childbirth. Back then, I thought that birth and prenatal life constituted, in large part, the origins of our experience. The archetypal and spiritual level were there somewhere, but not defined in any way.

At that time I had been preparing women and their partners for childbirth, and had founded an holistic birth centre, where couples were encouraged to have their babies in the most natural, empowering and fulfilling way they could. I learned in those years about the great pain that results when women are prevented from giving birth in the way they feel they want to, and congruent with their instincts, and when their choices are denied them. I learned about the suffering endured by mothers and their babies when the birth experience was not as they expected, and there had been interference in the natural process. Most of all, I came to understand not only the powerful impact on the mother of giving birth, but also the formative nature of both life in the womb and the birth experience on new babies.

I know that at that time, the focus of my attention had been drawn there for a purpose: to help create more soulful birthing conditions for mothers and babies by highlighting the sacred and spiritual dimensions of childbirth.

My work with childbirth led me to further examine the origins of human consciousness, the formative impact of early life, and the nature of the psyche, and I undertook studies and training in psychoanalytic psychotherapy, which resulted some years later in my qualification as a Jungian psychotherapist.

My clinical practice, together with further studies in the fields of consciousness research and pre- and perinatal psychology, suggested not only that birth and prenatal life are formative experiences affecting later life, but that such memories could be recovered. As I continued exploring the roots of human experience, I found my explorations led me increasingly to the spiritual and archetypal dimension of human existence.

If life is a continuum, and the soul or 'spirit' of each person is eternal, what memories might we bring with us into the world? What if, as evidence anecdotal or otherwise seems to suggest, our individual consciousness goes further back than conception? Could the roots of our soul lie beyond what we generally accept as the start of human life? And if so, what kind of memory might we have of a time in spirit when our souls had not yet incarnated?

I found my training inadequate to contain the kind of experiences that were presenting themselves to me. As an evolving therapist, trained in traditional psychoanalytical methods and theories, there was no frame of reference for the material flowing into my consulting room. I sensed something greater was needed, and felt limited by my training thus far. Here were young women afraid to become pregnant and give birth for no reason apparent to us, and men suffering from a sense of disconnection that prevented them from relating, sons living their dead father's unlived lives and women carrying generations of other women's pain. Working with biographical material, as I had been taught, was often not enough to reveal the hidden messages of the soul in these clients' stories.

In one instance a young woman came to see me because she wanted to have a baby. She was happily married and there seemed to be no reason why she could not conceive. However, she was afraid to try. In the course of some sessions we worked through the pain of a former abusive relationship which had resulted in a pregnancy and abortion, but that did not seem to do it. Although travelling back to this time helped her release some of the pain associated with this relationship and lost pregnancy, it did not seem to shift things for her. It was not until I asked her about her family, her mother, grandmother and her female lineage, that we made a startling connection. She told me that her maternal grandmother (whom she had never met) had developed puerperal psychosis and had been incarcerated in a mental institution. She had never recovered and ended her days there.

In this young woman's psyche was a great fear of pregnancy. To her, pregnancy was equated with madness. Unconsciously, she carried her grandmother, together with a story of pregnancy and madness, so that they were indistinguishable. When we made this connection something was lifted and she was able to allow herself, in due course, to conceive a child.

It fascinated me that connections like this could be made with distant and sometimes unknown figures in a family history. It brought it home to me how intrinsically we are all connected, and especially how the history of our family and ancestors still live on in us; how we seem to carry unlived dreams and unlived lives of characters we have never met and who might have died before we were born. How does this all come about? Here is one answer.

## Soul Waves

There seems to be continuity in the soul. This sense of continuity was accepted widely in earlier times and Jung's archetypal theory and Myss' idea of sacred contracts both encompass this notion. The Sufi poet Rumi makes reference to our endless search to release the karmic imprints of our souls:

> We search this world for the great untying
> Of what was wed to us at birth
> And gets undone at dying.

Jung, referring to our archetypal heritage, also wrote that the story of those who have gone before continues to unfold in us. We are born into and inherit our chosen family's history, and the myths of that time. We call this our personal and archetypal heritage. Each child is born with the contours of its life already present in potential. This means that we are born with, and carry, memories of both our ancestry and our future destiny. Our archetypal heritage and our soul's choices will inform how we go on to live our lives.

We are influenced not simply by the archetype per se, but by the archetype as it has been constellated and handed down to us through our ancestry. In this way, a pregnant woman can be informed by generations of pregnant women before her, and influenced by imagery and conditioning from her female lineage. Trans-generational patterns are passed on from parent to child so that a daughter can unconsciously carry her mother's, even her grandmother's wounds, thoughts, expectations, disappointments and pain, and a son can give birth to his father's unlived dreams.

Jung describes it thus:

Man possesses many things which he has never acquired but has inherited from his ancestors. He is not born a 'tabula rasa'; he is merely born unconscious. But he brings with him systems that are organised and ready to function in a specifically human way, and these he owes to millions of years of human development. Just as the migratory and nest-building instincts of birds were never learnt or acquired individually, man brings with him at birth the ground plan of his nature, and not only of his individual nature but of his collective nature. These inherited systems correspond to the human situations that have existed since primeval times: youth and old age, birth and death, sons and daughters, fathers and mothers, mating and so on. I have called this

congenital and pre-existent instinctual model, or
pattern of behaviour, the archetype.[25]

We are all on an archetypal journey, and our soul contract ensures that we meet the right people and experience the right
experiences, in order to fulfil our soul purpose.

## Archetypes as Architects of Our Lives

Archetypes hugely influence us, they inform our thinking and
behaviour and are part of nature and the soul. This soul level
also embraces a social ethic so that we are concerned about
others and humanity in general. In the archetypal domain we
are all interconnected so that what we do influences others.

The archetypal dimension is also the spiritual dimension, our understanding of which helps us approach life phil-
osophically, and enables us to grow beyond the narrow view-
point of our own ego needs and desires. Thinking in spiritual
and archetypal terms helps us not only to heal our painful
past but also to connect with our inner selves. It returns us
to ourselves so that we do the work, rather than expecting
the answers to come from outside us, and expecting others
to heal us.

An appreciation of the soul level helps us transcend our
everyday life and our emotional wounds. Engaging with our
inner selves develops a soul stamina without which we cannot
change direction, engage in healing or take opportunities. It
is only when we release the past that a new part of us can be
born, thereby ensuring our spiritual evolution.

In essence, the archetypal level constitutes the roots of our
experience. Trans-generational patterns are passed on in prenatal life since it is in the womb the archetypes become humanised, and pre-existing trends or patterns begin to be activated.
It is not that we are already primed to live a particular life or
that our future is mapped out for us; it is more that we are

predisposed to experience life a particular way. Our archetypal and psychic inheritance, together with our early life experience, greatly influence us, but need not determine how we go on to live our lives. We always have choice, but we generally need to become aware of our unconscious patterns before we can exercise this choice.

In prenatal life, we learn about life through our mothers. Everything is filtered through her. If she feels loved, secure and happy then her womb will be filled with lovely endorphins, the love hormone. If she feels unhappy, or has persistent anxiety and fear, then the child will feel it too. A child's experiences in the womb will begin to flesh out that child's archetypal heritage, and the child will be marked by that intrauterine experience in such a way that unconsciously will affect the child in later life.

Later, after birth, the child will learn about father, about siblings, about the world, and more about love. In *Reclaiming Father*, I write about how it is through his father that a boy learns how to love a woman.[26] All babies and children learn about human love through their parents and early life experiences.

## Soul Contracts

> Before I formed you in the womb, I knew you
> Before you came to birth I consecrated you
> ### Old Testament Jeremiah cp.1

Before there is a child, there is a soul wishing to incarnate. And in the parents, there is often the thought or the desire for a child, whether this is conscious or not. 'You were still a glint in your father's eye', people often say to a child who asks where they were at a time when they had not yet been conceived. Many of us call our babies to us, but most often I think it is our babies' unborn souls that call to us from some place between the earth and the sky when they decide to in-carnate through us. Each child will have contracted to be born to you and your family as part of its spiritual destiny.

Caroline Myss, author in the field of energy medicine and consciousness, writes in *Sacred Contracts* that your soul con-tract consists of agreements you made before you were born. This includes choosing to be born to parents and into families that will best provide you with the experiences you need to fulfil your agreements. Your sacred contract comes through your particular archetypal constellation or pattern. Linking them with Jung's archetypal theory she suggests that:

> Just as the energies of your chakras work together to provide a map of physical and energy information, the collective body of your archetypes produces a view of the governing forces of your psyche and soul.[27]

Jung believed that all souls are connected in the collective unconscious where the history of all people and the univer-sal currents of life are held. As we saw earlier, archetypes are organising principles that exist in the collective unconscious. Archetypal patterns are in potential in each person and are given shape through life experiences. They operate as dynamic living energy and form part of our psychic heritage. Myss de-scribes them as the architects of our lives.

Functioning in the same way, our individual soul contract influences the people and experiences we draw into our lives, and some of the choices we make. Some souls are destined to meet, for example, and have certain experiences that are meant to further their soul's growth. Knowing that you have a sacred soul contract can help you understand why certain relation-ships and experiences are or have been necessary in your life.

As I have previously said, the archetypal level is the spirit-ual level and contains the roots of the soul. Archetypal patterns awaken in us our own divine potential. They tap into the great flow of the collective and the currents that contain soul contracts. Through them we can begin to access our own histories and the life challenges we have chosen to experience.

Myss sees archetypes as part of each person's spiritual chronology. Since they are ancient, prehistoric and primal in origin, they are trans-biographical and pre-date our own birth. She writes of our archetypal inheritance:

> It comes from our own energy origins in the divine, which is also the source of our sacred contract – the guided plan for our life. We co-create our contract with divine guidance, and it includes many individual agreements – or subcontracts – to meet and work with certain people, in certain places, at certain times.[28]

## A Sense of Essence

Many people wonder what their life purpose is, and would like to have access to their sacred contract. However, such information is not readily available – it is buried deeply in our unconscious. Most of us do not have a conscious memory of our own births, never mind further back. However, many people have been able to recall and relive their birth experiences through hypnotherapy, age regression, and other forms of therapy. Past-life therapy also brings people back to previous lives to connect with whatever archetypal energetic patterns are still influencing their lives now.

Memory can be locked in the cells of the body, as well as the psyche. Releasing these memories can have a powerful transformative effect on the person. Typically, clients move from the past life through the prenatal realm, where energetic patterns expressed in their current life begin to take shape. As I said before, the prenatal realm is a place of learning; it is in the womb that many pre-existing archetypal pre-dispositions begin to take root.

What about earlier? Do we remember anything of the time we were in spirit? There are indications that we have some inkling of existence before we took human form. In prenatal and past-life regressions it has been found that somewhere in the unconscious psyche, there is awareness not simply of birth memory and life in the womb, but also of individual essence, of energies, of emotions and imagery, particularly when the stage or just prior to the stage of conception is recalled. Often this comes through a sense or vision of colours, sounds and/or feelings. In essence there is recall of a spirit state, or a being-ness specific to that individual.

Four years ago, early one morning, I was in a dingy gymnasium in the basement of an apartment block in Puerta Vallarta, Mexico. Minding my own business, and exchanging the briefest of comments with a fellow gymnast on the bicycle next to me, he turned to me suddenly and said, 'Can you feel your essence when you are cycling?' After we both fell about laughing, we got to talk more seriously about one's essence and what it was. Leaving the gymnasium we continued our discussion over breakfast. We both knew that, without being able to describe it, we each have our own unique 'essence'.

We never met again after that particular holiday but it was a moment I remember well and probably the start of some search in me to go to a deeper level in my work. I believe that this essence, when we can connect with it, can tell us something of what our soul purpose is, and sometimes help us understand the tasks we have undertaken in this lifetime. An inkling of our soul's purpose can also help us heal our relationships. Understanding that all our relationships and love affairs contain spiritual lessons we need to learn from can help us heal painful emotional wounds we might carry from them, so that we are empowered rather than crippled by our past.

To recover our essence and our soul contract we generally need to go further back than our normal biography – before birth. It is possible that it is at conception that each person is most whole, complete, full of potential, and more in touch with his or her divine purpose and soul tasks. The incoming soul is as yet untouched by energetic or material influences from its parents. Is there at this time an awareness of the soul's code and purpose? And if so, can we recover it?

I have on occasion regressed my clients into womb life and conception, when it feels appropriate to do so. This is always done within the context of ongoing work, and an established therapeutic relationship. Sometimes we are guided there by the psyche of the client when we seem to be stuck and getting nowhere with regular psychoanalysis of childhood experiences. The unconscious may have come through in a dream or other kind of imagery, and when the indications to go deeper and further back are there, we proceed.

In such regressions, I have had startling results that have produced dramatic changes in the lives of those I regressed. Many people were able to connect with some aspect of their original soul's purpose and a sense of individual essence, which gave meaning to their lives. Sometimes connecting with one's essence, a person's soul tasks and purpose in incarnating into this particular lifetime are revealed or partly revealed. This knowledge can help a person in many ways and unlock hidden aspects of their soul.

\*\*\*

Jenny, a 43-year-old nurse, was burdened with the sense of having to look after others. Though she enjoyed her profession and found it fulfilling, she could never switch off. She never seemed to be able to let herself go and enjoy life. She had friends and a social life but had remained single and unfulfilled in love.

When she came to me first I was struck by her opaqueness. I can only describe it as a sense of layers and packaging!

She was a heavy enough woman but not physically fat. I had a sense of not being able to get at who she really was. Usually I sense energy around my clients and something of their essence typically radiates out, but Jenny was different. She seemed hidden somehow beneath layers of padding. And yet some small spark in her, the one that had propelled her to come to see me, was obviously alive and wanted to be discovered.

Jenny, approaching middle age, dearly wanted to meet a man and have a relationship. However, when anyone came remotely close, she clammed up. Because she was comfortable in the caring role, she generally chose men who needed her but who in turn could not truly give to her. Moreover, she was afraid of full sexual intercourse and had remained a virgin, which also caused a problem in her relationships. When I met her she had not had a relationship for many years. She longed to break out of this cycle and discover what the problem was.

'I can't seem to be able to let my guard down,' she told me. The eldest of three daughters from a rural family, her parents had since died. As the eldest in the family, her mother, who was often sickly, had relied on Jenny to provide the mothering she herself seemed unable to supply. On top of that, the girls were brought up very strictly indeed, particularly when it came to sex and love. Both parents seemed to have an obsession about pregnancy and the fear that one or any of their unmarried daughters might become pregnant. This shameful ethic around sex and the body was responsible for a great deal of shame, neurotic behaviour, and misery in the family.

After some months, Jenny asked me if I would do a birth regression. Her mother was so much part of her that we rarely seemed to be able to move on. It was as though she carried her mother around with her. She would get very upset thinking about her mother and remembering the suffering she perceived her mother had endured. She felt there was something deep down gnawing away at her and she wanted to get to it. Obviously she remembered nothing of her own birth except that her mother had always said that birthing and being pregnant were something she did not enjoy, but simply endured as 'women's work'.

Jenny settled on the couch, and I began the regression. At first all went in the usual fashion and she went back over time into her mother's womb. Then I asked her if she could see herself before she had been conceived. She became very quiet and appeared to be asleep. When I gently asked her where she was, she sighed and said:

'I'm up there, it's a wonderful light feeling. There's lots of sound and colours. I can see colours.'

'What colours can you see?' I asked her.

She became animated and began to shift on the couch. 'Lots of greens and light blues, oh, it's like a rainbow.'
'Where are you, are you there in spirit, can you see or feel your essence?'

I was close to her, taking notes by the couch as I normally do, and looking at her, I saw that a remarkable transformation seemed to have taken place. She seemed light and airy, and I could see the little blue/green light essence of her shining through. Joy, light and love seemed to be radiating from her.

After some time when I asked her if she could see her mother she became quiet again and then began to cry.

'What's the matter'?

'I can see my Mum, she doesn't know I'm here. It's so hard for her.'

'What's hard, what's happening?'

Jenny was so upset we stopped for a while. I asked again if she had a sense of why she had come down. 'Oh yes', she said, a weariness beginning to appear in her voice. 'I have come to help my Mum; she can't go through this alone. She needs help. I am here to help her.'

And with that Jenny was conceived and entered her mother's womb.

Later, when we worked through the material we had uncovered during the birth regression, Jenny remembered what her mother had always told her. That pregnancy and birth was women's work. But she also remembered her mother had hinted at the unpleasant surprise she had had when she discovered she was pregnant with her. As it turned out, Jenny's mother had conceived out of wedlock in a time when this was considered hugely shameful. And Jenny had contracted to help her mother.

Since this contract was buried deep in her unconscious and was later amplified by the reality of her early life as her mother's helper, Jenny was unaware of what imprints she was carrying. She was unaware that she carried responsibility for helping her mother, and that this was lodged in the cells of her body as a memory. Jenny was carrying layers and layers of suffering and responsibility that did not belong to her. Here too maybe had originated her fear of sex. Sexual intercourse can result in a child being conceived. And this was shameful.

\*\*\*

In many cases, regression work reveals an essential truth about a person. In this case what we uncovered helped Jenny to engage with her true nature, her essence. Engaging with this energy within her helped her release some of what she was carrying, and connecting with her colours seemed to give her a sense of place; a sense of home – a place she could always return to when things got hard and on top of her. It gave her a feeling of knowing herself, and it also helped her, in time, release some of the heavy soul bonds that were holding her back.

**Learning from Unborn Souls: a Spiritual Wisdom**

As we saw in Jenny's story, we all come into the world with a soul contract, and this involves being born to certain parents, and having certain lessons we have agreed to learn to further our spiritual evolution. Many souls come in with issues such as how to overcome abandonment, guilt and betrayal, to learn the difference between conditional human love and unconditional divine love, and many others. Still others come in to help their chosen parents learn some lessons. This is an area that fascinates me, particularly with unborn souls that do not make it to birth – babies that do not survive womb life or that die at birth. What might these souls be teaching their mothers? Or what might the short womb life they inhabited have taught them?

I lost two babies in early pregnancy and these experiences no doubt stimulated in me a desire to discover their purpose in my life. In deep inner work, I have connected with these little unborn souls, particularly my little daughter to be; at the time of writing she would now be twelve years old. I know she came in unexpectedly at a time when her father and I were not happy together, and unconsciously I held on to her for some time after I lost her, maybe as a way of not facing the loss or failure of my marriage. In time, through deep soul work, I was able to connect with both my unborn babies' souls, learn why they had come and gone, and let them go.

I consider both these unborn souls as gifts I was given – their presence and loss represented important spiritual lessons I had to learn. These experiences have also guided me to help other women who have lost babies before birth. I know that there is probably no woman alive who conceives and loses a baby, whether by design or accidentally, who ever forgets 'what might have been'. I still remember clearly that early spring morning, looking wistfully at the buds sprouting on the trees and bushes in my garden and thinking my baby never got the chance to grow into fullness. My child had been due in June.

What purpose can there be to losing a child early in pregnancy? All experiences of loss teach us something; however, the loss of what might have been is especially poignant. It is the loss of unfulfilled life and can draw us to heal a hidden, very vulnerable part of ourselves. Healing the loss of an unborn baby involves profound inner work and the courage to dialogue with the little unborn soul so that both mother and baby can understand the soul bond or contract between them. Releasing and letting go can only happen after truly integrating the experience and uncovering the lesson it carried.

\*\*\*

Tara was a lovely young girl: tall, bubbly and energetic. She came to see me because she was having trouble at home. The youngest of four, she still lived with her separated mother, who had a crippling dependence on her. Tara worked and had a boyfriend and would have liked to move on, but her mother's emotional needs always pulled at her so that she felt guilty about even thinking of leaving home. Tara had got pregnant by her boyfriend and had an abortion about six months before she came to see me. Brought up as a Catholic, she was riddled with guilt about this and needed to talk about it. No one knew her secret except myself, her boyfriend and the priest to whom she had been for confession. She was particularly concerned that her mother should never know.

One evening (I shall always remember it because of the way the late evening sun shone with particular brightness through the dirty windows of the rather dingy consulting room I rented at that time in west London), Tara and I began to talk about her unborn baby. By now, she no longer referred to it as 'the abortion' but rather 'the baby'. I was glad of that as I felt instinctively that this little soul needed to be heard. I have always respected the sacred nature of pregnancy and birth. Tara was in tears as she recounted yet again her experience in a day hospital where she had gone to have the abortion.

'Tara,' I cut in, 'why don't you try to talk to the baby? I think she is here, she will listen to you.'

Tara stopped and went quiet. We were both quiet and then it felt as though the light shone more brightly than usual in the room and there was a sense of light, softness and love. It is hard to explain, but it was a presence we both felt without words. Tara then spoke with her unborn child, and the child responded to her. I said nothing, and simply held the sacred space we had created in the room, so that the little soul and Tara could tell each other everything they needed to say. Tara told her what was in her heart, her guilt, her sorrow and her pain. She asked for forgiveness and I do not know what words or thoughts passed between them but when Tara had finished, she radiated a sense of peace and love. Touched by this sacred presence, we were both in tears, but I knew the healing process would now begin in earnest.

Later, Tara told me that her little baby had told her she had come in to help Tara separate from her own mother and be a mother herself; that it was time for her to live her own life and that, it was OK, she would return to her, when Tara was ready.

Tara was not yet ready to become a mother – she had work to do in releasing herself from her mother and her childhood bonds. But her pregnancy had represented an opportunity both to heal herself, and to move on.

Working with Tara in this way confirmed for me yet again the wisdom and presence of unborn souls and the sacred nature of pregnancy. It also tugged at memories I had of my own – memories of being involved in this work over many years, perhaps centuries. Had I been a midwife, a healer, in former times? I think so, because it is never difficult for me to communicate with unborn babies and to help mothers do so.

The importance of this story is that it represented yet another turning point in my work. Tara's experience of communicating directly with the spirit of her unborn child established that healing is always possible at the level of the soul. It confirmed beyond a doubt that unborn souls are part of us, and can lead us to a deeper knowing which we can either receive or reject. There is always a reason, a spiritual lesson to be learned from each experience, so that it is important to listen to the wisdom of unborn souls.

*** 

Communicating with unborn babies is a very important component to healing loss, and it is something I encourage and foster when a woman comes to me for therapy after losing a baby. Many mothers feel guilt when they have lost a child. Often, as in the case of an abortion, the guilt is buried along with other feelings and uncovering the feelings can feel threatening – it can feel like opening a can of worms. However, true healing can only happen when the emotions have been released and expressed. And such women need to feel they are accepted and supported in a non-judgmental way as they process their grief.

My experience with Tara confirmed both the spiritual dimension of pregnancy and the wisdom of unborn souls that is available to all mothers. Helping Tara work through her grief and guilt at having terminated her pregnancy confirmed too that healing between mother and baby is always only a heartbeat away.

This material may seem unrelated and removed from a book which deals with love and relationships. However, we all relate from our past, and some of our patterns in loving will stem directly from the pre- and perinatal period of our lives. Many women and men actively carry scar tissue from their own births and prenatal experiences because, as I have already said, attachment patterns are formed in our earliest years.

## Birth as an Initiation for the Soul

Our births have a huge impact on our lives. To continue the journey into being, the new baby is about to be born, as a soul begins its journey into human life. It is said that when an earth mother rejoices a spirit mother mourns! Being born is a normal biological process, as well as a profound archetypal experience. On an archetypal level we are all primed to be born. We expect it; it is part of life and the human condition. The physical struggle involved in birth is mirrored on many levels and connects us with nature.

Birth is a major learning experience. Although birth itself should not necessarily be considered a trauma, a birth where there has been emotional wounding can hugely impact on the new baby and mother's relationship, which in turn influences that baby's choices and ability to love and be loved later in life. Birth represents a struggle, the incoming soul's first physical initiation into life. A baby has generally to work very hard to be born, and indeed the way a child is born creates a strong energetic and psychological pattern that is carried into later life.

I have already written about the various forms of initiations that represent different ways of being born in today's world. Caesarean section, for example, involves the interruption of a work in progress, or the natural order, and this creates particular energetic patterns.[29] Sometimes, far too often, due to painful and invasive birth practices becoming the norm in modern childbirth, birth can represent the incoming soul's first betrayal of love and trust.

Sometimes birth can be our first love wound

How is the child received? Is it roughly handled, blinded with bright lights or worse, pulled out with iron grips (forceps) on its tender skin so the marks of this violence remain physically for some time and emotionally a lot longer? After being wrenched from its mother, is it then put away in a dark place, alone, separated from the one person who can console it for the pain it has endured in the struggle to be born? Or is it received with tenderness and care, and with full awareness of its delicate sensitivity and placed in warm, loving arms?

The birth experience propels us into a world of uncertainty. We do not know how we will be received and as my previous work demonstrates, we can often be deeply wounded by the manner in which we come into the world. *Songs from the Womb* bears witness to the suffering and trauma inflicted on many due to the over medicalisation of childbirth. Many mothers and their babies suffer deep soul wounds because of a lack of respect for the human soul and the exquisite sensitivity of the new baby.

Birth into an unwelcoming world is the first betrayal of the incarnating soul. It is a betrayal of love. It is a primal wound, and one that is hardest to reach because of its deep nature. Soul wounds inflicted at a very early stage in one's life are always the hardest to heal because they are so deeply embedded in the unconscious, it can be hard to find them.

That being said, it is important not to overly define and limit soul wounds. When we understand birth as an initiation and spiritual task of empowerment, it both heals and frees us. Seen from the perspective of the soul, our struggles can refine our purpose. Rosie in our previous story had a difficult birth and we saw how this predisposed her to experience life (and love) in a particular way. We could say one of her soul tasks was to learn how to overcome abandonment and the betrayal of love. We could also say that her birth experience represented her first challenge. Birth trauma may be part of a person's wounding but will rarely be the fulcrum of it.

One thing we can say is that Rosie's initiation into the world was a difficult one that activated energetic patterns within her, and set in motion her soul contract. Separated from her mother after birth, and spending many weeks in an incubator, love was not something she encountered or could ever then count on. The primal experience of physical intimacy was also denied her so that perhaps she did not know how to be intimate. Her later love experiences with men further opened her initial heart wound so that, in time, she ceased to believe that love existed as other than an ideal which she relegated to her dreams and fantasies.

## Birth and the Human Energy System

The birth experience also has an impact at a spiritual level, and the manner of birth will have a resonance in a person's energetic system. Every human (and living thing) is known to have an 'aura' – an energy field. Additionally, there are central energy centres known as chakras, which each person possesses. Myss contends that the chakra system is, in actual fact, an archetypal depiction of individual maturation through seven distinct stages.

The first or root chakra is about our birth into this world. In spiritual empowerment terms, the root chakra represents tribal power: birth into our family of origin.[30] It represents group archetypal identity. We are interconnected with all of life and with one another.

The root chakra rules the base of the spine, spinal column, rectum, legs, bones, feet and the immune system. It is the foundation of emotional and mental health. From a psychological perspective this is why it is said that we need a loving, stable and emotionally sound beginning in order to function well in the outer world and later life. Emotional and psychological stability originate in the family unit and early social environment. To put it another way, love is something the new being needs in order to not simply survive, but to thrive.

People who have had difficult birth experiences can have root chakra imbalances. These are expressed energetically as not being adequately earthed – not being well grounded. Psychologically this could mean not quite feeling connected to others, finding it hard to adapt to some of the demands inherent to living, and sometimes behaving in an inappropriate manner. There may also be fears relating to physical survival, and emotional and physical security. People who have had difficult birth experiences often have fears relating to their physical well being and their ability to overcome adversity.

First chakra energy has trouble interpreting things symbolically: it takes things at face value. In adults it presents as a tendency to be very concrete and literal about life and a difficulty in seeing the bigger picture. Those with root chakra imbalances will be very focused on physical and emotional security, and often find it hard to trust in the world, since they can be dominated by fear of not having what they need to live life.

Rosie, for example, worried that she would not be able to manage her life when things got difficult. At a fundamental level she felt herself without the inner resources necessary to live life. She constantly sought security through the men she chose, who she imagined could support her financially and provide for her.

The physical act of birth can affect the balance of the chakras. The crown, or top chakra, of the baby is open at birth, since physically the baby's soft skull bones have not yet closed so that they can be compressed in order for the baby to pass down through the birth canal. The crown of a baby's head is called the fontanel and is very sensitive. The fontanel, through which you can see the baby's pulse, is still partly open at birth and for some time afterwards. It gradually closes over time but it represents, I believe, the baby's connection with the spirit.

Some years ago at a conference in Russia I learned with great excitement that in old people the crown chakra and the fontanel begins to open again just before death. It is said to be the way for the spirit to exit the body! Hearing this filled me with awe and also with trepidation since I know that frequently the baby is born through violent means, often involving tremendous force to its head, surely traumatising the crown chakra so that a further closing happens in all of the other energy centres. If the crown chakra closes through trauma then generally all further energy centres follow suit. A violent or invasive birth will need healing at an energetic level and there are, thankfully, many therapists now who specialise in healing birth trauma.

What happens to the little soul's capacity and memory of love? I believe that if the baby is received in a way that is not conducive to making him/her feel secure in this new, uncertain and perhaps fearful world, then he/she begins to subtly close down or something latent in him/her may not grow. As I said, a primal love wound can originate at birth, and set up resonances in later life and love relationships.

## Birth and Separation

Birth is also significant as the first physical and emotional experience of separation. At birth, we are separated from our mothers and womb life, thereby activating what psychologists term 'separation anxiety'. However, I do not believe birth to be our primary separation. At a soul level, we already hold a memory of wholeness and of having lost this wholeness. The added significance of birth is that it triggers the original separation of our soul and oneness, when we lost something so integral to our spiritual well being that we spend our lives trying to return to the state of union we once had.

As we saw in the chapter on love and the soul, we are always inwardly driven to find what we lack, and falling in love fuels the illusion that we will find it.

From a psychological perspective, however, our original love affair is with our mothers, so that what happens before, at, and immediately after birth, in relation to our closeness to her, is important as it sets down or activates dormant emotional patterns. We know that babies and mothers find separation very painful, and modern thinking has accepted that separation of mother and baby in the first formative hours and days after birth is not conducive to the bonding process. Bonding is necessary for the healthy emotional development of the child and his or her ability to will form healthy attachments later in life. Crucial bonding and attachment patterns are forged during pregnancy and birth, when the child is coming into being.

How does our birth experience then prepare us for love and influence where we will go to find it? Our birth experience will certainly affect the path we will take to return to this place of wholeness, of soul. Every time we find ourselves involved in a love experience we are re-enacting the lost wholeness that goes back to our earliest moments. To our love affairs we undoubtedly bring moments of memory of our first separation. We are not aware we do this; it is an unconscious impulse created by our need for healing. The soul hates to be fragmented, and always seeks wholeness, and trauma of any kind tends to fragment us.

In an earlier chapter I wrote about how difficult and complex the reception of love is; how somehow deep inside us, we find it hard to be loved, to receive love. I feel sure that our modern way of life and of birth has contributed to this difficulty because negative or painful life experiences can damage our self-esteem and contribute to our sense of unworthiness.

Our first relationship is with our mothers and fathers, and this relationship becomes the template for all future relationships, most particularly intimate ones. The heart is learning all this time about love. People that feel loved glow, and are generally able to give and receive love more easily than those who feel intrinsically unloved. As I said, babies are naturally primed to love and be loved. If the outer world responds to the new human being, the natural opening of the heart will remain open for life, and the corresponding power becomes an integrated part of the psyche. Others will have to work at it.

## Chapter 6

# Days of Becoming

Avoid contributing material to the drama that is always stretched taut between parents and children; it uses much of the children's energy and consumes the love of their elders, which is effective and warming even if it does not comprehend. Ask no advice from them and count upon no understanding; but believe in a love that is being stored up for you like an inheritance and trust that in this love there is a strength and a blessing, out beyond which you do not have to step in order to go very far!

*Letters to a Young Poet:* Rilke

Our early life holds the key to understanding the way we relate and the kind of relationships we have because we are always marked by our childhood experiences. As we saw earlier, our first relationship holds a template for all future relating because attachment patterns are laid down in prenatal life, infancy and childhood. Early days are days of becoming, so that we are simply–we are learning to become who we will be. Through relating to our parents and/or siblings we are learning what love and relationships are all about and we build the foundations of our life.

There is something incredibly beautiful about coming into being; about creation and the various stages involved. The act of creation is a mystery unfolding. It is a mystery which we are witness to every day, in nature, the arts, children and even our own hearts. Anyone who has had children will remember the incredible miracle of birth, of the first smile and of watching the child take its first steps unaided. First words are treasured, as are, in some cases, the baby teeth grown and shed with varying degrees of discomfort. I am one of those mothers in whose dressing-table drawers can be found small envelopes yellow with age, containing random baby teeth of my children.

Most mothers will remember the feeling of awe they felt when they first see their babies, freshly emerged from the womb. I remember lying all day on my side in bed facing the little cot where my new son (and first child) had been placed after being born. I stared and stared again, marvelling at his tiny, perfect hands, five fingers on each. I wondered how it could be that I could produce from inside my body this perfect little human being, and marvelled at the power of nature that had helped him grow, step by step, into this little baby boy. I wondered then what I had done to receive such a gift. I felt blessed as I did on each occasion I gave birth to my children.

If we are open to it, there are miracles of creation and nature every day that we can marvel at. It is also a great privilege to be at the birth of a new soul, and in my capacity as birth teacher, I have attended many births. There is something so sacred about the labouring to bring a new soul to the world that it behoves all of us involved in the process, in whatever capacity, to stand in awe of this power, this act of creation.

**A Womb with a View**
> I am not yet born; rehearse me
> In the parts I must play
> from *'Prayer before Birth'*: Louis McNiece

The drama that Rilke so beautifully suggests is 'stretched taut between parents and children' is very real. It is the start of the play, the start of the story that the child, when it emerges from the womb, will begin to live out of. Life in the womb and birth are the rehearsals for the life that is to come. As Jung suggests, 'man brings with him at birth the ground plan of his nature' so that by the time the new child has emerged from the womb, it already has a story to tell and many experiences behind it. They will have experienced good and bad, love and pain and a great many other emotions.

As I said earlier, pre- and perinatal psychology, consciousness research and observational studies confirm that both life in the womb and the birth experience are formative. The unborn baby is not merely a developing biological organism but a sophisticated evolving human being of immense sensitivity and capability. The child in the womb has been shown to be capable of learning, memorising, dreaming and even socialising! Studies have found that unborn babies have innate personalities, as well as likes and dislikes, and that there is continuity of behaviour in post-natal life. The sum of this work indicates that unborn babies are 'conscious' and profoundly affected by their womb-life experiences.

Since life in the womb is where the archetypes and our soul contract begin to be activated, it is worth referring to material I have covered in earlier books. In the womb, unborn babies begin their journey into embodiment with the parents they have chosen while in spirit form. It is important to note that at this time the unborn child already begins to take part in the family drama, whatever that may be.

Though it used to be thought that life in the womb was idyllic, where we experienced a kind of cosmic unity abruptly severed by birth, this is not necessarily so. Babies can suffer in the womb, and frequently do. However, because life in the womb is a kind of rehearsal for later life with its ups and downs, this is not always a bad thing. A child learns in the womb, most particularly through its mother, so depending on how she feels during her pregnancy, the child can internalise feelings of love or anxiety, and so on. Unborn babies react to changes in their womb environment whether as a result of the mother's emotional state, or as a result of substances ingested directly by her. Babies also have reactions to intrusive medical procedures and chemicals introduced into the womb.

Unborn babies are intimately aware of their mothers. They are inextricably linked, as observed by English paediatrician D.W. Winnicott who observed that there are no babies, only mothers and babies. For nine long months as the baby grows inside its mother, the baby grows used to her frequency. The child learns its mother's heart song, her rhythm, and responds accordingly. By the time that child is born, it will know its mother in a way that it will know no one else. The baby has resonated to her vibration and tunes in to her – the child has to do that in order to survive.

An unborn baby responds to its mother's moods, feelings and thoughts as well as to her physical space. A baby feels and experiences the womb space with its histories and its energies. Most babies will seek a womb with a view and often receive a dusty answer, for they will inhabit a womb space that will have its own particular brand of nuances and echoes from the past. Perhaps this womb has already housed a sibling, and her song still resonates inside its walls. Perhaps this womb has suffered previous death, and so sadness permeates its cells. In *Songs from the Womb* I wrote about a baby who grew inside her mother in an atmosphere of fear, created by previous deaths. This early conditioning stayed with her so that as an adult she was 'drawn towards death'.[31]

Perhaps the most important point here is that unborn babies absorb parental expectations, and just as children are destined to live out their parents' unlived lives, babies in the womb are marked by their parents' thoughts and feelings. Spirit permeates matter to create new life, and the womb is a place where psyche is given form. This form we then take with us out into the world.

If, for example, a mother wants her unborn baby to be a boy, she wishes this all though her pregnancy. She has expectations about what this boy will become and her unborn baby will be aware of this. If her baby is, in fact, a girl, she may be amused, upset, or confused by this expectation. She will be affected, albeit unconsciously so.

Sheila first came to see me because she had some difficulty with her sexual orientation. In the course of our work together we uncovered, through birth regression, that her parents had conceived her with the thought, 'let's try for a boy'. Parents of three girls, they wanted their fourth child to be a boy. Sheila's confusion regarding her sexual identity originated in the womb. She was a woman but her womb experience taught her that she should have been a boy!

Often parents have ideas as to what their child will become: a great artist, a musician and whatever. These expectations are part of the drama stretched between parents and children that already begins to unfold once the child is conceived. Children can carry these expectations well into adult life and not know what hampers or pulls at them so they never feel content in what or who they are.

The teenage girl who trudges home from her music lesson with her violin under her arm may never understand why she lacks enthusiasm, and why her heart does not sing when she plays. Similarly, the 35-year-old accountant, who has grown used to the dull ache he feels inside every time he gets up to go to work, may never ask himself if this is what he really wants. Somewhere deep inside he will have a sense that this is what was expected of him, just as the teenage girl wants Mummy, who always wanted to play the violin but never did, to be happy.

The womb is a child's first school. Unborn babies learn in the womb. This knowledge has encouraged prospective parents to communicate with their unborn babies through massage, touch, sound and even thought. Mothers know that thinking in a positive, loving way about their babies produces a sense of harmony that the child feels and enjoys. Many mothers and indeed fathers will talk to their unborn babies. I knew one father who every evening read poetry to his little unborn daughter.

Communication between unborn babies and their parents is not something new. As we saw in the last chapter, the soul of the child can also communicate with their parent's soul. This can happen in many ways; sometimes the child will come through in dreams the mother or father might have before the child appears.

So what are parents communicating to their unborn babies? They are communicating their dreams, their fantasies and their expectations. They are also communicating, through their relationship with each other, about love. If a pregnant mother feels loved and nurtured by her partner then her womb will be infused with endorphins, the love hormone. The baby will bathe in this sunshine, and feel warm and happy. If the mother feels hurt, abused or abandoned by the father of her child, then this too will be transmitted to the unborn baby because her womb will be filled with anxious, dark and tangled feelings.

Ample research indicates that pregnant mothers with supportive partnerships generally have better births and a more harmonious early relationship with their babies. The support a father offers before birth is like a nest. The father, supporting and holding the mother and baby safe, represents the outside of the nest that has harder, thicker twigs that hold fast to the tree. In this way the mother can relax, knowing things are taken care of in the outside world, leaving her to her task of growing and nurturing the baby in the feathery softness of the inner nest. If this inner security is missing, the mother will feel anxious.

## Learning about Love: Early Days

How do we learn about human love? We arrive into the world with an innate capacity for love. How the child is received into the world, however, will create a lasting impression. And the new soul, fresh from its sojourn in spirit where love is unconditional, may be in for a rude awakening.

Whilst it is still in the womb, the child will be totally dependent on its mother, whereas after birth it will be open to various other influences. It will begin to experience what human life is, the colour and taste of love or the lack of it, hunger and the gratification of that hunger. It will experience lack and need since its immediate basic physical needs will not be met in the same way as they were in the womb; loss, impatience and a myriad of other feelings and physical sensations.

It is well established that the basis of emotional and mental health is rooted in infancy and early childhood. From a psychological perspective this is why it is said that we need a loving, stable and emotionally sound beginning in order to function well in the outer world and later life. The attachment patterns we form in early life stay with us, and are generally re-enacted in all later relationships, most especially intimate ones. A person's ability to allow and enjoy intimacy is based on how he or she has experienced his or her first love object, his or her mother.

A sense of being loved is fundamental to our emotional health as human beings. Paediatricians and psychiatrists, such as John Bowlby back in the last century, found that babies die if they are not loved. He studied babies and children in nurseries, hospitals and orphanages: institutionalised children. Babies and children separated from their mothers suffered a great deal. Though physically cared for, some of these infants pined, as though somehow they had lost the will to live. What these babies suffered from was described as 'failure to thrive', which really meant collapsing due to a lack of love.

Bowlby's work, and those of others such as psychoanalysts

Donald Winnicott, Daniel Stern and the Object Relations theorists of the last century, all established that emotional life is a crucial component in our make up and, further, that emotional neglect affects our development and well being. All psychologists highlight the importance of early bonding between mother and child, together with a positive holding environment and the central emotional presence of the mother, to the future development of that child. This means that in effect it is the mother who enables her baby to 'come into being' through interaction with her.

Winnicott, who was also a paediatrician, believed in the need to avoid interference in the natural process of mother and baby bonding, and although he did not develop this idea, it is clear from his writings that he believed that fostering the natural process was to be encouraged. He believed, moreover, that every woman was innately equipped with the ability to be a good enough mother and thus provide the right environment or medium within which her baby could grow. He thought that babies are born with certain ego facilities, but that these are disorganised, and relied on the mother's capacities to provide the right environment in order to develop in an organised way. In other words, the mother, by virtue of her abilities to be there and perform certain tasks, enables her baby to come into being.

This ego organisation happens through the workings of what Winnicott termed Primary Maternal Preoccupation, in which the pregnant mother begins a process of internal change, which continues after the birth, and which means she can adequately identify with her baby. It is by this mechanism that a mother learns to do what is best for her baby, or to give meaning to her baby's actions. In this way, by her constant and consistent responses, she enables a relationship to take place out of which the baby gradually forms a sense of me/not me. Thus:

> From my point of view the mental health of the
> individual is being laid down from the very beginning
> by the mother who provides what I have called a
> facilitating environment, that is to say one in which
> the infant's natural growth processes and interactions
> with the environment can evolve according to the
> inherited pattern of the individual.[32]

In the psychoanalyst Daniel Stern's model, the sharing of
experiences is crucially important to the healthy development
of the baby. Mother must be available to enter into her baby's
experiences, in order to validate them as it were. If there is lack
of attunement (or mirroring) by the mother to the infant's experiences, such as in the case of a depressed or over-identified
mother (who cannot see her child as separate to herself), then
the infant will react by developing a compliant or false self,
as opposed to a true sense of self. The mother's own needs,
thoughts and preoccupations will impinge upon her infant's
experience, because she remains unavailable then to enter into
those of her baby, and to share them. This results in loss of creative development for the baby.

All this psychological theory is based on the simple fact that
as we are coming into being, we rely heavily on our parents to
provide for us an environment in which we can develop. It also
means that we are affected by our primal and early experiences
in such a way that we form patterns out of which we live. This is
especially so in relationships. If we have never experienced true
bonding, or the sense of being loved and held as an infant, then
we will develop reactive patterns to this lack, and may find it
hard to establish secure attachments later in life. Our loving will
be laced with fears of abandonment, and our sense of lack may be
internalised as an unworthiness we may not even realise we hold.
We will tend to recreate our original wounds and go looking for
love in places we are unlikely to find it.

Early experiences hold an emotional charge that can be so unconscious we only become aware of them when they are activated in later life and relationships.

We all know that the presence of loving parents and a secure and happy infancy and childhood are not givens, and that many of us do not experience them. What we need to remember, simply, is that we were learning – that our early life experiences form us and create emotional patterns that we recreate in our adult relationships. Whether we choose to be crippled by our past or be empowered by it – the choice is ours.

So early days are always days of becoming, when we will begin to learn the life lessons we have chosen for our spiritual evolution. If we have chosen to come into this life to learn how to deal with neglect or abandonment, for example, our first challenge may be to overcome an emotionally stark infancy and childhood, where love was in short supply; or we may, for any number of reasons, have to endure a lengthy separation from our mother at a time when we need her most.

Alan, who you will meet later in the book, experienced abandonment early in life. Since he was a sickly child he was frequently taken from his mother and placed in hospital, sometimes for long periods of time. This little boy, at the age of five, used to wait long hours, days and weeks that turned into months, to be taken home again. With only the words 'you'll be home soon' to hold to his heart, little Alan sat and waited, and pined. He watched painfully as other little children on the ward would be taken home, and wondered when it would be his turn.

Alan carried this abandonment in the cells of his body, so that as a handsome adult man, who had no trouble attracting admiring women, he found it hard, impossible even, to form lasting attachments. Any relationship that went beneath the surface and touched his heart would awaken this early pain, and would make him run. To love, to allow his heart to open again, would mean reliving a pain he felt would be too much to handle. And yet, it is only by going deeply into his heart and enduring the suffering again that he could be healed. A part of him knew this but it takes a huge leap of faith to go to that place in oneself and trust that we will survive and overcome such trials.

And Rosie. Rosie who had been torn from her mother's womb when she had only been there seven months, and was then placed in an incubator, never knew what bonding was, let alone intimacy. Rosie carried that sense of abandonment deep within her, so that all future attachments were laced with fear and insecurity. Abandoned at birth, Rosie never saw herself reflected positively in her mother's eyes. When a mother cannot or is not present to receive and love her child at and after birth, the child is wounded and pines inwardly for this love. To be loved, and to have that love reflected back, is a primal need, without which we suffer. Lacking this primary love experience, such a child can spend the rest of her life looking for that reflection and, as a woman, may imagine she sees it in every lover she encounters.

## Humanising the Archetypes of Mother and Father

Mother and father are basic and primeval archetypal figures. A child is not born as was once thought a 'tabula rasa', a blank slate ready to be imprinted on; the child is born knowing. The child knows about many things.[33] He knows to expect that there will be a mother and father and other guides to help him make his way in life. He will have a sense of these things because his archetypal heritage ensures that when a child is born, as Jung says, he brings with him the ground plan of his nature.

Even if there is no father present, for example, the child will have some kind of inner knowing about fathers and he will feel a lack. He may not be aware of what is lacking, but unconsciously he will try and find ways to fill it. He will draw on other things and people to clothe a skeleton father.[34] You could say that the archetype is a skeleton waiting to be given flesh. An archetype is drawn into human life and activated through experience. In other words, life experience clothes and gives form to the archetype. In this way the father archetype, for example, is humanised through the personal father the child experiences. So the child learns about the father, he learns what this dim or indistinct feeling of father is through his experience of relating to his own father. This is what we mean when we talk about humanising the archetype.

All of us need to have the archetype of the mother and the father humanised and embodied in our own parents in order to feel our way into life as secure human beings. This is very important. The less a mother or father is 'present' to give us this experience of being parented, the harder it is for us to find our way as human beings. In essence, it will mean we lack guidance, and have to learn basic life skills the hard way – by trial and error.

Additionally, accepting that birth is a soul experience means being mindful that the soul of the child is already very aware. The unborn baby will, in line with the soul contract, have chosen his parents as the ones most likely to offer it the conditions necessary to fulfil it. The child will not only seek out a mother but it will also seek out a father.[35] These images are archetypally imprinted in the psyche of the child, therefore the father's role in the process of the child's coming into being is extremely important, like the mother's.

## Masculine And Feminine Made Real

Parents also humanise the archetype of the masculine and the feminine for their children. This means that a child's parents make real that child's idea of what male and female is.

A child's healthy psychological development involves identification with parental figures. A girl needs to identify with her mother to gain access to her femininity, to clothe her bones and draw her female soul into the world. A boy needs his father to fully incarnate as a man. If his father is absent, then the boy will use, as a reference point, other male figures and he will draw on the dim memories of his grandfather and great-grandfather to give flesh to his indigenous maleness. He will also draw, as a matter of course, on his mother's animus or male side. But he will have a father hunger.

The same also happens with girls. If a young girl loses her mother early in life she will draw on other female figures as mother substitutes. She will also be influenced by her father's inner feminine, but she will have a mother hunger. This mother hunger will drive many of her actions and, unconsciously, influence her life in many ways. A mother hunger will lace her adult relationships with fears of abandonment and a sense of insecurity because, at base, an un-mothered child seeks mothering.

A child needs guidance. An incoming soul needs and seeks out parents to guide it on its journey. Without these flesh and blood human figures as role models a child will have to rely on remoter parental substitutes, and internal parental imagery. Since mother and father are the child's first experience of male and female they will therefore act as internal models of what being a female and being a male is. This image, in turn, will guide them later in life in their search for a sexual partner, and love. Suffice to say at this stage that parental models and early life experience influence greatly the kind of partners we choose, and the kind of lovers we make.

We could say that our early life is a preparation for later love relationships.

## Animus and Anima: Inner Guides

The archetype of the animus and the anima, the contra-sexual aspects in women and men respectively, are profoundly important since they are the main guides to forming love relationships.

A boy learns through his mother and other female figures in his childhood what a female is, and this becomes his inner image of the feminine; a girl learns through her father and other male figures in her early life what a male is, thus forming her inner image of the masculine. We are also influenced unconsciously by the collective images we individually hold of the masculine and feminine.

These inner images have an importance in two ways: not only do they guide us in our choice of partner and behaviour towards the opposite sex, they also – since a part of them belongs to the collective unconscious – form a bridge between inner and outer reality, the personal and impersonal, the conscious and unconscious. That is why when I am working with a man in my capacity as a therapist I am relating in large part to his anima since this is his link with his inner life. In the same way, as a woman, I constantly have to negotiate with my inner man, my animus, because he is my guide in understanding my unconscious.

These inner personalities behave in ways compensatory to the outer personality, and exhibit characteristics that are lacking in the outer, manifest personality. In a man, these are feminine characteristics; in a woman, masculine. Both masculine and feminine are normally present to a certain degree in everyone and, as I have said before, they are not gender related – they should be thought of as universal energies present in every human being.

Nonetheless, both these archetypes are very important and seminal to our development as men and women, and how they have been humanised for us will depend on our parents. The animus or inner masculine is responsible for our creativity and more specifically, our ability to bring that creativity to life. Emma Jung, in her book, *Animus and Anima*, says of the animus:

> If a woman does not adequately meet the demand for consciousness or intellectual activity, the animus becomes autonomous and negative and works destructively on the individual herself and in her relations to other people. This fact can be explained

as follows: if the possibility of spiritual functioning is not taken up by the conscious mind, the psychic energy intended for it falls into the unconscious and there activates the archetype of the animus.[36]

Jung suggests here that the animus represents the spiritual aspect of the psyche. Acting as a counterpart to our instinctual nature, a certain amount of animus or 'spiritual' energy is necessary in order to become conscious. Ego consciousness involves a degree of differentiation from nature. If we did not become conscious we would be unable to function in the world, remaining, instead, fused with our instincts. In plain English, ego consciousness means developing one's mental capabilities and the ability to see the bigger picture, so we are not acting purely instinctively.

Developing the animus is important as a counterpart to the feminine as it helps us gain perspective. This balance is important so that we do not get overcome by feelings. Jung suggests that the animus represents clarity of insight and the ability to focus. My own interpretation of this is that the animus has to do with the ability to be self-reflective. When we are led too much by the anima, we are caught up in our emotions and we cannot think straight. If, on the other hand, we are connected to our feelings and also able to enlist our mind, then we are in balance, we are acting with a sense of clarity and purpose. Often, however, there is confusion in us, caused by our emotions, and we lose that reflective ability.

The animus is responsible for the activation of creativity in our lives. In essence, human beings need both emotional and mental capabilities. If, as women, we connect with a positive animus, then we are able to act with clarity and focus. We are able to use our minds to sort out our feelings and make sense of them. We are also able to give birth to our creative endeavours because we will have thought them through and made the necessary moves.

Developing the anima, which is more to do with relating, is just as important because, in a man, the anima represents everything to do with relationship; his relationship to himself, the world of love and emotions – how he relates in general. The anima, in contrast to the animus, is always about relating, and in a man is usually about relating to a woman. This woman can be an inner woman (his anima) or an outer, real woman.

The anima figure, however, is characterised by the fact that all of its forms are at the same time forms of relationship. Even if the anima appears as priestess or witch, the figure is always in a special relationship to the man whose anima it embodies, so that it either initiates or bewitches him.[37]

In contrast to the animus, which is more connected with spirit, anima essentially represents nature, and a wounded anima always reflects in difficulties with relationship because in essence, the anima is about relating.

An example of how these inner figures influence us can be seen with Tara. Tara's father was weak and disempowered. He did not spend much time with Tara during her childhood, mainly because he had a drink problem, and Tara's mother had a difficult and conflicted relationship with him. Their constant conflict gradually eroded any love there had been between them so that, for as long as she could remember, Tara's parents had ceased to be intimate with each other. Tara's mother used sexual withholding as a way to control her husband, since she felt unloved by him, and he in turn, feeling rejected, turned to drink and occasional violence. A vicious cycle was thus played out and Tara, being the youngest, usually took the brunt of this conflict, since her mother used her as a physical shield against her father.

Witness to both her father's physical violence and her mother's emotional pain, Tara's inner image of the masculine was of a weak man and a tyrant. She identified with her mother and her mother's pain and sense of being unloved, and this made it hard for her to have any relationship with her father. Thus her male side, her animus, was wounded. Tara had a very tyrannical inner masculine, which is how the animus becomes when it is weak and undifferentiated. By the time she was 23, she had got used to the fact that somewhere deep inside, there was no male figure to help her on her road to life, because one of the father's main functions and roles is to help the child separate emotionally from the mother. If, however, a mother feels unloved and has a fear of abandonment, she can use her children to fill her emptiness. She then becomes the 'negative mother', negative because her emotional stranglehold pushes her children into reactive behaviour, activating their mother complex. We all have complexes – I will explain these more fully in a later chapter.

The negative mother complex in both men and women is responsible for many difficulties and complexities in relationship. Tara was caught in the dark web her mother cast over the family because, without the father to mitigate the power of the emotionally devouring mother, the child stays trapped and cannot grow up. Since it is her positive animus that she calls on to help her negotiate the world, and hers was unavailable, she remained trapped in the negative mother complex and could not move on. Her outer life reflected this in the way she lived alone with her mother from whom she could not separate.

Ben's mother, on the other hand, was stern and controlling, which meant Ben found it hard to reach his anima, his inner woman. You will hear more about Ben later, but essentially he grew up in a household dominated by his mother. Since she was emotionally distant, Ben never got the love and affection he craved. Instead, he feared his mother. He perceived his father as weak since he seemed unable to stand up to her moods. Ben was also witness to the humiliation of his father by his mother. Since children pick the imponderables in their parents' hearts very easily, and humiliation can be as subtle as a tone of voice or a constant insidious 'putting down', Ben's mother, in a way, emasculated his father in the way she both spoke to him and treated him.

To witness this type of humiliation is very painful for a boy, because he looks up to his father and seeks to emulate him. In his father he sees the man he will grow up to be. Similarly, a little girl looks at her mother and sees herself as a woman. And if we perceive our mother as controlling and somehow stronger than our fathers, then we imagine that being a woman is to be stronger than a man, and that men somehow are not to be relied upon; men will let us down so that we will have to compensate by always remaining in control.

Isabel grew up in a family that was dominated by her mother's emotional needs and outbursts. Isabel's mother fundamentally never felt loved. She was constantly seeking her husband's love, but because of emptiness in her from her own childhood, and his emotional inability to show his love for her, she never got what she needed. Particularly susceptible to her mother, Isabel unconsciously learned from her that being a woman was to feel totally wounded because what a woman needs above all is to be loved, and a man cannot provide this. To inhabit the body of a woman therefore was to be a priori wounded.

This internal image in Isabel was responsible for how she went about finding love, and the kinds of men she chose later in life to give her this love. She invariably chose men like her father, emotionally unavailable, who could never give her what she hoped for. In this way she played out her script with principle actors that she chose herself. Isabel chose well; her destiny and childhood wounds guided her to these men so that she could complete her tasks and learn her spiritual lessons.

## The Inner Image and Love

Our internal images of the masculine and the feminine are the cannons that fire our passion and lead us into the battlefields of love. Ultimately, we are always seeking wholeness and this means the balance of the masculine and feminine within. In Jungian psychological language this is termed, as we saw earlier, the 'inner marriage'. Our internalisation of this balance is based not only on the inner images of the masculine and feminine as they are handed down to us, but also on how we have experienced the relationship between our parents.

It is always my practice to ask my clients how they experienced their parents' relationship with each other (as a child), because this will give me a sense of where the balance of the masculine and feminine is in the client. Was mother viewed as stronger, or was father? Did father love mother and perhaps sought more from her than he ever elicited? Or did mother always reach out for father and find little? Any number of variations are possible.

I worked with a man once whose father embodied all the qualities of love, tenderness, and nurturing that are normally associated with the feminine. His mother, by contrast, had been the disciplinarian, stern and unyielding, embodying the more masculine qualities. What this did to him was confuse him. He had problems with his sexual identity, was always seeking a soft feminine presence, and felt unable to be the strong male he wished to be. He remembers desperately wanting his father to be strong, and to stand up to his mother. He hated the way his mother constantly put his father down. In a strange confusion of emotions, he felt tied to his mother through his anger, and tied to his father because he wanted to protect him. Yet at the same time, there was a dim awareness in him of the betrayal that he felt at the hands of his father because, in his mind, a father is meant to be strong.

During our sessions, he found himself incessantly angry and frustrated. He felt disempowered; that he was only operating on three cylinders, not quite up to speed. Like a rusty engine, he merely limped through life. He had lost his spirit, his driving force and his zest for life. When I asked him to describe this feeling, he said it felt as if there was a mattress pressing down on him. He associated this feeling with his mother.

When I brought up the subject of his father, Peter became emotional. In touch with his father's gentleness of spirit and his tender heart, Peter recalled his father with love. In Peter, the inner masculine and feminine were out of balance and confused somehow and we needed to straighten it out, so that he could find his inner strength as a man capable of engaging in a mature relationship with a woman. He needed to connect with his anima, which in his own words 'feels like a bridge to the world'.

We always seek what we lack, and we always seek balance. The soul never likes to be fragmented and the masculine and the feminine energies within us need to function together. In fact, this union is essential to the spiritual well being of every individual, which is why we are most often compelled to find this union in outer relationships.

## Anima and Animus: Architects of Love

In essence these two archetypes are the main architects of any love affair. Women project the animus onto their partners, and men the anima. Falling in love is very much a state of projection, where one sees in the other what is latent but undeveloped in oneself. This projection happens through a process called transference, and it is something that occurs naturally between all human beings engaged in relationship. Transference is also addressed more particularly in psychodynamic psychotherapy. However, Jung writes:

> Projection means not only the transference of an image to another person, but also of the activities that go with it, so that a man to whom the animus image has been transferred is expected to take over all the functions that have remained undeveloped in the woman in question, whether the thinking function,

or the power to act, or responsibility toward the outside world. In turn, the woman upon whom a man has projected his anima must feel for him, or make relationships for him.[38]

In modern language we call this a co-dependent relationship, wherein partners play an essential role in such a way that there is a currency exchange between them. I know many husbands who have little or no friends of their own, because it is their wives who do the relating and socialising for the couple. Similarly, I know wives who would be incapable of sorting out their day-to-day practical affairs, money, bills and so on, leaving all that to their husbands. Most intimate relationships have a healthy element of co-dependency. However, when the projection of the anima and animus remain unconscious, no psychological growth is possible.

Our inner images, formed through childhood, and primed by our soul's choices, will guide us as we move out into adult life and begin to engage in intimate relationships. These same inner images, the anima and the animus, are the unconscious forces that propel us to interact with certain people and will dictate how we are in relationship. As has already been said, we are always in search of what we lack so we will gravitate towards the person who embodies these qualities for us, so that we may feel complete. How often do we hear from lovers, 'I can't live without you'?

By the time we reach adolescence, our personalities and characters are pretty much established. We will have certain ideas and expectations about the opposite sex that will guide us in our choice of partners later in life. We will be attracted to certain people that reflect the inner qualities we have internalised. Most of all, we will be guided to heal early wounds, thereby furthering our spiritual evolution and completing our soul contracts.

So what kind of lovers will we make? And what drama will be played out as we enter the battlegrounds and theatre of love? Will we have a strong male side and choose gentler, softer men we can direct? Will we choose a strong woman who will bring out the strength we seek in ourselves? Opposites attract and are drawn together like magnets so that each can become whole. When the fierce energies of the unconscious magnetise each other in our most wounded hot spots, it is impossible to resist!

PART FOUR

# LOVE STORIES

## The Little Tin Soldier and the Ballerina

Oh, once in a town in the Black Forest
A little white toy shop stood
And a little tin soldier with only one leg
Lived in a castle of wood.

And across the room on another shelf
Stood a little glass case
And a tiny ballerina lived in there
All in a dress of lace.

From where the little tin soldier stood
They could see each other so clear.
And the little tin soldier watched over her
With a love that was so dear.

Then one day sadness came;
The tiny ballerina was sold.
The little tin soldier was thrown away
And into the gutter he rode.

The waters carried him to the sea
And many far off lands.
He made many children happy
As he passed through their tiny hands.

Then one day they met again
In a house in the land of Ire,
And when the clock on the wall struck the midnight hour
They jumped into a fire.

And in that fire they shall stay
Forever and a day;
For the fire lord is the fire of love
Just like the peace of dawn.

\*\*\*

Ben entered the hotel lobby and walked straight through to the bar. It was late evening and the best time to sit and have a drink, as the light from the setting sun glowed softly through the palm trees lining the patio. Ben had for a long time wanted to visit this hotel. El Colunia was renowned for its location by the sea and its excellent cuisine. Despite being a tall man blessed with romanesque good looks, Ben, at this moment in time, did not feel tall inside. His overburdened heart appeared to pull him inwards so that his shoulders had begun to stoop in the manner of overburdened coat hangers. Though he held himself bravely and smiled a lot, there was a great sadness about him which seemed to keep people from getting too close.

There was only a scattering of people in the bar and Ben, tired after his long drive, sat down heavily and ordered a beer. After a while he began an idle conversation with the man drinking next to him.

Katya sighed as she closed the door somewhat loudly on the room she shared with her two travelling companions, and went down for her usual pre-dinner drink. Her elderly companions were in the rather vulgar habit of having their drinks in the room and Katya despised this, finding the dragging around of gin bottles and lemon slices squashed into plastic bags almost offensive. It was her habit to get dressed up for dinner and go down to the bars of the various hotels they stayed in, leaving them to it. El Colunia was a beautiful hotel and Katya, inclined to romanticism, allowed herself the luxury of imagining herself a princess or at the very least a woman of noble descent as she descended the marble stairs, head held high. Her silk skirt swished around her legs in a way she found sensual and exotic; she knew she looked good, the sun was still warm, and you never knew who you might meet.

Katya was getting over a broken heart. Like all heroines

of the past who were sent away to get over a lover affair, she had packed up her job, rented out her house and left. She had been travelling now for four months, was running out of money, and due to go home in just a few weeks. Though she still thought about him, her lover, every day, the pain had lessened considerably and lately she had begun to feel lighter. Besides, being an explorer at heart, she loved travelling and meeting new people, and encountering new cultures.

Ben's attention was caught immediately. He saw her enter the room and settle on a bar stool some distance away. Not only did he think her beautiful, it was something about the light that radiated around her that drew him. Though small and neat of figure, she carried herself with courage and pride. She was confidently ordering a drink and he could hear by her accent that she was foreign.

Ben suddenly began to despise the grey little man next to him and wished he would go away. Though he was normally good with small talk, all of a sudden he was impatient, and tired of this aimless chattering to an uninteresting male stranger. Ben, a shy man, felt compelled to talk to this exotic woman. He had to talk to her. There was something about the way she held herself that seemed familiar to him. A million and one feelings tumbled around in his heart as a dim memory began pulling at his soul. Who was she? Did he know her? What was this strange feeling of familiarity he felt when looking at her? How was he going to get to talk to her?

Ben was begining to feel sick with worry that she might leave before he plucked up the courage to say something and, nauseated, he ordered another beer, even though he didn't want it. By this time he could see that she had almost finished sipping her cocktail and he grew desperate for something to happen. Then, as though his prayers were answered, the man next to him got up and left, and Ben saw to his great relief that there was no one between him and the foreign woman. She sat about four stools away and was, by now, happily chatting to the barman about the French cocktail she was in the habit of asking for, and he had obliged her by making this evening.

I was sad but not surprised when Ben did not show up for his appointment. We had been making good progress, I thought, but I knew he tended to keep away when he became depressed, something which, I was not tired of telling him, defeated the purpose. I had grown to love this big, shy man whose good looks and socially polished manners seemed at odds with his inner lack of confidence. Like an enthusiastic youth as yet unaware of how to be and where to place himself in the world, his woundedness seemed out of place.

His wife of twenty years had left him and, after a few minor relationships and brief encounters, he had fallen in love with a foreign woman. That she also loved him was not in question; the problem was that the geographical distance between them made for a complex relationship. It created a false impression that they were eminently suited to each other since they never spent more than a few weeks together at a time, and it also masked in each of them a tendency to avoid fully committed relating by having a relationship 'at a distance'.

Now, the relationship was under huge strain and in danger of breaking altogether. After two and a half years of commuting to each other's countries, Ben had made the verbal commitment to emigrate. Katya had made it plain she did not want to live in the USA and Ben did not want to live without her. They had passionate reunions every few months or so and, in between, they dreamt of a life together, the home they would create, the life they would lead.

With the safety of distance, Ben poured his long-held feelings out on paper. Emailing long, romantic letters to Katya, Ben opened his heart and poured his longings, his soul searching, his pain and his love into their communications. In them he discovered he was a lover at heart, a poet and a dreamer. He secretly hated the world into which he had been catapulted, a world where he had to put aside his dreams and his heart to be succesful and run a business. An accountant by profession, he was quick with figures and had done well, but in recent years and, since his long acrimonious divorce, things had been going downhill for him financially. He dreamed of a new life with Katya, a dream she also shared, since her heart was similarly ravaged by loss and a sense of wanting to start a fresh life.

Dreams were big in Ben's life and, when depressed, which was not infrequently in recent years, he took refuge in them and in the words and lyrics of the songs he wrote. Though on the outside he radiated optimism and enthusiasm, much of this was bravado. Inside he was a loner, who found life and relationships difficult, and his poetic heart sought and had failed to find a home. A lonely soul searching for true love, Ben's whole life lit up when he met Katya. He thought his search was over and when he sent her a card on their first Valentine it read:

Long before we met, I could see you in my dreams—I knew you were my love. I carried your image in my heart and I searched for you, looking for you in every passing face. And when at last we met, I knew my journey was over.

He had found his soul mate and they would be together forever. But the unthinkable had happened, was happening. They were fighting. Try as they both did to remain harmonious, after a few days together they would start bickering. After the novelty had worn off, when Ben and Katya were together for any length of time, they argued. Something seemed to pull at each of them and tear them asunder. They got at each other, and fundamentally did not agree on many things each felt was important. She was a liberal and he a conservative, she was free spirited and pioneering, he a follower of tradition who liked to toe the established line. She was a rebel and he a follower. He felt threatened by her need for freedom. On top of all this their cultures seemed to clash somewhere.

But the worst was what happened to him as he opened his heart to her. Big, smiling, affable, happy Ben became sullen and stubborn, like a sulking child, when the slightest whiff of conflict caught his nose. Loving her seemed to loosen dark feelings which he hated himself for, but could not contain. He felt a need to control her, her free-spirited nature threatened him. What if she went off with other men? She was so attractive and high spirited, like an exotic bird, Ben wanted to keep her in a cage so he could have her for himself. He was insanely jealous.

Yet he knew somewhere that she did love him, and had never given him any cause for jealousy. However, there was something he wanted from her that he could never get. This longing gnawed at him like a sore that refused to heal. There was something unavailable about her. If the truth were told he felt she still loved her old lost lover; perhaps this accounted for the part of her that appeared unavailable to him. Though she seemed to open herself to him, he wanted more. He loved her, and she loved him, so why was he torn asunder by these ugly feelings, he wondered?

And then there was the money. He had none–his divorce having wiped him out completely. There was part of him that hated that; it made him feel useless. What did he really have to offer her? If a man has no money he has not proved himself worthy of a woman's love. In her company, though generous by nature, Ben became parsimonious on occasion, when the memory of his ex wife who had plagued him incessantly about his lack of success in providing the family with money, came back to haunt him. At those times he saw his ex in Katya, even though they were so fundamentally different, and Katya had no need of his money, being independent.

Ben felt stuck in a hard and dark place, and when he felt this way he retreated. He withdrew into a small, narrow world, where he could feel his boundaries and know he was safe. His self-constructed little world, where perhaps only five minutes of freedom were allowed a day, kept him out of harms way. He would get up every day at the same time, do his exercises to a precise timing, have his shower, drive to work, get coffee on the way, work through the day without a break for lunch, drive home late and pick up something to eat in a take away; watch TV for perhaps half an hour, attend to his emails and go to bed. Any attempted interference in this self-imposed internment would be met with impatience and dismissal. Little, if any, deviation would be allowed except at weekends when the routine would vary to include 'relaxation time'.

Katya, whose heart was ravaged by loss had, by the time she met Ben, long ago given up on love, and relegated it to her dreams and her fantasy life. There it existed because she and her true love were able to hold hands over the tangled mess of the real world. Souls can transcend the narrow confines of the flesh and join together easily. Ben was so beautiful, she thought of him as a pure, untainted soul. Somehow he radiated a kind of youthful enthusiasm which her jaded soul appreciated. Somewhere deep she sensed his woundedness, though she knew he was unaware of it himself. He projected his hurt onto her, seeing her as a fragile butterfly and tiny dancer that he must heal through his love.

When he told her frequently that he wanted to look after her, Katya began melting. The glass exterior she had constructed to protect her heart began unfreezing, and this frightened her. She grew to love him for the largeness of his heart and the way he was not afraid to voice his deepest feelings. No man had ever opened his heart this way and expressed it to her so openly. In the beginning, Katya wondered whether his frequent 'I love yous' were a cultural thing, and not to be taken seriously, but as she got to know the depth of his heart and his need for love, she began to believe he truly did love her.

When they were together for any length of time, however, his narrow views and controlling behaviour irritated her. Eager to make it work though, she tried not to let him get to her, but he got on her nerves so much the strain of holding back would finally push her into overreacting, and a row would start. Her free spirit felt confined by him, and the more she felt this, the more he pulled her back, so that she would feel she was in prison and walking on eggshells so as not to upset him. Katya walked an uncomfortable tightrope then between keeping him happy and maintaining a modicum of self reliance and control over her own life and needs.

Ben, sensing her desire to escape, grew more and more controlling and dark. He would go into one of his moods and Katya dreaded these because they could last days; long dark days when he would lope around with a sinister threatening aura around him, refusing to talk to her, refusing to eat, refusing everything. Katya was frightened of his moods because she sensed in them a silent violence, and knew that Ben retreated to a dangerous, splintered place neither she nor anybody else could reach, and only time seemed to bring him out of.

Something had happened to their beautiful dream and the image they both projected of the perfect couple. They made a handsome couple, good looking and well dressed, they liked the same things—going out to dinner, drinks on the terrace, followed by a romantic night stroll under the moonlight. Having met the way they did, both far away from home, there was a fairy tale romance about them, which both played into. But underneath that image there were flaws, and it seemed those flaws became large cracks which threatened to erupt into full-size volcanoes, destroying the dream they were attempting to make real.

Katya saw that there was a huge gap between Ben the golden, beautiful, pure soul, and Ben the dark, angry tryant. It frightened her that this gap was so large, because when he came out of these moods and she tried to talk to him about them, he denied them. This was another difficulty between them; she was able to rationalise much more easily than Ben, who lived mainly in his feelings, so that when these feelings erupted, he was overwhelmed and the dark tryant took over.

Ben was in despair because he thought he had finally found the woman of his dreams, the woman who made him feel complete, in a way his wife never had, and yet it was not working. He could not understand it. He felt as though some dark and fractious energy were pulling them apart. He idolised her and put her on a pedestal; she was this great wise being, this tantalising butterfly, his beautiful wounded dancer. But when she ceased to fit the special robes he had dressed her in, she toppled from her pedestal and he looked on dismayed, as his dream shattered to the ground.

When Ben returned to therapy, their relationship had ended, abruptly, after a difficult patch when he had been to see Katya and discussed the practicalities of his proposed emigration. Things had not gone well; they fought almost incessantly and Katya finally told him she did not want to live with him. Rejected and abandoned, he left her and his dream at the airport and boarded a plane for home.

Chapter 7

# Once Upon a Time: Stories We Live By

Far out into the sea, the water is as blue as the petals of the most beautiful cornflower, and as clear as the purest glass.

But it is very deep, deeper than any cable will sound; many steeples must be placed one above the other to reach from the ground to the surface of the water. And down there live the sea people.'

From *The Little Mermaid*

Like all children, I loved stories. There was no story that fascinated and touched me as much as *The Little Mermaid*. I would make my aunt read it to me over and over again, and I can still see the sad pictures in my mind of the little mermaid holding in her arms the unconscious prince she loved so much but could never have, the shipwreck, the sea witch and other scenes. I remember feeling the pain of the little mermaid as she took one step after another, on legs that felt as though 100 sharp knives were piercing her. It seemed to me then that a terrible price was to be paid to win the love of a mortal man, and that love was surely out of reach. I cried bitter tears for the little mermaid, for whom love seemed unobtainable, and I remember something lament deep inside me, and a resonance in my deepest being.

This fairy story had an impact on me then which, only now as an adult woman, I am beginning to understand. Was I destined to grapple with love, with finding my soul mate and life partner? Is part of my sacred contract to learn about life and the wisdom of the heart through relationships, and the search for a true soul mate? What is sure is that this story resonating, as it did at a deep level within me, revealed a lot about my little girl's heart and soul, and maybe about my life's journey.

It is thus for many of us. A particular fairy story or myth can hold some essential truth about our soul's journey and sacred contract. A myth or fairy story can also reveal aspects of a person's unconscious life and underlying relational patterns.

Ben and Katya, for example, were living out the tale of *The Tin Soldier and the Little Ballerina.*

In essence, the tin soldier and the little ballerina is a story of the unification of opposites, the inner marriage, love and wholeness. The tin soldier has only one leg, which means he is wounded. Legs and feet symbolically represent our ability to make our own particular stand in the world, and he only has one leg – he is incomplete. The little ballerina he loves so much represents his anima, his love, his heart and his ability to relate, which, as we can see, is also wounded and out of reach.

Though very beautiful and fine, the little ballerina is untouchable – she is in a glass case and he cannot reach her. Glass is cold and hard, and both protects and keeps away – it repels.

The little ballerina is also wounded and, curiously, also stands on – rather balances on one leg in a dancer's pose.

Katya, as the untouchable and beautiful dancer, fitted perfectly into Ben's anima image. Ravaged by loss and with a history of broken love affairs, Katya had placed a protection around herself. Searching for love, she was at the same time terrified of it, especially when it came close to her. She kept herself safe in her glass case. In close relationships, Katya would feel claustrophobic and easily pinned down. At a deep, fundamental level, her childhood experiences had been such that she felt herself unloveable. Furthermore, she feared that if she opened up, she would be hurt.

The tin soldier and the little ballerina survey each other from across the room; they love at a distance. That way they are safe from the gradual erosion of dreams by everyday living, and the continual chaffing of differences. Both Katya and Ben felt safer having a distance relationship, and yet when they were apart the longing to be together pulled at them both, because we all have a desire to try and make our dreams real. However, it is only when the lovers find each other again after being separated, and jump into the fire, that their love is transformed and they can be together.

And when the clock on the wall struck the midnight hour, they jumped into a fire.

Fire always represents transformation, and midnight is that special 'bewitching hour', when Cinderellas everywhere run home before their ballgowns change into glad rags and their dreams are shattered by a return to reality.

Reality broke into Ben and Katya's dream of union, and neither was able to bear it. In the same way that Katya as the little ballerina represented Ben's anima, his wounded inner feminine, the tin soldier in Ben represented Katya's animus, her wounded masculine. Both have wounded counterparts so that neither of them can step out into the world. Little ballerina is surrounded by glass and trapped in a case and tin soldier is missing one leg. The feminine and masculine need each other in order to form the inner marriage and become complete. Like the tin man in *The Wizard Of Oz* he is missing his heart, and she is trapped in the wounded feminine and cannot get out. They need each other.

Ultimately, each love affair activates the archetype of wholeness, and the choice to be empowered and learn from the experience is always there. In their relationship, the tin soldier and little ballerina story formed a basic inner drama out of which they related, both to each other and the outer world.

## Myths and Stories We Live By

There is something essential about myths and stories that mean something to us. Stories are the universal currents of history and contain archetypal energies that we resonate with at a deep unconscious level. This explains the popularity of certain epic type mythic movies like *Troy* and *Gladiator*, as well as classic tales of love and integrity embodied in stories by the Brontë sisters and Jane Austin, to name a few. We can identify with the hero and heroine's struggles, aspirations and life challenges.

Although we are influenced by archetypal and universal images, we are also simultaneously creating our own stories. On a spiritual level, I believe that we are co-creators in our life. This means that we create a story and that we live out of that story; stories that our soul carries with us into this incarnation; stories that come alive at night in our dreams when sleep encourages their emergence out of where they lie, hidden in the unconscious. Our inner drama – our story – is also an expression of how we have chosen to live out our soul contract, so that we will be drawn to those that express particular challenges we have to face and lessons we have to learn.

Relationships, and love relationships in particular, bring out and activate our stories, which is why they offer us the greatest opportunities for soul growth. We are largely unconscious of what story we might be living, but if we do not work at becoming conscious, we identify with the drama, so that we live, act and behave as the characters we identify with. This means that like the little mermaid, for example, we might imagine that we will never find love or that love is simply out of reach.

Often our inner drama is reflected in a favourite fairy tale that was read to us in childhood. In the last few years it has been my practice to ask clients if they have a favourite fairy story or myth; a story they liked or were most drawn to as a child. If they have, or can relate to one in adulthood, it serves as a road-map for our inner work. Fairy stories often underpin a person's psychological make up. These stories will have a resonance in their soul. In people that can recall them, there is usually an intensive relationship between a particular tale and that child's psychological development. Children identify with different figures in the fairy tale, so that the tales can be a bridge to the unconscious. This happens during the developmental stage in childhood, when the archetypal and mythical imagery is close to the child. Fairy-tale figures are usually personifications of a person's unconscious complexes. Identifying with stories, along with their experiences, is how children learn about life, about its struggles and its joys, and the rewards for the successful accomplishment of life tasks.

Why is a child drawn to a particular tale? There is something in the child's soul contract and early life experience that finds resonance in the fairy tale. *Rapunzel* and *The Little Mermaid*, for example, are tales of attempted development of the female ego out of the dominance of the mother archetype. Both heroines are in search of their counterparts, their animus or masculine sides. Union with their inner man creates wholeness and allows them to come into psychological consciousness, and also to relate to an outer man.

In the foreground of the fairy tale plot of both those stories is a yearning to connect with the masculine, personified by the prince. In *The Little Mermaid*, there is furthermore, a failed attempt at a love relationship, due in no small part to the girl's inability to verbally express her feelings. Being 'dumb', the only way of expression for the little mermaid is through dance, a more primitive and unconscious form of articulation. The little mermaid needs human legs in order to have a chance with her beloved prince. Feet and legs represent our standpoint in life, our ability to assert ourselves and establish a relationship to reality. But the price is too much for the mermaid to bear, for in exchanging her voice for human legs, she loses her ability to communicate her feelings, and thus her chance to find true love.

At some level, we all live out of a story or belief system. I have discovered this through *The Little Mermaid*. That I am a therapist, and now many years later writing a book on love and relationships, says something about how far along the road I have come in terms of the tale! It is, of course, a sad story of impossible love.

Particular fairy tales, like archetypes, can play a big part in a person's life, as I was to realise myself. At the end of our first year in psychotherapy training our tutor gave us an assignment. When I was told we were to write a 5,000-word essay and hand it in by the last day of term, I grumbled and protested. However, when the assignment was explained to us, I perked up considerably. My interest had been stimulated; we were to choose a fairy story (or myth) of our choice and write an interpretation of it from three different psychoanalytical perspectives: the Freudian, Jungian and Kleinian.

It was an interesting and challenging task, and one I enjoyed particularly because, along with most of my colleagues new to this way of thinking, we were more or less unaware of how this would reveal our own inner worlds. By our choice of tale, we unconsciously revealed ourselves!

I am still amused when I think about how myself, along with my unsuspecting friends and college mates, poured our intimate stories out on paper, thinking we were merely exposing how much theoretical material we had retained throughout the year. We never suspected that into our renditions we had put our own soul's story, thus revealing much more than we intended! In actual fact, our choice of fairy story or myth was not really a choice. Nudged by our unconscious, we were compelled to reveal and repeat our own inner dramas through the stories we wrote about and interpreted.

Sometimes you find that a person is living out of a fairy tale. A favourite fairy tale can have a parallel to a person's unconscious psychological dynamics.

## A Life without the Gods is not Worth Living!

Why do myths and stories have such an impact on us? Because they reveal universal forces that are in all of us – they are about us. We cannot really understand the mystery of love and human relationships without including the mythological aspect. Myths and fairy tales offer a transcendent dimension to human experience. Mythological characters and their stories symbolise for us the journey of the human soul, with its many trials and tribulations. Myths are a way of telling a story that has a universal appeal. It has been defined as something that never was but always is. There is something about myth that transcends race and culture, and touches what is essentially human in each of us.[39]

We need to have a symbolic approach to life when we are dealing with the soul. And relationships are all about soul.

With the help of the first psychoanalysts, Western culture has moved from a literal to a psychological understanding of the world in only a hundred years. Everybody now more or less accepts the existence of the unconscious and unconscious processes. But now, I believe this is not enough; we need to move further still if we are to meet the demands of our souls. We need to move from the psychological view of things to a symbolic or mythological view. Understanding psychological processes can help us become more self-aware, but to heal our wounds we also need to develop symbolic sight. Symbolic sight is a way of seeing and understanding life in spiritual terms, where healing, change and transformation are always possible. This is more difficult for us, as it involves the sort of double vision that develops from dialogue with the underworld of our souls, and it involves the ability to be without the reassurance of certainty. Symbolic vision is able to live with questions and with paradox, and to stay with the unknown until it becomes clear.

The symbolic way of thinking and seeing is more challenging; it is not concrete, literal or quantifiable. It demands more of us. Developing symbolic sight helps us build the soul stamina necessary to connect with our inner selves and live soulful lives.

The marriage of psychology and spirituality is one of my main focuses, because the time has come when our evolution demands it. No longer satisfied with a purely concrete, causal or literal approach to psychological problems, people are being driven to seek healing within, through deep inner soul work. We need to move from the psychological view of things to a symbolic or mythological view. Understanding psychological processes can help us become more self-aware, but to heal our wounds we also need to develop symbolic sight. Symbolic sight is a way of seeing and understanding life in spiritual terms, where healing, change and transformation are always possible.

## Each Love Affair Dramatises a Myth

Love affairs offer us a unique opportunity to find out who we are, what we are, and what stories we are still living out of. Usually, as has been already said, we choose principal actors that fit into our life script and symbolise what we want to learn, overcome and achieve. As human beings we are always searching for our perfect love, our soul mate.

At the very core of a fairy tale, just as at the core of a love affair, is a vision of wholeness. This is very important and cannot be overstated. Most, if not all, fairy tales separate the masculine and feminine, which is unnatural, and yet necessary, if they are to find each other and be united. There is often a king without a queen, or a princess without a prince, and obstacles have to be overcome and challenges met in order for union to happen. The prince has to find his princess, the king his queen and so on. Their struggle to come together represents the struggle towards consciousness, and their union represents the outer union as well as the inner marriage we all seek. The prince needs to find his princess so that they become king and queen and as such, reign over their happy kingdoms.

The king and the queen represent conscious individuation and the fulfilment of the inner marriage. Princes and princesses are kings and queens in waiting – they are searching for their equal, the one who will recognise how special they are, how unique. Their union symbolises our potential sense of wholeness. The princess seeks someone who recognises her for who she really is, a special one. The prince seeks a princess worthy of him, who also recognises his majesty and his potential to become king.

## The Nightingale and the Rose

Oscar Wilde's *The Nightingale and the Rose* depicts the yearning for love and a failed attempt at finding it. I am including it here because it has a lot to tell us about our search for love; the sacrifice that is demanded of us when we seek to grow, and through love achieve spiritual fulfilment, and outer union with another. It also painfully and beautifully describes the human struggle to reconcile the opposites within us, the masculine and feminine principles.

'She said that she would dance with me if I brought her red roses,' cried the young student, 'but in all my garden there is no red rose.'

From her nest in the holm-oak tree, the nightingale heard him, and she looked out through the leaves and wondered.

The nightingale, who sang every night about love, was impressed by the student and saw how he appeared to be suffering for love. This young man was in love with the professor's daughter. The student weeps and the nightingale's tender heart is touched – she vows to help him.

'Here, indeed, is a true lover,' says the nightingale. 'What I sing of, he suffers: what is a joy to me, to him is pain. Surely love is a wonderful thing?'

The little nightingale, who understands the student's sorrow, and who often thinks about the mystery of love, soars into the air and goes in search of a red rose. She stops at two different rose bushes, one white and one yellow and finally, tipped by the others, flies to the rose tree that grows beneath the student's window.

'Give me a red rose,' she cried, 'and I will sing you my sweetest song.'

But the tree shook its head.

'My roses are red. But the winter has chilled my veins, and the frost has nipped my buds, and the storm has broken my branches, and I shall have no roses at all this year.'

The nightingale tells her she only wants one red rose, and the tree goes quiet and then replies, 'There is a way, but it is so terrible I dare not tell it to you'.

'Tell it to me,' said the nightingale, 'I am not afraid.'

'If you want a red rose,' said the tree, 'you must build it out of music by moonlight, and stain it with your heart's blood. You must sing to me with your breast against a thorn. All night long you must sing to me, and the thorn must pierce your heart, and your life – blood must flow into my veins, and become mine.'

The nightingale hears these words and trembles a little, but declaring that love is better than life, and that the heart of a man is worth more than the heart of a bird, flies to the student who lies weeping, and tells him to be happy – that she will build him a red rose out of her music and heart's blood by moon light. In return for this terrible sacrifice she asks the students only one thing: that he be a true lover.

Though the student listens, he does not understand what the nightingale is saying to him, because he only knows about love from what is written in books.

That night, as the student lies sleeping in his room, the nightingale flies to the rose tree, and she sets her breast against the thorn. As the crystal and cold moon shines down, the little nightingale sings. All night long she sings, and her song is so beautiful the moon and stars listen, enthralled.

The nightingale sings of love, of the birth of love in a boy and a girl, and as she sings the thorn goes deeper into her heart.

'Press closer little nightingale,' cried the tree, 'or the day will come before the rose is finished.'

So the nightingale pressed closer against the thorn, and louder and louder grew her song, for she sang of the birth of passion in a man and a maid.

She presses the thorn against her heart, and feels a sharp pain as her life's blood begins to fill the beautiful delicate rose a rich crimson colour. Her cries grow fainter and fainter, and as she begins to die, her cries become wilder and wilder, until finally, 'She gave one last burst of music. The white moon heard it, and she forgot the dawn, and lingered on in the sky'.

"Look, look!" cried the tree, "the rose is finished now"; but the nightingale made no answer, for she was lying dead in the long grass, with the thorn in her heart.'

The student, who has been asleep all this time, next morning, opens his window and sees the rose. Exclaiming his good luck, he plucks it and takes it to the professor's daughter. She rejects him, telling him the red rose will not go with her dress, and besides, the chamberlain's nephew has given her real jewels, and everyone knows they cost more than flowers.

The student angrily and ungraciously flings the red rose into the street where it is run over by a cartwheel.

'What a silly thing love is!' he exclaims, 'and not half as useful as logic, for it does not prove anything, and it is always telling one of things that are not going to happen.'

He flounces back to his room and takes out a big book and begins to read.

## 'Yet Each Man Kills the Thing He Loves'

This beautiful story is about a search for love and the inability to find it. It is about a sacrifice that comes to nothing. In psychological language it is about a failed initiation into love, and an attempt at individuation. I use Oscar Wilde's own words, immortalised in his poem 'The Ballad of Reading Gaol' as a heading to describe what happens in this story, and what can happen to many of us, as we seek to live our lives and find love.

Sometimes we kill off the thing we love. We shut down our hearts and, maybe too, our potential for spiritual growth because of our fears of change.

The little nightingale represents our soul, our feminine, our anima, our ability to love and to transcend the limitations of our ego-driven personalities. In a man, the student, who is versed in logic and inhabits a uniquely *logos* (rational) world, the nightingale is his anima, the part of him that falls in love and that can put him in touch with his soul.

When we meet the student he is still trapped in an infantile emotional state where he feels safe, but which prevents him forming a fulfilling love relationship. He is safe and comfortable in a world that does not involve his feelings.

Birds symbolise spirit, and as creatures of the air, have the ability to communicate with the gods. In Celtic and other traditions, birds are considered messengers of the gods, and often accompany the hero or heroine on their quest. They are frequently helpers and can mediate with humans, offering helpful advice from a spiritual or higher source. In this story the nightingale is a kind of ambassador for the soul, looking to help the man integrate his anima so that he may know love (and get the girl!).

It does not work.

First of all, there is no red rose in the student's garden, meaning there is no feeling, no heart. A red rose signifies love and passion. Living in his head, in a life filled with books, this man is out of touch with his feelings. Being attracted to the girl though, there is a chance that his heart can be opened if he goes with it. But he must suffer, and sacrifice a part of himself that is no longer useful and is inhibiting his growth. Essentially, he has to let go of his childhood, and take steps out into the world.

Sacrifice is always demanded when something important happens upon us, giving us the opportunity to change and grow. In this case, the student must sacrifice his old, overly-rational ego. He must move from a safe, ordered and contained reality to the terrain of the soul, where nothing is certain but where love resides. In simple terms, the student is a man who is out of touch with his heart and his feeling nature, and he must take the leap of faith necessary to leave behind his old life if he is to find love.

There is also an obvious parallel with the author. Wilde wrote his stories in the 1880s, Victorian England; a time when art, poetry, love and anything remotely connected with the pleasure principle was considered unseemly and duly repressed; an England where the emphasis was on strict moral discipline and a conservative way of life; an England where poets and the arts were considered frivolous. To this England came a wild Irish man steeped in the Celtic tradition of the poets and bards – a man full of creative potential and free spirit.

We know what happened to this 'untamed' spirit. Wilde survived the only way he knew how, by developing the wit, irony and cynicism for which he became famous. We also know he suffered greatly, and his works are testimony to this fact, and to his sensitivities and his inner struggles. Wilde was ultimately a man of heart, who felt betrayed by life, by love, and by the world he inhabited and created. He was a lover in the wrong time and place. The story of the nightingale and the rose tells us something of how he suffered, and how he viewed life. Perhaps he was in search of his soul, but from his writings we can see he was certainly a true lover and a man who loved deeply, and struggled to reconcile opposing forces inside himself.

The symbolism of the red rose is important. The rose is both heavenly perfection, and earthly passion. In alchemy the rose represents wisdom since it combines and unites duality, spirit and earth. The student needs to possess the rose because it symbolises both human feeling and eternal, transcendent love. This is the love we search for, that every human searches for. To possess a rose and gain it through awareness or consciousness is to possess the key to individuation, to inner union.

However, since it is a red rose, it demands a sacrifice. Although associated with passions, sensuality and seduction, the red rose also signifies death, mortality and sorrow. Its thorns signify blood, pain and martyrdom, and it is this duality that is significant in the story. To gain such a rose demands a price.

And our hero does not pay this price. The student throughout remains unconscious. Apart from moaning about his lack of a rose to present to his love, he does little. The little nightingale speaks to him but he does not understand, as his heart is still closed. And all night long, while the nightingale sings and dies a slow and agonising death with her heart against the thorn, sacrificing her heart's blood to form the red rose, he sleeps. Oblivious of the sacrifice and suffering involved in producing his desired red rose, he merely plucks it and then, when he is rejected, throws it into the road. He has no regard for this beautiful flower, this feeling, and treats it with disrespect, returning again to his safe and bookish world.

We see in this tale then the failure to make the move necessary to find love. Unaware and unappreciative of the sacrifice that created it, the student leans out and plucks the rose; so Eve plucked the apple from the tree of knowledge in the Garden of Eden. With the plucking came the birth of consciousness/knowledge. There is no such birth of consciousness in our tale, therefore no change happens. The student goes back to the life he led before.

'What a silly thing love is, it is not half as useful as logic, for it does not prove anything and is always telling one of things that are going to happen and making one believe things that are not true. In fact, it is quite impractical and as in this age to be practical is everything; I shall go back to philosophy and study metaphysics. So he returned to his room and pulled out a great dusty book and began to read.'

And what of Wilde himself? Though his wit and irony was undoubtedly brilliant, behind it, if you look carefully, you can see the hurt and despair of a man disconnected from his true spirit, from love, but who keeps it alive by writing about it.

## Saving Damaged Lovers: the Healing Dimension

The story of the nightingale and the rose carries another important element, common in many relationships. It contains the notion of sacrificing oneself for the other. There are many lovers who enter relationships with someone who is wounded or who cannot love them, because they are drawn by the challenge. 'I'll change him' turns into 'I'll love him so much, I'll help him open his heart', or 'I'll save him'. These are words that some women think about when such a dynamic is present in their love relationships. Men also can be drawn to love a woman they perceive as wounded and unable to love.

There is a healing dimension in love that is usually activated in a love affair. To be drawn to a lover who cannot return love is a particular type of dynamic present in many relationships. This element is usually unconscious, but surfaces when the relationship gets deeper and more established, and one partner wants more from the other than he or she is able or willing to give.

There is something very painful about this kind of relationship because often the lover, like the nightingale, will be totally tuned into the lost or damaged part of their partner. To help that partner unfreeze becomes the prime goal. A woman can personify a thus wounded man's anima, for example, and identify with the part of his soul he cannot reach. She will embody the archetype for him and if she remains unconscious, like the nightingale, may sacrifice herself for nothing. If this happens and she identifies with the archetype of the lost anima, she may lose touch with herself, her own life and soul, and therefore lose all.

Blanca was in love with Jose. Introduced to him at a friend's party, she initially thought little about him. A lanky, intellectual kind of man, Jose looked as though love was a stranger to him, and it seemed to Blanca that if love were a coat, it would not fit him. Awkward in his body, yet housing deep intelligent eyes, his quick wit and stimulating articulate conversation nonetheless drew her to stay and listen. Very soon she saw the effect she was having on him. With her physical beauty, wild open heart and easy manner, she fascinated him. And this pulled her in even more, so that when, a short time later, he called her, she happily went out to meet him.

Thus began a love affair that turned into a marriage that ended painfully after only six years. Blanca was young, innocent and inexperienced, but she was very hurt, since as a child she had experienced abandonment. She hated being alone, and craved the security a wealthy, steady man like Jose seemed to offer. But Jose was very damaged by his own early life and had, a long time ago, closed down. A deeply sensitive soul, he had been farmed out as a child and spent many of his formative years in boarding school. Since he was not physically strong, and did not fit into the sporty male boarding school ethic, he was frequently bullied, and suffered greatly. He survived on his keen and active intelligent wit.

Shortly after they met, Blanca wrote this poem. In it, she reveals how she identifies with his lost and trapped soul, and seeks to heal him.

The room was full of people,
There he was over there
The man I came to meet.

Awkward, long and dark,
Is that him I thought?
Not very good looking.
Later I noticed his eyes
A boy's eyes,
But it was what I saw inside them
Made me stop and stay awhile,
The child lay naked, somehow young for his years.

Later, deeper still, I saw the lost hungry soul
Yearning for he knew not what.
It should have been simple, but somehow it
Got twisted,
The restless soul, trapped in a crippled body,
Born damaged yet alive and
Burning with the will to succeed.
His spirit leaping out and far beyond the
Confines of his maimed flesh,
Destined to grapple endlessly with a
Force too big to rest even for a moment.

A tortured hungry soul
Longing for the life he felt but could not grasp,
A spirit's flight
Pure and full of love.
A false brashness didn't draw me
Away from the inner softness
For somewhere, somehow deep inside,
I saw and recognised the wound,
Felt it in me,
And back, back into a time
I never knew but felt,
I saw my brother hold my hand and cry.
Long, long ago,

Two spirit's trapped down by pain,
Unable to fly and soar above the harsh
Cruelties of things twisted by man's
unenlightened hand.
And being free, I cried for him his tears of despair,
And smiled a girl's smile as I watched my
brother walk
Free from the force that almost destroyed him.

Blanca lost herself in this relationship, and almost literally died when Jose left her abruptly for another woman. Terrorised at being alone, and ravaged by grief and pain, she spiralled quickly into a deep depression. She ceased to eat, lost the will to live, and was unable to care for herself. Like the nightingale, Blanca had sacrificed herself for love. But, like the student, Jose was unworthy of such a sacrifice, since remaining totally unconscious, he did not appreciate or value Blanca. Not willing to engage with, or understand his own anima, he remained trapped in his infantile mother complex, moving on to another woman on whom he projected mother.

Blanca herself housed a very needy little abandoned child, and she housed a damaged animus. Instead of being her inner king, capable of standing up for her and protecting her, her inner man was wounded and disempowered. If her animus had been healthy she would never have got involved with a man who was destined to betray and disappoint her. But she thought she could save him and herself, by turning him into her Prince Charming.

Many of us travel down the wrong roads looking for love, especially if we are wounded and needy emotionally. We may choose emotionally unavailable lovers, and imagine that through our love we will change them. What we need to remember is that in seeking to save our lovers, we are really trying to heal our own wounded hearts. If we do not make an effort to remain conscious at all times when relating then we can, like the nightingale, end up sacrificing ourselves for nothing.

And we can end up alone.

## What Story Are You Living Out Of?

Healing from within means you must identify your story so that you can begin to unravel and understand your patterns. Think about what story you might be living out of. Remember, if there was any fairy tale that impressed you as a child. Are you a Cinderella who waits for her prince to save her, or are you a Rapunzel, who remains trapped in your mother's world, waiting for the Prince who is daring enough to brave the forest and climb the tower to rescue you? Or you may be a Little Mermaid who surrenders her voice so that she may win the heart of her prince and gain an immortal soul. You might even be the prince who feels he has to rescue his princess and finds it hard to let her fight her own battles. Or you may be the Peter Pan who flies about and does not want to grow up or make a commitment?

It is a useful exercise to do, to spend some time writing a story about yourself and your relationship.

Begin with 'Once upon a time …'

## A Love Began

It was late and I was preparing to finish up for the day, close my computer and go downstairs for the evening. The phone rang. I answered it instinctively, something which I wondered about later since I normally always leave it on answering mode.

'Hello, is that Benig Mauger?' A mellow, deep male voice asked. Upon hearing to the affirmative, he then asked if he could come and see me. He had read my books and had only just got my number. He wanted to consult me on an urgent matter. Despite the fact that I was tired, and in fact had no spaces in my practice I cared to give away at the time, I agreed to see him the following week.

As I shuffled around the kitchen preparing my supper, I found myself thinking about this stranger. What, I wondered, was so urgent that it couldn't wait until morning? In the little he had said (I had encouraged but the briefest of exchange), I had detected not simply the desperation that often drives people to call a therapist, but a kind of fire, a passion that cannot be put on hold. A passion to have his questions answered maybe? Or maybe a compelling need to tell his story.

My life and work have taught me that the desire to tell one's story is very much part of a healing journey. We are engaged in this task all the time really. The only difference a therapist brings to the situation is that the story is heard. Somehow, bearing witness to the telling seems to validate the story. But healing does not happen overnight because the story is told; telling and listening takes time. It takes time to unravel the complicated bundle that is someone's inner life. Maybe then, for the lack of telling, this man's inner life had now swollen to an unbearable degree, infecting his outer life – and he could no longer wait.

All this was normal in the course of my work, but I wondered what it was, nonetheless, that made me answer the phone, and offer an appointment when I had resolved to keep any free time I had for myself. And why had this man chosen to call so late?

Sighing, I pushed the call to the back of my mind and turned on the television.

On Wednesday, the doorbell rang at the appointed time. I hurried downstairs and opened the door to a tall, middle-aged man. With white shoulder length hair and striking green eyes, he would have been handsome but for the extra weight he carried. Not simply physical weight; psychological weigh, if you can call it that. I immediately felt a sense of hurt, over laden by a very strong masterful force of personality.

He followed me upstairs to the consulting room, as is the norm.

'Thank you for seeing me so quickly,' he said settling himself down on the couch. Sitting opposite him I noticed his polished black shoes and saw he was dressed immaculately. He also had a strong presence. I often feel the energy of my clients and his was very strong, radiating a long distance around him. It drew me in by its force and, as I was later to discover, it also at times pushed me away.

As soon as he entered, the room was filled with sounds, colours and lots of activity. There was even a sense of majesty, as though with a swish of his hand he was not removing his coat, but adjusting his cloak. Looking at his face, I also saw that he knew this. In some far-from-conscious place, he knew his majesty, but it set him apart rather than helped him. He seemed ashamed, and this was at odds with his otherwise confident appearance. At some level, I sensed that this larger-than-life character felt he was nobody underneath the immaculate clothes and polished manners. Worse, he was a worthless wannabe, a poseur, not really deserving of the good things life had to offer. Carrying his shame like a protective mantle, he was certainly not aware of his inner beauty. It hindered rather than helped him.

Time passed, and as the story unfolded, the princely character disappeared to reveal a small, frightened, lonely boy who shifted uncomfortably on the couch. As I looked, I saw this handsome man shrink to a five-year-old sick child. The confident jaunty look in his eyes was replaced by a tearing vulnerability. And fear. In his eyes, I saw the man wrestle constantly with the boy, and gain ever so slightly, the upper hand. But not before I had glimpsed the terror and the pain.

*My name is Alan but I like to be called 'Alain' which is the French for Alan. Why? Because I loved to read, and early on had learnt French. Self taught from books I borrowed from the local library. It appealed to me; I somehow imagined as a boy, that I had lived there once. And that really I did not belong here. And when I visited France later as an adult, I felt at home.*

*I was born into a large, working-class family, in the city centre. Since my father worked on the railways when he could find work as a casual labourer, we often did not have enough to eat. Times were hard. My mother was constantly either pregnant, sick, or both. I don't remember her ever being anything other than exhausted, and that being so she had nothing to give. I hardly saw my father. I think he thought of us children as nuisances, and his marriage as a trap. My mother and he had married young, because at nineteen and seventeen, they had found themselves expecting my older sister.*

Alan switched back into regal mode and told me, in answer to my question why had he come, that he had no choice.

'What do you mean?' I asked, slightly irritated. 'Everyone has a choice and if a partner had sent him, then I didn't …'

'No, I wasn't sent,' he interjected cutting me off in mid thought.

I settled in to listen.

Alan told me that he had been married, and was divorced. He had had three serious relationships in the last ten years: and in between times, women, many women. But they all left him hungry. Ah, another Don Juan, I thought. I'm used to these.

'It's not as though I'm a Don Juan,' he cut in again. 'I really do want to relate. I just can't seem to. I don't know how. Or is it that I am afraid? I don't know. But I need to find some answers, so here I am.'

'Why now?' I asked. 'Why come to me now?'

'Because it is time,' he replied. And then he hesitated, before adding, 'I've met this woman, you see …'

Ah, I thought. So that's it. Cupid has hit again. Even in the heart of this man who had been 'hit' many times before and gradually gone cold, love had resurfaced. This did not surprise me, because I knew that love is, in fact, irrepressible; it is such an integral part of life that we actually cannot live without it. Those without a partner often pour that power, that energy, into domestic pets, animals such as dogs and cats. Others pour their love into their children, grandchildren and family. Still others into their work, hobbies, sports and pastimes they became passionate about. And some, of course, have given up.

Perhaps this was the case too, with Alan. But then he would not be here. A man like Alan, who thought he knew all the answers, would not have condescended to come to therapy. Suddenly the puzzle of the late phone call and my response was solved. In one go, I worked out why the hurry, and why my response. This man bowed to no one, his 'wish' was my command! And I had fallen into it. I let the realisation sink in and then settled to what would be a difficult challenge.

Over time Alan, or Alain, told me his story; little by little, piece by piece, we unravelled the complicated bundle of conflicting feelings and emotions that made up his life: and his loves. And with the unravelling came slowly a weaving together, of a particular soul's human journey, so that it began to make sense.

An excerpt from his journal

*I met her at a book launch. I wasn't intending to meet anyone, but if the truth were told, I was lonely. My last relationship had broken up over a year ago, and I was still smarting. Though I had brief encounters since, I was not fulfilled. Sex no longer distracted me as it had. I wondered was it my age? Had I suddenly become too old and tired for love, for sex even?*

*I love women. I have always loved them, but after a while, I get restless, bored, and either I leave them, or they leave me. Often they leave because I will not make a commitment.*

*Lately, my therapist asked me if I was afraid of commitment. I couldn't answer her. I had told her that I had the impression that every woman I had met wanted to put a cage around me. It was then she asked about the commitment. She pressed me, and seemed irritated when I added, 'They expect the relationship to be forever and ever'. Well, it's true isn't it?*

*But then she said, 'Doesn't everybody? I mean when you start a relationship are you already thinking about its end? Could it be you have some sort of agenda, Alan?'*

*I told her I would have to think about that.*

*Anyway, back to the book launch. I was introduced to this woman, and liked her. I was immediately drawn to her, not just because she was quite beautiful and indeed sexually alluring, but because of her vitality. She talked openly about loneliness and pain, without being dragged down by it - as though it was the most normal thing in the world to be lonely and going through a blue period.*

*What attracted you? my therapist asked.*

*Thinking about it, it was her femininity and the way she radiated something I had never felt, but long to feel.*

*I can only describe it as a sense of well being, vitality and wholeness. We began to talk and then one thing led to another. Very shortly afterwards we became lovers, but very soon too, I began to feel constrained. Though only a few weeks had passed, I felt she wanted more from me than I could give her. I was, as ever, reluctant to move, to commit. We argued over little things and I told her I did not want to be in a relationship; that is, a committed relationship. I found it was too difficult for me, I knew I couldn't really give her what she wanted.*

*And so, I know I will lose her. As well as that, my heart is still smarting, and try as I might, I cannot forget my past and move on.*

I could see that Alan carried his life story around with him all the time, that he never really relaxed and that being so, there was little room in his heart for anything or indeed anyone. I saw that each new woman he encountered and tried to engage with would get the same response.

Alan was filled with something that he called self-hate. I saw that he had a very conflicted and painful relationship with his anima, what we call in Jungian psychology, his inner woman, his soul mate. A man's anima is based on his first experience of relating to the feminine, usually his mother. So Alan was like many men, emotionally still mother bound. Separated from his mother for long periods of time as a sickly child, he had never broken away from her emotionally. He could not break away because his attachment to her was conflicted. He hated her for abandoning him but he longed for her love, and so he still sought her in his heart. And she, exhausted and running on empty as she was, had had nothing to give him. So instead, he sought to heal her.

Since our first relationship forms a template for all future relationships, most particularly love relationships, leaving our parents emotionally is an essential part of growing up, and moving on. The degree to which we have done this will be apparent in how we relate, or don't relate. Ultimately, all men have to leave their mothers, and all women face the very same task in relation to their fathers. If we do not make the emotional break from our initial love object (our parents), then we can spend the rest of our lives searching for someone that doesn't exist.

Emotional maturity and the capability of engaging in healthy intimate relationships are dependent on having worked through and emerged from the cocoon of childhood. Life demands that we move from a place of dependency to one of responsibility. So that when we are missing something, we learn to find what we are looking for on the inside first.

Alan was a passionate man who wanted to love, but he was also very conflicted in that he hated his needs. He wanted to love and be loved but, he said, he always ended up giving himself away in relationships. I asked him what he meant by that. He gave too much, was always in the supportive role and ended up feeling used. He said the women in his life never took responsibility, and he carried all the emotions. I doubted this, but recognised this is how he saw it.

Time was up. We arranged to meet again.

Lucie drove home in a terrible state. After her night with Alan, her heart was in tatters, yet again. What was all this about? She had only known him a few weeks, but already she felt she loved him, and so his break up of the relationship, such as it was, devastated her. Moreover, she could not understand it. Their relationship was still so young, it was only forming, how could it suddenly and abruptly end? They would spend endless evenings together, which usually ended up with lovemaking. They were passionate lovers. They walked on the beach, they went dancing together, and they visited art galleries. They had fun.

But partings were a problem. They would talk on the phone

in between times, and then the arguing would start. This still perplexed Lucie because, when she examined it, there was no real argument. Phone calls would be long, painful and protracted. Alan would pick something she said and take offence, and very soon an innocent remark ended up as a full-blown insult. She was abusing him, he said. He read dismissal and impatience into everything, until Lucie felt paralysed into fear of saying anything at all, and always ended up pacifying him. Not wanting to get caught in his endless negativity and criticism, she bit her tongue, and would say whatever she thought would placate him.

She knew placating him was wrong because she was not being honest, but she was afraid. And she wanted to keep the love there. She wanted to love him and be loved by him. At some level, this man challenged her, and she did not know how to respond when he behaved in this way. Besides, she had a very inquisitive and open mind, as well as heart, and she was willing to learn. From relating to him, she had already learned that she was quick and was reminded of her impatience. She must talk to her therapist about it.

So why did you let him get away with that? Her therapist asked, tapping her fingers impatiently on her writing pad. Lucie's therapist always had a pad in front of her, which she used to write down Lucie's dreams and other things. "I don't know," cried Lucie 'That's what I want you to tell me'.

Lucie was forty-eight, had been married and divorced, and had like Alan, at least three long-term relationships that had failed under her belt. A vital, articulate and strong woman, she still housed a small girl, who would do anything for love. Lucie's path to find love had so far taken her to many unsuitable places; places where she was unlikely to find what she was looking for. Lucie's abandoned little girl had, in the years of therapy and soul work, grown up considerably, but could still be counted on to rear her head when a man came into view and love was a possibility. Only her therapist really got to see her vulnerability, however. Lucie's vulnerability was, in fact, her strength. But she had yet to grow into that, or live it comfortably.

Lucie was a writer, and moderately successful. Graced with sparkling, if classical, good looks and a trim body that had given birth to two children, Lucie appeared to have it all. But she was lonely. Like Alan, she loved men, as he loved women. And she regularly fell in love, often with the 'wrong type'. She craved a relationship that would last, but they all seemed to come apart. In Jungian terms, Lucie had what you would call a well-developed animus, meaning she had a strong male side. This often compelled her to choose feminine or artistic men. In them she would seek something of her own latent feminine qualities, some vulnerability that she wanted to heal.

Invariably though, her lovers let her down. They were rarely forceful enough for her. She looked for strength in them that they did not have, and that she ended up providing. Structured by nature, it exasperated her when, making up for her lovers lack of firmness, she had to make the moves. She remained in control of her relationships.

'I'm tired of being in control,' she told her therapist. 'I want a strong man who will let me be my own person, and yet with whom I can share my life. Why do I constantly choose men that are somehow weak, and that let me down?'

'Why do you think that is, Lucie? Perhaps you are trying to find and relate to a part of yourself you have not yet accepted. What part would that be?'

'Well, maybe I am trying to relate to a vulnerable, wounded side. I don't know. It's not what I want though. I want a strong man who comes for me. I want him to make the moves. I don't want to have to drag a commitment or an engagement out of him.'

Lucie was, in essence, a very feminine woman. She was also quite spiritually aware, and over the last few years, had been drawn to follow a spiritual path. This was something that lay well with her and that seemed, over time, to have helped her grow. She was at ease with her physical self and, increasingly so, with her soul. But, as yet, she still sought a home, a place where her heart could be at rest. Lucie, at a deep level, was restless. It was that restlessness that had ended her marriage and many other situations in her life. She constantly sought change.

Despite her many lovers, Lucie was not yet fulfilled in love. Because of her spiritual bent, the kind of men she met were often similarly engaged, and had a conflicted relationship to the physical world, imagining they could only pursue a spiritual path if they were alone. Caught up in the spiritualisation of the material world and the feminine as a representative of this, they feared the power of the feminine, and were often not at home in their bodies, or their physical desires. Lucie, with her strong embodied femininity, threatened them. They both desired and feared her.

Alan had now been coming to regular sessions for six months. He was beginning to lose interest. In reality, he feared the commitment involved in the process. Using lack of money as an excuse, he began to miss sessions, and then asked me if he could come every other week. I did not comply with his request but instead challenged him.

'Are you afraid of the commitment?' I asked.

'No', he replied, 'but I don't feel I need to come any more. It's not getting anywhere.'

We had reached a place in his therapy where he was beginning to be exposed; or rather his inner, very wounded self was being exposed, and Alan did not like this. He did not like any woman seeing this side of him, so he began criticising the work and, by inference, me too. Gifted with unusual insight and intelligence, he used it as a defence, and began to subtly attack the process. I was not using the right technique; he was better able than I to interpret his dreams and so on. When that did not seem to work he switched quickly into princely mode, where he felt safe and in control. He was paying for the sessions; he was employing me. It was for him to decide what he should do with his life.

Yes, indeed it was.

Alan looked at Lucie as she entered the hotel lobby. They had arranged to meet here, before going on to a concert and dinner. As usual, his heart rose when he saw her. She was so beautiful and she was coming to meet him. Him, she had chosen him, when she could have had any man in the world. He watched her cross the room towards him and felt pride but, almost as soon, another darker, tangled feeling came in. He tried to squash it, but it rose as sharply and as fiercely as an arrow in battle. He hated her; she had everything, good looks, successful career, money, and worse, she was at ease with herself. Despite his own good looks and his immaculate dress, he felt ill at ease. No amount of well-cut garments and expensive aftershave could hide the degradation he felt inside. He was ugly deep within; he felt this and he hated his body. It was a body that had given him nothing but pain and anguish. And it kept love away from him.

Yet here was this lovely woman, ready to love him. And tonight, no doubt, they would make love. They had become lovers just recently, and Alan was beginning to feel for Lucie. This would not do. Sex was one thing but love another. Alan's heart was conflicted as he watched her cross the lobby towards him.

Laden with bags from her shopping trip, Lucie walked into the hotel. She did not see him at first, and looked around. It was early evening, and people were beginning to come in for pre-dinner drinks. He was sitting at a table in the corner of the lobby, a half empty glass in front of him. Her heart lifted. There he was, such a handsome and well-dressed man! She had been looking forward all day to this meeting – had dressed well, and had her hair done earlier in the day.

'Hello Alan,' she said. He stood up and bent to kiss her,

his manners as impeccable as his dress. Alain beckoned to the waitress to attend to her. *I feel good to be with this man, I'm glad I got my hair done.* Lucie knew she looked good and was longing for her new lover to say so. She also knew that he was not a man who gave compliments easily, so that when he told her she looked beautiful, Lucie glowed even more. She felt like a goddess. She was falling for this man.

On only their second meeting, Alan had called her 'princess'. And with that she was hooked! Lucie was a sucker for good-looking men, and especially those who joined her in her fairy-tale game. Part of her was a goddess, the goddess of love naturally, and part of her was a Princess. Alan, himself a prince, of course, was able to pick up on this and together they played well.

And loved well, when it stayed at this level. Part of his attraction was his ability to read into her, to know her, to recognise her. It moved Lucie that someone, almost a stranger, seemed to know her. And his very soulfulness also seduced her. Alan was very 'tuned in' at a deep level and this always attracted women because it made them feel special. And somewhere too, Lucie tuned in to a strength in Alan, a raw male power he himself had not yet integrated. He challenged her, and though it frightened her somewhat, because it made her feel uncertain, she welcomed it. At some level, Lucie felt she had met her match. Here was her prince, ready to take her and make her his queen.

Now it had all vanished, the fairy tale had ended.

# PART FIVE

# ANATOMY OF RELATIONSHIPS

# Chapter 8

## Inner Landscapes of Love

The minute I heard my first love story
I started looking for you, not knowing
How blind that was.
Lovers don't finally meet somewhere
They're in each other all along.

*Love's Bewilderment:* Rumi

Most of us long for a soul mate. To love another soul is part
of the way in which the divine plan expresses itself within us.
And relationship, whether with another person or with one's
own inner nature, or even with one's work and calling in life, is
essential to individuation. Whether our search is for that 'other
half' as Plato calls it, or the one that will complete us and lead
us to the divine mystery, we all seek wholeness. It is this drive to
inner wholeness that compels us to seek a soul mate.

Loving another person can open our hearts and bring us
to experience compassion. However, there is a confusion about
love. We have a tendency to imagine that it is outside of us
– it is out there in the world and if we are lucky we might be
loved, or someone might love us. We do not see that it is inside
us, that we are love. It is the projection of love 'out there' that
ultimately makes us unhappy. We do not see that when we fall
in love, for instance, it is with someone who embodies the soul
qualities we desire and have not yet activated in ourselves.

A man I knew complained bitterly that he could never

find a woman who truly loved him. All his relationships ended after a time because he never felt satisfied that he was loved. One day I said to him that the challenge was not to find love but to be able to give it. 'How much are you able to love?' I asked him. He had never thought about it this way – it was a turning point in his life.

We are all connected, as we saw in chapter one, and being part of the spirit of the world means we are all part of each other. In this way, our soul mates represent split off parts of ourselves. You could say that this 'significant other' is, in essence, part of our separated selves, and together we form a whole. As the great Sufi poet Rumi wrote, 'Lovers don't finally meet somewhere, they are in each other all along'. Our search for union and for wholeness guides us to our 'other half', to our soul mate. In essence, we are being guided to become more conscious, and to become more whole within ourselves. Inner union is essential to the spiritual well being of every individual, which makes the desire for relationship so compelling.

From a spiritual perspective, learning to love is part of the challenge of human life. We are offered the gift of love, and the challenge to open our hearts. Accepting and enjoying human love is part of our spiritual growth. Enduring the joys and conflicts of the heart will ultimately propel us to encounter our divine natures, and to unite the opposites within us. Experiencing profound love and heartbreak is also the conduit to learning to love unconditionally and to experience compassion.

## Soul Mates: Mirrors of the Self

Relationships, however, contain challenges. The struggle to overcome these challenges presents opportunities to become more conscious and, ultimately, more whole. Seeing our lovers and partners as a mirror is helpful when trying to understand the inner dynamics of our intimate relationships. We can ask, what does my partner reflect back to me about myself? What do I see in him or her that I do not see in myself? What pattern am I acting out in my choice of partners and my way of relating?

We do not love by accident! There is always a greater plan at work in our lives and relationships. We saw earlier that we are drawn to have relationships with certain people because of our soul contract, and certain agreements we made before birth. We also know that we are guided in our choice of partners by not only our soul destiny, but also the tapestry of our family and archetypal heritage. On top of this, we are influenced, as we saw earlier, by certain archetypes as they are humanised for us by our parents. Our early life and our relationship with our parents influence how we will relate later in life, and have a huge impact on our love lives. All of these factors mean that there is always something to be learned in each relationship we have, no matter the outcome.

If you want to see yourself, look at your partner. In him or her you will view parts of yourself, unconscious aspects of your personality you need to recognise and integrate. The soul hates to be fragmented, so it will generally draw you to a partner who will complement you. In relating you will gradually, if you are willing to engage with the process, become more aware.

In Jungian psychology we talk of the 'shadow'. The shadow is that part of us we repress, and also that we have in potential. In other words, our shadow represents unconscious aspects of our personalities, and includes our latent qualities. When we relate, particularly in intimate relationships, we usually project these aspects onto our partners and those closest to us. When we project unwanted qualities or patterns we consider unacceptable, we will be irritated by these very things in our partner.

Katya, for example, had great trouble coping with Ben's slowness. Impatient by nature, she could not understand how Ben would take hours to get ready in the morning and always seemed to be dawdling. He would spend endless time completing a task she felt could be done in jig time. He, on the other hand, hated her impatience, and the more she urged him on and got irritated by him, the more he dragged his heels. If they were on an errand for instance, she would march on ahead of him, which he felt as a dismissal. In actual fact, Katya needed to learn patience, and Ben needed to recover some of his strong, purposeful male energy and to speed up a bit! Katya's impatience with Ben could be seen as a reflection of her impatience with part of herself, her animus, her inner man.

The same process applies in the positive. When we fall in love, we project positive, beautiful qualities onto our lovers, so they embody all the beauty our soul desires. Isabel, for example, fell in love with the joy and creativity she saw in James and needed to find in herself. He, conversely, loved her depth, and her ability to nurture and be open and loving. He needed to heal his wounded feminine nature so that it nurtured him instead of castigated him. And Isabel needed to recognise and incorporate her inner creativity, her wounded masculine.

This process of mutual projection means there are always inner forces at play in our relationships. Becoming aware of what these inner forces are is helpful so as to maintain an equilibrium, and work through conflicts within the relationship. As I said previously, our engagement in intimate relationships offers us a unique opportunity to know ourselves. Understanding something of our own inner landscape in relationship will help us relate with more consciousness, and eventually to cease repeating patterns that may be destructive to our well being and that of our relationships. It will also help us heal our emotional wounds.

## Complexes

Looking more deeply into this inner landscape, we encounter our complexes. Most people have heard of complexes. The father and the mother complex are perhaps the most commonly known. Our shadows contain our complexes. Jung and other psychologists consider complexes, like archetypes, to be central organising principles in the psyche, in that they are dynamic and responsible for feelings and outer behaviour.

Complexes consist of emotionally charged memories from different periods of our life that resemble each other in the quality of emotion or physical sensation that they share. Emotionally relevant memories are stored in the unconscious in the form of complex dynamic constellations. Each complex generally has a basic theme, such as say, abandonment and betrayal, or humiliation and shaming. In the negative, these experiences have damaged our self-esteem and ability to trust, for example, and since they are buried deep in our unconscious, are responsible for reactive behaviour at ego level.

Since there exists a dynamic interplay between these systems and our external world, at some stage, our complexes are activated. This means that external events will trigger internal dynamics that will bring to life our complexes. Our activated complexes will push us to recreate their core themes in our lives. Intimate relationships offer a unique and perfect setting for the activation and working through of complexes. Often, couples will be drawn together with similar complexes, so that they have the opportunity to heal and to grow. In their relating, they will be challenged to transform and heal their complexes, a necessary part of the journey to wholeness. Looked at from the perspective of the soul, we are always tested to see how we will deal with the obstacles placed on our journey, so that these challenges represent spiritual tasks of empowerment.

A woman with a particular father complex, for example, will often choose a partner who will in some way mirror it back to her. If she has experienced a very dominant and tyrannical father as a child, she may choose a man she thinks she can dominate, or who will, as their relationship unfolds, dominate her; or she may find that her partner has a complex with a similar tone, so that in the rubbing together of their complexes, a dynamic energy gets activated which has the potential to make both partners more conscious. Whatever way the father complex energy gets activated in the relationship, it will surface and act as a conduit to both consciousness and healing, if the partners are willing to engage with it.

## Archetypes as Architects of Love

There is always an archetypal core to a complex, and uncovering the multiple layers involved in a complex is a regular part of normal psychoanalytic work. The archetype, per se, is usually neutral. At the primordial level, the archetype is neither negative nor positive, since it is life experience that gives the archetype its emotional energetic charge, thus forming the complex. Earlier we saw that two archetypes, the anima and the animus, are particularly involved in intimate relationships, acting as architects of love. The anima in the man and the animus in the woman will act as guides in the choice of partner, and also determine how they will relate.

Our archetypal heritage informs our psyche in the form of imagery and conditioning, and our early experiences flesh out the archetype, giving more shape to our soul. The roots of the soul have a resonance in our lives in that they give rise to our experiencing the world in certain ways. We may be predisposed to experience love in a particular way, for example, or to imagine we can never find love; or we may have a conflicted and painful relationship with love and commitment to another soul. We may be pulled by conflicting emotions, such as the need to love and be loved, and the fear of being controlled and losing one's identity within relationship.

Our inner landscape will house particular archetypes, and they will influence how comfortable we are in relating, and indeed how we relate. According to Caroline Myss, there are four archetypes in particular that have a great deal of influence on our lives, and that walk with us. These are the

Child, the Victim, the Prostitute and the Saboteur. They are our main survival archetypes and, as such, our intimate companions in life. They form the basis out of which we live, and determine largely how we relate to others and ourselves. As the architects of our lives, how each archetype lives in us is determined largely by the manner in which they are humanised for us by our early life experience. Our first relationship with our parents and siblings, for example, provide a template for future relating.

It is important to remember that each archetype has a negative and positive aspect. The positive aspect of an archetype means the gifts that a person may develop as a result of experiencing life as an orphan, for instance, and the negative represents the shadow aspects, or places where such a person may remain stuck. I have heard this dynamic described as benefits and baggage!

The gifts of the Orphan Child archetype are the ability to endure and persevere in difficult circumstances, and the development of independence and trust in their own ability to overcome obstacles and thrive. The shadow, or negative, aspects of the Orphan Child manifests in the inability to grow up and shake off the feelings of abandonment and rejection. The scar tissue from family rejection pushes such orphans into always trying to find surrogate families and structures or groups where they can fit in. Feelings of abandonment can propel the orphan into inappropriate relationships to experience a sense of belonging.

## The Inner Child

The Child archetype embodies innocence and purity. Everyone identifies with the Inner Child. As children we are meant to be learning through playing, living much of the time in our imagination and dreams, only gradually developing our own separate egos. We are still partly in spirit, gradually learning about life and dependent on caregivers to provide us with basic security, and to guide us. There is a belief amongst Tibetans that it takes seven years for the spirit to fully incarnate in a child. Learning the challenges involved in human living takes time so that, generally, childhood is meant to be a time when we are gradually introduced to the world from the security of being loved and nurtured.

When children are forced to take on too much responsibility in early life, then their spiritual development is disrupted, such children have to grow up too quickly. In essence, this means that the child is robbed of his or her innocence. Many children are born into difficult circumstances and families where their spiritual growth is disturbed due to emotional or physical neglect, lack of love or abuse. Since a loving home and parents is not a given, many of us will have suffered as children, and we can suffer deeply when we are deprived of those special years, when we are supposed to be innocent and living in our imaginations.

Our Inner Child will guide us in how we relate to our intimate partners because in relationship, we re-enact our first relationship with our parents. In adapting to our partner's personality, we mirror the adaptations we made to our parents, teachers and other authority figures. For example, if we have experienced abandonment as a child, then we may behave to our partner as a child in relation to a potentially abandoning parent.

Isabel frequently fell into this pattern when there was conflict with James. In order to keep him happy so that he would not leave her, and she would not feel abandoned, she would often compromise herself and her integrity. Fearful of the moods he could get into, she would endure bad behaviour and, rather like a battered wife, would excuse him and return for more, grateful that she had his attention, if not his 'love'. Operating out of fear, she would not be able to assert herself, and ended up placating him instead.

When such feelings are prominent, then the resolution of

conflict within a relationship is difficult, because one partner has regressed to the Child, and relates to the other as a parental figure. Many, if not most, arguments escalate into a position where both partners are 'complexed', meaning they are acting and reacting out of their complexes. When this happens, neither is really listening to the other. And since being complexed means to be in the grip of strong and possibly overriding emotion, maintaining perspective and clarity necessary for the resolution of conflict is impossible.

When complexed in this way in their arguments, Isabel, for instance, became the insecure, needy Child, fearful of being abandoned, and James, who had a lot of activated Divine Child energy, became the tyrannical omnipotent child. The Divine Child is another aspect of the Child archetype and we will discuss this in detail further on in the chapter. When a child is felt to be special by its parents, it often projects this energy outwardly – in the negative, with feelings of being special and superior to others. James would shout and stamp, as a spoilt angry child, and frighten Isabel's needy little child into submission. Since to his mother he had been a magical, special child, James expected to get his own way. The Magical or Divine Child archetype also has its gifts and its challenges.

As already mentioned, each archetype has its strength, its gift, as well as its shadow side. When a particular archetype is active in a person we refer to it as being strongly constellated. One's childhood experiences generally have a lot to do with which archetypes will be active in us. A strongly-constellated child archetype will mean the person can be endlessly creative and innovative and will have the courage, as children often do, to follow their own path, to explore. In Jungian psychology we call this eternal child energy the Puer or the Puella archetype. This young Peter Pan energy has a creative and free-spirited side, always ready to break existing boundaries, to create something new, like a child, discovering life for the first time. The negative or shadow side of this, of course, is the desire to remain a child, and an inability to grow up and take responsibility, or make a firm commitment, to anybody or anything. The shadow of the Puer or Puella is the desire to avoid responsibility or accountability.

## The Orphan Child

The Orphan is an aspect of the Inner Child. Many of us can relate to the Orphan, especially if we have had emotionally stark or wounded childhoods. It is often recognised that un-mothered or abandoned children, or children who have experienced a lack of love and holding, can be unusually intuitive, and are often gifted. Like the ugly duckling that becomes a swan after it has been ostracised from the group, it appears that most gifts come to us after a period of suffering. Separation and abandonment by our tribe – our families – can have such an effect on us, so that we learn to be resourceful, and to find our own way in the world.

A degree of separation from our families is essential to grow up. At some level, we have to be separate in order to develop our own individual identity. Separation from our parents and familial values, and an experience of aloneness, are necessary in order to develop our own individual values and integrity. A period, or periods, of time alone and abandoned by our 'clan' provide us with opportunities to develop certain gifts, such as the ability to trust and to survive alone. In general, group identity, important in early life, hinders individual development, and it is necessary to break away, as adolescents naturally do from parents, in order to truly individuate.

If the archetype of the Orphan Child is strongly constellated in you, you may feel from birth that you are not part of your family, including the family psyche and tribal spirit. Like the Little Mermaid, Cinderella, the Matchstick Girl and others, you will feel different. Myss describes it thus: 'The absence of family values, attitudes and traditions inspires or compels the Orphan Child to construct an inner reality based on personal judgment and experience. Orphans who succeed at finding a path of survival on their own are celebrated in fairy tales and folk stories as having won a battle with a dark force, which symbolically represents the fear of surviving alone in this world.'[40]

Many of us can relate to the Orphan Child. This seems to be particularly so in the healing or caring professions. Having a strongly-constellated Orphan Child myself, I have learned the hard way to be independent and resourceful. However, I am also keenly aware of the need to move on from feelings of abandonment that originate in my early life experiences. I have learned to recognise when my abandoned Inner Child dictates my feelings or actions. I know how easy it is to become overwhelmed by such feelings, and I have worked hard to transcend Orphan wounds.

The shadow of the Orphan archetype is the tendency to remain stuck in childhood wounds. The genesis and flowering of a culture of 'woundology', where people are directed to uncover, confront and heal their childhood wounds, may have played into this tendency, so that people find it hard to move on. Remaining wounded can be preferable to being healed if it is more profitable. Myss suggests that cultural attitudes have now extended beyond appropriate healing measures to become hypersensitive to the claims and demands of victims. The social message here is surely that wounds are a means of profit; healing earns you nothing.

In my therapeutic work, I am more and more drawn to helping people see how they can remain trapped in childhood through identifying with their wounds. Facilitating the movement from enduring the suffering of early painful experiences, learning from them and transcending them, I consider one of my main tasks as a therapist.

## The Divine or Magical Child

If we have experienced abandonment and a lack of nurturing, then we will have a wounded, insecure Inner Child, whereas if we have been 'the apple of our mother's or father's eye', we might carry the Divine Child archetype. The Divine or Magical Child is the 'special child', who can also be wounded because, in essence, from being overvalued or spoilt, they are unprepared for a life where they are not central figures. They need to learn that the world does not revolve around them. Such children may also be hurt because they have not been valued for who they are, but rather what their parents want them to be.

The gift of the Divine or Magical Child is the ability to see the potential and sacred beauty in all things. It is the part of us that is both enchanted and enchanting to others. When we have this gift, we are able to see the beauty and potential in everyone, but the pitfalls are that we may be blinded to the negative, or caught by the fantasy rather than the reality of a person or situation. The shadow of this archetype is also the belief that no action or energy is necessary for growth, so that there is a retreat into fantasy. Such children may also have been spoilt or 'looked up to' by their parents, which reinforces the attitude that they will be taken care of, without any effort or involvement on their part.

## The Wounded Child

Many people can relate to being a Wounded Child. This person holds the memory of the suffering, abuse, neglect and other traumas he or she experienced as a child. The Wounded Child pattern is very common since it is generally the focus of therapy, and childhood trauma is considered the raison d'etre of adult suffering. The Wounded Child in you will draw you to experience adult life a particular way, and influence how you behave and, most particularly, how you relate. Many people blame their Wounded Child for their subsequent dysfunctional relationships. Blaming, however, does not facilitate healing.

The positive aspects of this archetype are that the painful experiences in one's life can awaken a deep sense of compassion, and a desire to help others heal such experiences. Spiritually, a wounded childhood sets you on the learning path of forgiveness, and can open your heart to compassion. The negative or shadow aspects of the Wounded Child are the tendency to blame others for your current situation and shortcomings, and also to wallow in self pity. When this aspect is constellated in your psyche you will find it hard to move on, because you blame all your shortcomings and problems on your past, and you remain stuck in self pity. You are then crippled by your past rather than empowered by it.

## The Inner Victim

The Victim archetype embodies self esteem and deals with issues of personal power. Again, how this archetype manifests in our lives is largely dependent on how we have experienced our formative years. Have we built up a good sense of self and a healthy self esteem? The core issue for Victims is whether it is worth giving up your sense of empowerment to avoid taking responsibility for your independence. Sometimes a child has been kept in a childhood paradise for too long, and does not want to take responsibility for his or her own life. Parents sometimes keep children bound to them. They do them no favours because those children find it hard to flee the nest when the time is appropriate. Such children make conflicted adults who have a hard time taking responsibility for their own lives, and who expect others to provide for them.

Developing a sense of personal power is very much dependent on how a person feels about him or her self. A healthy self esteem is necessary to be able to take one's own power, and to stand up for oneself. Taking responsibility involves the willingness to give up dependency on others to meet your needs. Independence, true independence, requires that you take responsibility for your own life, and for your choices. So the victim archetype mediates in you a sense of your own power, and is about evaluating your relationship to power. Honesty is very much at stake here because a victim generally always blames others for their difficult life situations.

A man I knew, who was divorced and living on social benefits, spent the whole time complaining that he was the way he was because of his ex wife's demands and behaviour. Even though they had had a difficult marriage, with endless conflict, he had not ended the marriage, she had. And he had always given everything to her, whilst she had taken everything and so on. Listening to him, it was as though he had absolutely no part to play in his marriage, or the ending of it. He had merely reacted to her. He could not see that he had, by his own life choices and his own behaviour, had a hand in his present situation. An archetypal Victim, while he felt like this, he remained in a prison of poverty; a narrow prison of his own making.

Being a Victim is to have no sense of personal power, or the ability to make self-empowering choices. The beneficial side is that when properly recognised, the Inner Victim can be a great help in intuiting situations where we might be in danger of being victimised. It can also help us see how we might be playing victim for personal gain in the form of sympathy or pity. To work with our Inner Victim means to also become aware of our tendencies to victimise others. Healing the Victim involves working towards a stronger sense of personal power, which comes naturally when there is healthy self esteem.

The Victim archetype will be seen in our intimate relationships by how we deal with issues of power and control. If we have a strong Victim energy, we will often then try and control our partners through passive aggressive or other behaviour. Passive aggressive behaviour refers to the inability to confront issues directly and to use more subversive, covert ways to control others. Emotional blackmail is an example of passive aggressive behaviour. We will have difficulty confronting problems and dealing with issues in a direct way; or we may feel 'victimised' by our partners and not be able or willing to stand our own ground. A Victim feels powerless, and will never stand up and take his or her own power in a balanced way. The polar opposite of the Victim is the Tyrant, who can become tryannical in an attempt to control.

Passive aggressive behaviour in a person in relationship is a particular way in which the Inner Victim comes through. The person is usually very fearful of taking responsibility for their lives, their choices and life decisions, and so projects this forceful energy onto their partners, whom they then berate for having the power in the relationship. The Inner Victim can also come through in obsessive compulsive behaviour, which is designed to keep the person in a safe place, away from having to face life's struggles. An obsessive compulsive person is compelled to engage in habitual behaviour repetitive actions or both. Obsessive compulsive behaviour is a defence against inner chaos and change, and represents a regressive move to perceived safety.

## The Inner Prostitute

The Prostitute archetype embodies and tests the power of faith. If you have no faith that you will be looked after, or that you can look after yourself, then you will sell yourself for physical, emotional or any other security. On the other hand, if you have faith, then no one can buy you. If we have experienced illness, or a difficult and shaky beginning, or if we were abandoned or separated from our family in our earliest years, then we may have a strong Prostitute energy. Lacking faith that we will be looked after, or that we can look after ourselves, we will do anthing to buy love since as children we are dependent on our parents' love to provide us with physical security, a home, food and so on. The Prostitute in us is insecure, and has to sell him or her self in return for physical security, love and the promise of emotional and economic security.

A basic lack of trust and faith in life means that our Inner Prostitute has great difficulty being alone, or imagining they can survive without a partner. Prostitute interactions make us confront our fears of survival, and represent the most painful type of relationships. Though more commonly recognised in women, the Inner Prostitute can also be present in men.

The Prostitute archetype is about mediating and confronting our fears of survival, and in our relationships, will often mean we compromise ourselves in return for emotional and/ or physical security. Our Inner Prostitute in intimate relationship will imagine she cannot manage her life, or even survive without her partner, and so she sells herself. She may sell her body, her soul, her integrity or all three. It can be that she offers herself up as a sexual or emotional healer to her partner, in return for physical or emotional security. Choosing a particularly wounded or damaged man, she may imagine she can help or save her partner, and therefore becomes the 'carer' in the relationship. In doing so, while still remaining unconscious, she is selling her soul.

Many women prostitute themselves in this way in their marriages, to men who may make good providers, but bad partners. We saw this earlier in the story of Blanca and Jose. These women may be internally very unhappy, and feel used and demeaned by their husbands, but they are afraid to leave because of a fear of being alone. Men can also be held hostage by their Inner Prostitutes in unhealthy relationships and feel unable to leave or make any changes, because of a fear of abandonment.

Sometimes, a woman sells herself to men as a sexual or other object because she is in search of her positive animus, her inner man. She will look for him in every man she meets and offer herself to him in return for the protection and emotional or physical security she craves.

A woman married a rich man whom she knew was not capable of truly loving or respecting her because, left with four small children and very little money after her first husband moved out, she felt alone and vulnerable. Doubting her own capabilities and feeling utterly abandoned, she married for security and thus sold her soul. She suffered greatly in this situation since, at heart, she felt she had made the wrong decision but felt trapped by her fears.

The Prostitute archetype can also constellate in artists, or anyone who sells themselves, or their work short, in return for material or other rewards. Marketing, media and publicity concerns necessarily bring up the possibility of prostituting one's work in return for commercial success. Thanks to my strongly constellated child or free spirit energy, I have never yet succumbed to this iniquity, but it is something that every artist at some point has to grapple with. It is part of the shadowy side of life every human being has to struggle with at some stage.

Confronting the Prostitute archetype within ourselves transforms it into its opposite, the Guardian archetype, so that we feel secure and happy that we can manage our lives. When we develop trust in ourselves and in the universe to provide all we need, then we can mitigate the Prostitute, and become stronger and more confident in our own abilities. We rely less on others to meet our needs, which in turn frees us to be ourselves. When we allow ourselves to tap into divine guidance, and realise that everything we need for our life tasks will be provided, we transform the Prostitute into the Guardian, and we are able to look after ourselves. We are at our strongest when we do not look to anyone for approval or happiness.

## The Inner Saboteur

The archetype of the Saboteur embodies and represents how we deal with choice. As the name implies, the Saboteur in us will be responsible for disrupting our lives. The core issue for the Saboteur is fear of inviting change into our lives. Change requires that we respond positively to life opportunities that could shape us. When the Saboteur energy is strong in us, it resists change and the opportunity to grow and develop. It makes its energy felt through disruption, so that we sabotage our opportunities for advancement, and may even reject relationships that are good for us. The Saboteur is the mirror that reflects our fears of taking responsibility for ourselves and for what we have created in our lives.

In intimate relationships, the Saboteur makes itself felt through behaviour that is disruptive of change and growth. Engaging in endless conflict and arguments can be a way that the Saboteur breaks up a relationship, or the chance of harmony, love and happiness that the relationship might represent. The Saboteur in us is responsible for spoiling our chances of happiness, and is usually based on fear of responding positively to opportunities that shape and deepen our spirit. Basically, the Saboteur is responsible for self-destructive behaviour.

A woman who craved a fulfilling intimate relationship with a soul mate and life partner, and who had searched many years for such a partner, sabotaged her chance of happiness. When such a man came into her life, and seemed to offer her the committed relationship she so desired, fearing the closeness and commitment involved, she pushed him away. As the relationship developed, she began to feel claustrophobic, and her fears of closeness and intimacy surfaced so that, panicking, she told him she did not want to live with him. He took this as a rejection, and since his own Saboteur was also constellated in their relating, gave her ultimatums that he knew she could not keep. This couple, though their love for each other was without question, spent much of the time in argument and discord until finally, they split up.

Responding positively to change requires courage and conviction, and the desire to grow. It requires letting go of fear, particularly of the unknown. Inviting change into our lives requires surrender to the future, being in the moment, and the willingness to let go of the past. It also requires a leap of faith.

The Saboteur can be strongly constellated in a person who has been too sheltered as a child. Such a person remains unconsciously bound to childhood and has a fear of moving on, taking risks and making life-changing decisions. The leap of faith required to respond to life-changing situations and to deepen the spirit seems too difficult to take for such a person, who prefers to remain in the comfort he or she knows. 'Better the devil you know than the devil you don't know' can be the Saboteur's dictum!

Conversely, the Saboteur can be constellated in a person who had no secure, loving home and who, in the hunger for love and security, created his or her own home. Built on strong defences, fences and the sign 'keep out' are usually posted there, so that no intruders are likely to disturb this self-made, narrow world. Change is not welcome, so that all opportunities for growth and positive experiences are met with suspicion, and rejected. The Saboteur prefers to stay put, and thus loses out on opportunities to develop and move on.

Engaging your Inner Saboteur means that you will gain the ability to recognise situations when you are in danger of being sabotaged, or of sabotaging yourself. In this way you will learn to read the signs, and stop yourself repeating mistakes and patterns that will ultimately cause you grief. If you dialogue honestly with your Inner Saboteur, you will gradually learn to be able to take the leaps of faith necessary to be able to make life-empowering (rather than destructive) choices.

## Loving from a Wounded Place
We come to love, and we come to a relationship, with our survival archetypes in place. The Inner Child, Prostitute, Victim and Saboteur, will all be there. We unconsciously carry into our

relationships our childhood conflicts and wounds. In most relationships, each partner's Inner Child is constellated, which activates the healing dimension within the relationship. Though our greatest challenge as human beings is to learn to love unconditionally, our childhood conditioning means that we love conditionally, and we generally expect our lover to meet our needs and heal our wounds. As we saw earlier, if a soul contract involves relating to a particular person so that certain lessons can be learned, then powerful forces will magnetise these two souls together.

We enter relationships because, at a conscious or unconscious level, we want to grow. This is a natural part of our spiritual evolution, and our soul will guide us there if there is a particular experience or experiences we need to learn from. However, we may or may not be conscious of our Inner Child and its wounds and cries for healing, and so we may invest our lovers and our relationships with tremendous power to heal, or hurt us. Fear of abandonment, as we saw, will mean we have a tendency to compromise ourselves for love. This could mean staying in abusive or unhealthy relationships rather than making the positive choice to leave, or it can mean we have great difficulty establishing our boundaries within the relationship.

If the healing dimension is strong in a relationship, there will be many hard challenges, some very difficult to bear, as activated wounded Inner Children and complexes make for demanding relationships. Our Inner Child may be wounded in a particular way and, in relationship, it will be awakened to its need for love. We want our lover to be different, to meet our needs, to be there for us no matter what. Often we are disappointed, because he or she has let us down, and is not what we expected. If we refuse to look within, and continue to remain unaware, we may leave that person in the mistaken conviction that we have made a mistake, and we can find what we need in another.

We will continue seeking in vain, for we need to see that what we seek in the other is, in fact, what is missing in ourselves.

## Look for the Hero Inside Yourself

Looking within is ultimately our most important and vital challenge. It is vital if we want to heal our hearts, take responsibility for our lives, and evolve. It is all too easy to project everything onto others: our sense of inadequacy, our lack of self esteem, our anger at our early unmet needs, our wounded hearts and our need for love. If we continue to do this we will always be unhappy, because ultimately we are expecting to receive everything from outside of ourselves. The catch phrase 'love yourself' is so clichéed as to be often dismissed, yet is nonetheless an important reality and essential truth. We need to understand and learn that love is not something that lies outside of ourselves; it is within us.

We need to look for the hero inside ourselves.

However, many of us do not grow up knowing we have a hero inside ourselves. If we have had difficult or unhappy childhoods, we might feel we are lacking in some way, and do not have what it takes to be happy, or to create happy lives and relationships. If our self esteem is unstable, we often look to others for approval and confirmation of identity.

In our Western culture, we are not, as children, taught much about our hearts, and how to handle love. A young teenage girl stood up at the end of one of my public talks and said, 'I wish we were told in school that one day your heart will be broken, and how to deal with that. Instead of spending so much time learning to sew and do mathematics, we need to be taught about our emotions – our hearts.' I was alerted by the simplicity and truth of what she said. I was moved to hear such an essential truth from a very young person.

But it is true. How often are children and adolescents taught about heartbreak, and emotional needs? Very rarely. In fact one of the difficulties and challenges facing many young people today is how to deal with love, feelings of neediness, and desire for love and relationship. Children and young people are taught sex education, not love or heart education. When young hearts are broken, as they can be when a first relationship breaks up, the result can be devastating. It appears that for boys in particular, this is a problem. An initial heartbreak can last a lifetime.

Emotional isolation in young people, particularly in boys, was something that became apparent when I was writing and researching my book, *Reclaiming Father*. In our culture, boys seem to have a harder time than girls when it comes to love and matters of the heart. Perhaps boys, and men, are less equipped than girls and women to deal with heartbreak. As I wrote then, the cultural and social climate in which we live tends to make it harder for boys to admit to having a heart first of all, and to needing help when they cannot bear the pain of their hearts. There is simply nowhere to go when it hurts.

Growing up, we are not taught enough about our hearts and our emotional lives. And yet, without a heart (symbolically and actually) we would die! We are not generally taught to value our feelings, and to understand that these feelings, and how we manage them, will determine the flavour of our lives. We are not taught that love is the greatest challenge and the greatest truth, and that we may endure painful experiences in our search for love. Perhaps if we understood that when we fall in love we activate powerful inner forces and patterns, it might help us better deal with heartache, and ultimately with our relationships.

Yet relationships, and our ability to love and receive love, form the core of our lives. Writing this book, I met with, and talked to, many people about love and their experiences of relationships. It surprised me how many people volunteered that their first love relationship and experience of loss had deeply affected them, and their subsequent relationships. I learned that the first heartbreak can be so devastating, that some never quite recover.

## Sex and Love – Another Split

Another complicating factor in relationships is the split between body and mind, or the divorce of our emotional lives from our thinking lives. In our modern world, sex is often divorced from love. There are many reasons for this. One of these is how we view love as external to us. We learn that if we are lucky we might find love, but it is often at the cost of giving away something precious. This precious thing, in young girls especially, is giving their body before they are emotionally ready to experience physical love. Instead of a spiritual initiation through love, our young people are often initiated through sex.

In our modern culture the sexual behaviour of young people is a cause for concern. Adolescents, children really, are being initiated into sexual experience now much too soon. In Ireland this is exacerbated by a 'drink culture' where tolerance for alcohol abuse is high. It is sad to see the little girl inside the made-up woman that is only twelve or thirteen years old, teetering on high heels, wearing a short skirt, shivering in the cold on an evening out. It is painful to realise that it is likely that the same girl, on the brink of womanhood, will a few hours hence either throw up from excess alcohol consumption, or be sexually initiated, or both.

One imagines that many young people may confuse sex with love, thereby setting up a further fragmentation of the heart, which they will seek to heal in later relationships. The initiation into adulthood, and into sexual love, is a very delicate thing. Robert Bly writes about the great disappointment of the adolescents in our culture who were promised that something wonderful would happen when they grew up. He writes: 'There is evidence from many cultures that an opening toward spirituality arrives around fifteen or sixteen. Many cultures support and respond to this natural spiritual opening through religious ceremonies or simply family and cultural rituals celebrating spirit or soul.' On the other hand, in Western culture, writes Bly, 'the adolescent sees posters advertising sexual energy ... he or she hears his sexual urges constantly alerted by sitcom, talk shows, movies, hears the strong beat of the sexual chakra in rock music'. 'Average twelve year olds,' he goes on, 'know more about sex than the average sixty-year-old knew in 1890.'[41]

He is right. What happens is that when sex fails to deliver this wonderful thing, and when the marvellous ecstasy a young person is primed to expect does not come, what arrives is not a spiritual awakening but a great disappointment. Bly believes that the adolescent feels horrific despair when the sexual chakra does not deliver the ectasy he or she has expected. Sex is brief and flat.

And love gets lost. Perhaps love and sex are confused so that girls imagine that to find love, they must give their bodies to the boy before they are ready. And after the first flush of excitement and bravado that accompanies a boy's first full sexual experience, the boy feels empty.

What we need is an initiation of the heart instead: an understanding of the inner landscapes of love and our hearts. The hero inside lives there.

# Chapter 9

## Outer Loving

And think not that you can direct the course of love,
For love, if it finds you worthy, directs your course.
*The Prophet:* Kahlil Gibran

Our inner landscapes affect the way we love. Love itself, however, is not something we can control. When we fall in love with someone we are infused with something special, an energy or life force, which has nothing to do with being rational. And when we enter a love relationship, a part of us is also not in control. Even if we wanted to, we cannot 'direct the course of love'. As we saw in the last chapter, there are inner forces always at play in our love relationships, and these forces will have an enormous impact on how we relate. Our inner archetypal patterns will dictate how we behave, and determine the degree to which we find relating and intimacy challenging.

Loving always brings up unconscious forces within us, and if the healing dimension is an important component of our relationship then the challenges will be greater, since our partner will act as a mirror to force us to see ourselves, or aspects of ourselves, that we may need to heal and change. Love relationships, in particular, offer us an opportunity to heal childhood wounds and to reconcile conflicting forces within us.

### Falling In Love
It is important to bear in mind that when we fall in love we are

not in control. We are immediately in the realm of the soul. We are opened to a new, magical world, where everything seems possible. We are taken out of ourselves and our everyday reality. The feelings associated with falling in love can induce a state of euphoria. We are propelled into a world much more beautiful than we normally inhabit. We notice how the sun shines and the way the light falls on the trees, casting a golden aura around everything. We talk to the stars and whisper to the silver moon, and our dreams are suddenly filled with a mysterious light.

Something wonderful happens to us when we are falling in love. We feel and often act differently. Our thoughts are interrupted constantly by feelings and thoughts about him or her, and at night our dreams are full of love imagery. If the attraction is strong, it pulls compellingly at us day and night and we are likely to have erotic, sexual dreams about our lover. Fantasy and dream life increase, with the love object as the main focus. Our longings tug at us so that we have no choice but to follow them in fantasy, if not in reality. We have a great desire to connect with our lovers, and find it hard to be apart.

There is always a creative element to sexual attraction, whether we recognise it or not. Unhappily, the split between body and soul has impacted on our lives in that love and sex, as mentioned in the last chapter, have become separated. In terms of falling in love, when our sexual energies get activated, we are seeking to connect with our own and the other's life force.

Sexual relating in dreams is symbolic of the desire to connect with life, with one's creativity and life force. The irrepressible push of new life is part of nature and if it finds us, then it means we are being drawn to move into new life within ourselves. Falling in love with another person is one of the most pleasant and exciting ways we do this.

Sexual imagery is very symbolic. It is interesting to note

that after a traumatic life event such as a bereavement, it is common to have dreams of physical love. When these dreams begin, it is the psyche's way of alerting the dreamer to the fact that healing has begun. These dreams signify the stirrings of renewed life, and always suggest that the soul is healing and seeks to grow. Sexual relating in dreams symbolises the desire to connect with new life.

When something, or someone, comes into our life and exerts a strong power over us, it is pulling us to experience something new, often to heal something old. Falling in love only happens when we are ready. This is why mourning an old loss or love wound is necessary before one can really love again. To be able to fall in love, we have to be in a state of readiness.

When we fall in love, we open both our psyches and bodies to receive a new energy. This is totally involuntary. I had an interesting example of this opening in my own life. Some two years after I had suffered the break up of my marriage, I attended a healing workshop. We were set into pairs in order to practice healing techniques based on intuition. The woman who was paired with me reported afterwards that as she was working on me, she could feel a strong energy emanating from my heart. She described it as the bursting of spring in a garden, as though a million spring flowers were ready to bloom.

Later I understood why. Just two months previously I had met a man I liked, and though our relationship had not yet come into its fullness, there was a great anticipation of love and fulfilment in my heart. It further transpired that on that very day, hour even, he was thinking of me and missing me, also anticipating our next meeting.

Falling in love has nothing to do with the intellect and rationality. Thinking is suspended, as we allow our hearts to be propelled by our soul's needs, to take us into a different world. Love takes us into a deeper terrain. It takes us into the realm of the soul. The feeling of falling in love opens new channels within us and we enter a transcendent space. When we are in this space, everything becomes possible. Our feelings for the beloved propel us into new heights. Our hearts are full and everything seems different. Falling in love alters our consciousness so that it is often compared to madness!

## The Descent

To fall into something is to 'descend' and all descents herald a change in our status quo. Psychologically, a descent signifies a lowering of consciousness, so that the ties of the ego are loosened to make way for new consciousness from the soul. A descent happens when the ego is flooded with a wave from the unconscious. In this space, we enter soul. A similar dynamic happens when we fall into a state of depression. In the fall and the descent, the ego, with its desires and its need for control, is shaken. This has to happen in order for change to occur because the ego does not like change. For new consciousness to happen, there always needs to be a loosening of ego control.

In the descent associated with falling in love, our ego loses its will to power and makes way for soul. What often then follows, is a power struggle between our ego, which wants to maintain control, and the needs of our soul. Our egos hate to lose control yet being in love does just that. When power is present, then love is not. Jung speaks about the battle between love and power in this way:

> Where love rules there is no will to power: where power predominates, there love is lacking. The one is the shadow of the other.

Falling in love is one of the ways our soul alerts us to the need for inner change. When we are in love we see through the eyes of our soul. Often these eyes are rose tinted or may even be blind! Infused with our inner image and our need for wholeness and healing, our lover will be dressed in the clothes of kings and queens or prince and princess. He or she will represent everything our soul at that time desires.

## Getting Real

The twilight or liminal period of falling in love soon passes, however. Then the challenge starts, as we begin the work of truly relating to the loved one. 'First we dream, then we make real', becomes a reality as we remove our rose-tinted glasses and start to relate.

After a while, we begin to see more clearly the person our soul has chosen. The prince becomes an ordinary man, and the princess an ordinary woman. The man might be balding, and have an irritating habit of closing all the windows that drives her mad. The woman may be heavier than he thought and have all sorts of eating behaviour that irritates him. Later, she notices that every time she goes out with her friends he sulks, and he remarks on how uninterested she is in having his mother to visit.

As they engage and begin the real work of relating to each other, lots of other characters from their respective inner landscapes enter the relationship. She may discover that when she goes out without him, for example, his Inner Orphan Child feels abandoned; or he learns that her attitude to his mother is dictated by her Inner Victim or Saboteur who feels threatened.

Every love affair and relationship re-enacts an inner drama.

In short, each person's inner landscape begins to infiltrate the outer relationship, so that the shadow and individual complexes get constellated. Each partner's Inner Child, Inner Victim, Prostitute and Saboteur, together with childhood wounds, are loosened and awakened. Since most relationships represent an opportunity to heal previous painful experiences, each person's unconscious co-operates by activating their complexes.

Intimate love relationships offer us a unique opportunity to heal childhood wounds and overcome the scar tissue of our past. We cannot actually do this in isolation. Some people think that they can only do inner work and pursue their soul's calling if they withdraw from engagement with others. But, as an eminent workshop leader on relationships once said, it is easy to become conscious alone. But return to relationship and that consciousness is constantly challenged. We can heal a certain amount by being alone and sometimes that is appropriate, but we cannot grow in isolation. The consciousness of relating to another opens us to union and wholeness that is not possible any other way. It is only through the constant chaffing of differences that we learn to deal with otherness. Through this acceptance we move to inner wholeness.

Part of the growth potential of relationships is developing the ability to accept the 'otherness' of a person, and to love that otherness. This cannot happen outside of relating to that person. Sadly, however, it is often the 'otherness' of a person that becomes the grounds for separation. 'I love him but I cannot live with him' is commonly said. And whereas I am not advocating staying in unhealthy relationships, sometimes leaving when the going gets tough curtails a process of growth within the relationship.

Some people leave a relationship because they cannot seem to live with otherness. Part of the problem is coping with the fact that at some level, they begin to realise that the person they have chosen is not all they thought they were. Then they might feel guilty for the feeling of disappointment that comes with this realisation. Our ability to look beyond, to the true essence of the person we fell in love with, is dependent on how strong we are, and how willing we are to stay with the delicate paradox of life where good and bad, perfection and imperfection, exist simultaneously – and how tuned in we are to our soul's needs.

Jungian writer and analyst Pinkola Estes states that 'the desire to force love to live on in its most positive form only is what causes it to die'.[42] Being prepared to live with, and accept, the shadow side of our partners, and see beyond the difficulties, can help us deal with the less positive feelings in the relationship. It is likely, however, that if we persist in demanding and expecting perfection, the relationship will either end or spiral downwards.

Leaving a relationship because it is not what we expected is unlikely to be beneficial to us, unless we have done the inner work necessary in becoming conscious of our part. If not, we are likely to find that the same issues will come up in subsequent relationships. It helps to remember that at the heart of every love relationship is a vision of wholeness. And engagement with the other is about healing the split within so that, in separation, it is likely that unless the issues that have divided the couple have been resolved, the same dynamic will occur again in subsequent relationships.

Many relationships end because one or other or both cannot negotiate their inner landscapes and their own hearts. For a relationship to work, both partners need to be able to take responsibility for their own feelings. Some relationships survive because they are based on more practical concerns, such as the need for emotional and financial security, the succesful rearing of children and so on. Other relationships function well because neither demands much of the other emotionally, so that relating is relatively easy. But many, if not most, couples are strongly engaged through the needs of their souls, to develop more consciousness. These sort of high-voltage relationships demand more of us, and from us. The desire of the soul is always for inner wholeness, and an intimate relationship is one of the most powerful paths to this wholeness.

It is very difficult to remain conscious when we are in relationship because love and loving opens a door to the unconscious, and allows in inner figures that have a life of their own, and often dictate how we behave. It takes constant inner (and outer) work to stay on top of what emerges. We may be taken unawares, for example, by the intense feelings of jealousy we feel when our partner meets a business associate who happens to be a woman; or we are shocked by the emptiness we feel when our partner goes away for a few days. We wonder where do these intense feelings come from. What is the matter with us that we feel so needy?

Inner conflict is always reflected outwardly, so that if you are fighting with your Inner Child, for example, dependency and nurturing will be important issues in your relationship. At ego level, you may abhor the snivelings of your needy Child, but your soul still pushes her out there to be heard. Ego says, 'Nonsense, of course he's not having an affair', but insecure Child says, 'He's not giving me enough attention'. 'You know you love her and need her', whispers your soul; 'rubbish,' responds your ego, who is obsessed with freedom and the fear of commitment, 'she'll tie you down'. And so you are conflicted.

When the ego and its desires become prominent, then the intellect tries to take control. Do not be fooled by this. Inner growth does not come from the intellect. In actual fact, integration always happens at the heart level, and without the intellect. There is no way out or short cut to achieving consciousness and self-knowledge. Rational thinking alone will not do it. Our Inner Child, for example, simply needs to be heard and recognised for healing and integration to happen. This is why living the questions, suffering the conflict and enduring the chaffing of differences can move us into soulful relating, and a deeper, more authentic place. From this place, we are then in a position to make empowering choices relating to ourselves and our relationship.

Struggling with relationships can mirror our life struggles, and overcoming obstacles in the relationship represents fulfilment and ultimately self-empowerment. It is in the work of relating, and the gradual erosion of dreams by everyday reality, that we struggle and grow. To dream is wonderful; to make real our dream, is even more so.

Relationships are the core of our lives, and as the source of our greatest joy and our greatest suffering, offer us a unique forum for soul growth. Enduring and battling with conflicting feelings helps us grow – it helps us build soul stamina. In heartache we get to know our hearts, and can grow to experience compassion and forgiveness. In loving, we can know courage and fortitude in the face of adversity. In giving, we learn the power of love to heal deep soul wounds.

## Nuts and Bolts: the Anatomy of Relationships

To help us work positively with our relationships, we need to be ready to look at how we are relating and identify some of our inner complexes and archetypal patterns. This awareness will help us, so that instead of becoming victims of the intense emotions that relationships can provoke, we become disciples of the profound soul-enriching potential of our relationships. Remember that healing always comes from within.

The basis of this work is to become more conscious, and in the next section of the book I have outlined a simple checklist that provides a framework for understanding how your past can shape your life by creating patterns that may be influencing your relationships today. Though our early life experiences often diminish our capacity to live from our essential self, they need not necessarily determine how we live our lives. Identifying and engaging your inner figures and archetypal patterns, will enable you to gain insight into your self-protective mechanisms and destructive patterns, for example, which push love away.

Inner landscapes affect outer loving. Look at how you are relating. Begin by identifying your inner archetypes, because these figures will be at play in your relationship. A more detailed description of these archetypes, which I described as architects of love, forms part of the last chapter, Inner Landscapes of Love. Refer back to this chapter to help you work in more detail with each archetype. This work is also outlined in detail in the later chapter Healing From Within, which I have included in the section dealing specifically with healing love wounds.

## Outer Loving: Common Psychological Patterns in Relationships

Just as we are compelled to live our lives according to unconscious archetypal patterns and our soul's contracts, we find that in relationship we fall into patterns of relating. Identifying and understanding your inner archetypes, your story and your attachment patterns, will also help you understand how you relate. Becoming conscious of your relational patterns will help you change destructive ones and make more empowering relationship choices. Here are just some of the most common patterns in relationships today.

### *Saving Your Partner*

Sometimes a woman or a man will be compelled to save (and heal) their lovers. The story of The Nightingale and the Rose embodied this dynamic. And Blanca also lived it out with Jose. When the energy of the abandoned, orphan or wounded child is strong in a person, then he or she might get into this situation. At base it means that the person falls in love with the potential he or she sees in the other. And the desire to heal the wounded other and bring him or her to fulfil this potential is so strong it overrides all other obstacles to the relationship.

Emotional wounds exert a very strong power on people. When the psyche is ready for healing, we often fall into a relationship that offers the potential for that healing. When a person unconsciously equates love with loss, for example, they will be fearful of getting involved, and find loving threatening. Love is always out of reach, and any attachment will be insecure, because the person imagines and fears it will be snatched away. This fear often compels such a person to choose emotionally damaged or unavailable lovers, and to try to heal them. In effect what this situation is saying is that you are ready to heal that hurt part of you, but you do not see it in yourself; you see it in your lover. In this scenario, all the hurt part of you is projected onto your lover.

There will usually be a glaring inequality in these relationships, because one partner appears to be getting very little from the relationship, and appears to be sacrificing her or himself for the other.

The film *When a Man loves a Woman* has something of this dynamic. It is about a man who loves a woman who is an alcoholic. He tries through his love to heal her, but when she seeks healing herself, and moves away from her dependency, it is he who has to face his dependency. He discovers that he is 'co-dependent', that he is invested in being the 'helper' in the marriage, which places her in the role of the 'sick one'. When she goes for healing and begins her recovery, he is left feeling bereft because he is no longer needed as 'the helper', and he had grown used to being needed. To continue in the relationship he has to be willing to look at his own wounds.

As said earlier, the power of love wounds is very strong, and hurt people often unconsciously fall into relationships that will help them heal these wounds. This is how it works: it is in the nature of things that what we crave most we often push away; a person who has a fear of love will often draw it into his or her life, so that he or she has a chance to decide whether or not to engage with it. When a man, for example, carries a love wound that his psyche is pushing him to heal, he will invariably draw into his life a woman who wants to love him, and relating to her will challenge him to open up.

James feared love because he had been hurt in the past. However, he drew Isabel into his life because at some level he needed to heal, and to learn to trust again. However, his hurt was greater than his ability or willingness to love, so that despite the fact that Isabel challenged him to open his heart, when the relationship got to a deeper level, he turned away. Isabel, who loved him, often wept in despair when her love was not returned. She knew he had the potential to love, and she wondered why he could not do so. She had fallen in love with his potential, and imagined that she could thaw him out through her love.

Waking frozen lovers appeared to be Isabel's destiny. She had experienced it several times in her life. When Isabel loved, she lost herself. She knew about frozen love, because her emotionally stark childhood predisposed her to experience it. It surfaced in her relationships once her heart was touched. When she opened her heart to her lover, Isabel's wound would open again, and a great need would be awakened in her. Craving love from emotionally damaged and hurt lovers, she would get lost in the storm of her desires. Love would be lost in her attempts to find it.

Desperate to be loved, Isabel would prize open her own wounded heart prematurely. She generally did this by choosing very hurt men. These men were destined to disappoint her because, more often than not, as with James, their fear of hurt meant they could not return her love, at least overtly. They were unable to express how they felt and she would get frustrated. The more she sought from them, the more they pulled away.

They needed time to thaw out. Isabel knew this at some level, but invisible strings from her heart seemed to pull her, and she ceased to recognise what she knew to be the truth. The messages from her heart confused her.

A wounded heart is like a crushed flower. It must be allowed to open in its own time, undisturbed, loved from a distance, as the rays of the sun help a plant to grow. Isabel remembered that James had, in his own words, told her this. In the kitchen, that spring afternoon, he had held her and asked her to wait, to let him grow to trust and love her. 'Leave it to me', he had said as he stepped back from the intensity of their relationship. 'It won't always be like this. I won't always have my walls erected around me.'

But Isabel found it hard to wait.

What she failed to recognise was that she was a frozen lover herself; that inside her own tender and open heart was a very wounded child, who did not know how to love without losing herself entirely. Deep down Isabel feared love above everything else, because it felt unsafe. She was so desperate to find love that she would frequently travel down all sorts of unlikely roads, and in the process, caused herself pain and humiliation. Her ceaseless search for love and validation blinded her to what she already had. It caused her to push love away when it came too close.

Isabel pushed James away with the kind of ferocity and tangled pain that is typical of hurt lovers' relationships. She tested and re-tested him until, exhausted, he fled from her relentless anxiety and her restless soul. When he fled, she suffered in the resulting emptiness. Then, finding no escape from the ceaseless and intolerable pain inside her, she also fled. She fled to a very small place inside herself. She withdrew from the world. At those times of pain, Isabel's world became too big for her to manage, and she would retreat from everything and everyone. Only the wind and the sounds of the sea could soothe her torn soul and her aching heart.

Lovers who seek to save their partners generally get caught up in relationships that are particularly painful, and ultimately, unfulfilling. Because essentially they have to work so hard to get their emotional needs met, they burn out. Preoccupied with healing their partner, these men and women deny or ignore their own emotional needs and spiritual growth, so that eventually a crisis may occur. Physical and/or emotional sickness may result if they remain unaware and unconscious of their part in this pattern.

These kinds of relationships are very painful because they are so unequal. Usually the one who sells herself or himself as the healer has little or no emotional boundaries so they may, unwittingly, like the little nightingale, sacrifice themselves for nothing. They may offer their souls, their bodies and their hearts, to someone who frequently cannot love. At the very least they will be compromising their integrity to find love. At worst they may be involved in repeatedly unhealthy, even abusive, relationships from which they cannot seem to leave.

## Loving Too Much

The popularity in the late 1980s of the book *Women who Love Too Much* tapped into another common archetypal pattern in relationships. There are similarities between this pattern and the saving of one's partner. In this pattern, one partner, often the woman, appears to be much more conscious or psychologically aware than the other. She thinks that she has enough love for both of them, and that she will lead him to love. Her open, generous heart is boundless as the sea, and she seeks to bestow some of this larger than large love onto her partner.

But such a love can be suffocating and may, in fact, push the other away – it leaves no room for the other. Over loving fills all the spare places in the relationship, so there is no longer any room for manoeuvre. The other partner will feel smothered and claustrophobic. The one who loves too much will be like a stifling, over-indulgent mother, who cannot allow her child to grow. Such over loving pushes others away because it is unhealthy and, ultimately, murderous.

This sort of pattern illustrates the challenges involved in

freeing oneself from the mother complex and generally evolves between two people that are individually struggling with the mother complex in its many forms. A common dynamic is that between a man who, in remaining tied to his mother, has an Oedipus complex, and the woman who seeks to break him of it so he can leave childhood and love her.

Another aspect to this pattern is the tendency in quite psychologically-aware and evolved women to choose either very (psychologically) young, or very wounded men as their partners. To all outward appearances, these women are marrying beneath them, or not marrying their equal. It can almost feel like a mother and son situation. The mother seeks to help her son/lover grow into the man she needs. In a convoluted way, these women are offering competing mother love to their lovers. In an effort to break the stranglehold of the mother, they are recreating it.

I discussed this with a woman friend who is also a therapist, and I remember what she said, since it represented a moment of clarity for me. 'Why do you think it is, that strong women fall in love with very psychologically young or wounded men much less evolved than they are?' I asked, one evening at dinner. My friend leaned across the dinner table and replied, 'Perhaps it's a maternal thing. It's like growing a man!'

I thought about this afterwards, and it certainly makes sense. Many women are also struggling to escape from the mother complex, particularly if they have not had a strong father to help them cut the ties with their mothers. These women commonly choose men with a similar complex. Such women will often appear to be very loving and mothering themselves, and will attract a man who seeks nurturing. Unconsciously, the idea is that they will, through their love, help this young man grow into the strong mature man they require to help them, in turn, grow up.

However, this miracle growth rarely happens. What happens

instead usually ends in tears and separation. The man, if he has remained a child and played his part well, will move on to the next 'mother' he finds. He does this because after a while, his lover/mother/wife becomes like the trapping witch of Rapunzel, keeping him in her tower, and preventing him from growing up. Feeling confined, he seeks to leave this over-loving womb, and moves out into the next one.

The woman involved in this kind of relationship needs to pull herself back from such over loving, and return to herself. She needs to attend to her own inner work, so that she becomes strong and independent, because she too is struggling to leave mother. She has a need to move out of the mother world and develop her animus, her male side. This is the animus she projected onto her lover, hoping he would do the growing up, and take her with him. She needs to become more conscious of her own inner world. Often, as I mentioned earlier, such a woman has lacked a strong father to help her separate from her own mother. This is the father's seminal role in childhood. When he is weak, absent, or not experienced as being actively present, the girl remains trapped in the maternal unconscious, and can later be found playing out the 'loving too much' role in her love relationships.

## Grounding Peter Pan

This is another very common dynamic that happens in relationships. It need not necessarily always be a woman seeking to ground a male Peter Pan; it can happen the other way around. There are plenty of women who carry the Peter Pan energy. In Jungian psychology, the term for the eternal youth archetype is Puer Aeternus, with the feminine version called the Puella.

This Puer energy embodies freedom from restriction, and the ability to break out of the mould. At its best, it is an attractive quality that can be very creative because, like a child, it is innovative, and likes to try new things. If harnessed positively, this eternal youth energy enables the individual to transcend the usual boundaries of tradition and cultural belief systems, and create something new. We all need a certain amount of this energy in order to overcome obstacles to growth and evolution. We require it in order to mature, and have the courage to change.

In *Reclaiming Father* I wrote a lot about this, because the shadow side of the Peter Pan energy is very common in people where fathers were experienced as absent. An unfathered man, for example, often becomes an eternal boy, a Peter Pan refusing to grow up, someone who drifts from one thing to the next, and from lover to lover, never putting down roots. He may be the eternal seducer, the Don Juan who flits from woman to woman, seeking more and more conquests, and dropping each one as the novelty of the chase wears off.

It can also happen with women. In *Reclaiming Father* I wrote about such a woman. It is worth repeating the story. Georgina complained that she could never find a man who would commit to her. A vibrant, career-orientated woman in her mid forties, she had ended her marriage to a wealthy stockbroker because she felt trapped and confined by the constraints of marriage. She had two children, now in their late teens. Since the break-up of her marriage, she had had several relationships with men, but they always ended after a time, when it appeared she wanted 'more'. The men would not make the final commitment to her. She railed against them, and wondered why it was just her luck to fall for one Peter Pan after another.

'Have you thought that perhaps you are not ready to commit fully to a relationship yourself?' I queried. 'That's nonsense,' she replied, indignant that I should suggest such a thing.

Georgie had been coming to therapy regularly, and had committed herself to our weekly sessions. Although she was strong and articulate, and very successful in her career as a journalist, in many ways she seemed like an adolescent.

Obsessed with the need to succeed in the outer world, she did not wish to be dependent on a man, yet a part of her craved intimacy. The call of nature pulled at her heart, the call of all women and men at some stage in their lives. She wanted to love and be loved, but yet she also feared it. She was attractive and bubbly and had no difficulty meeting men. At some level though, she frightened them. She was so successful, competent and together that she appeared to have everything a woman could want. What could they possibly offer her?

Typically, she chose men who were gentle and tender, and less successful in the outer world than she appeared to be. They were generally charming, attractive, creative types who, when it came down to it, had great difficulty making a firm commitment. They appeared to mirror her need for independence. Possessed of a tender heart, she opened herself to love, and usually fell head over heels in love with her partners. She would abandon herself to her lovers, throw herself at their feet and then wonder why they hesitated.

Invariably she was disappointed. Her partners then became hole-in-the-heart lovers, inadequate, when they could not fulfil her needs. She felt hurt and rejected.

The irony of her story was lost on her. She had initially found a man who had committed himself to her totally, her former husband, but at that time she had wanted to get away. She felt confined. Georgina's soul pulled her to a different place; she sought freedom; she wanted to play. At some level, therefore, she attracted men who were playmates, who also wanted to play. Perhaps they were all seeking freedom from the unresolved constraints of their childhood.

How we experience life whilst we are still forming our characters and dependent on our parents will shape how we are as adults. A strongly activated Puer or Peter Pan energy in a personality indicates that there is a part of that person that did not feel free to play when a child; or who felt thwarted or restricted in some way. Or it can mean that childhood was so idyllic that, like Peter Pan, the person does not want to grow up. In relationships if this energy is strong in one or other partner it means that person has great difficulty growing up and taking responsibility for their actions and behaviour. Such a person will not want to be accountable in any way that might restrict their freedom. This fear of restriction often transmits itself as a failure or a reluctance to commit to another person.

Georgina's dilemma is not uncommon. She wants to root herself with a male partner, and yet a small part of her is not ready to do so or fears commitment to another and what that entails. Consciously she seeks union but unconsciously, the story is different, and so her soul is telling her this by pulling her towards men who are, at some level, unavailable.[43]

In relationship this dynamic becomes particularly destructive when a polarisation occurs, so that one partner embodies the Peter Pan whilst the other one wants to ground him or her. In this case, the more one partner tries to move away and find space, the more the other looks for in the relationship. The more she seeks him, the more he moves away. He feels her as demanding, the mother witch who seeks to trap him. She feels him as immature, unavailable and irresponsible.

The marriage of Peter Pan and the Mother Witch is doomed to failure, unless both parties are willing to work through what has caused such a polarisation.

If you feel that this, or any of the above dynamics, are present in your relationship, look inside your own heart. Examine your childhood memories, and ask yourself whether some of these patterns come from feeling insecure or abandoned as a child. If you are the Peter Pan of the couple, for instance, ask yourself what you are afraid of. Perhaps you felt restricted as a child, unable to express yourself; or maybe because of family circumstances, you had to take on too much responsibility, which left you no freedom to play; or perhaps you were abandoned or neglected as a child, so that you never developed the capacity to trust you could be loved.

Healing from within is always about dialoguing with our souls, and self examination. The purpose of this work is to become more conscious of who we are in relationship. Outer loving is dependent on inner landscapes. If we work to become aware of what we are projecting onto our partners, then we have a greater chance of engaging in healthy and soulful, life-enhancing relationships. Engaging with our inner archetypes, and letting go of the stories we have built around ourselves, can help us to avoid repeating patterns – and can help us heal love wounds.

## Dark September

The first time I saw Áine, she was dressed entirely in black. She was in mourning, she told me. After fifteen years of marriage, her husband had left her for another woman. He had left suddenly, one weekend in September. Returning from a business trip, he had packed his bag, kissed the children and walked out the door.

It had rained all weekend, she remembered. She also remembered every detail of the few minutes it took to end her life as she had known it. She recalled with vivid detail the blue shirt he was wearing, and the shadow on his normally clean-shaven face. She remembered that his hair seemed longer, out of place. Most of all, she recalled with acute precision the few words he had spoken and the way he had said them. 'I've met someone else. I love her. I never loved you, I only thought I did.'

Áine recalled how suddenly she seemed to be hovering over her body, able to hear but unable to respond. Frozen with shock and numbed by intolerable pain, she remembered staring at him as he spoke. The icicles of his words immobilised her. Surely this wasn't true, it was all an awful dream, she would wake up in a moment and laugh at the absurdity of it.

She did wake up, but not before her husband had closed the door of their house for good, taking most of her with him.

Áine was in bits for a long time afterwards. She was shattered and too fragmented to feel. Tiny pieces of her lay scattered like broken glass on the empty table of their marriage. When the initial shock of her husband's departure wore off, she began to feel. When reality kicked in, so did the pain.

For a while, she consoled herself with the idea that he would return. He would realise what a mistake he had made, and would return to their home. She had sulked, of course, and would make him pay for the pain he had caused. Locking herself into denial, she delayed facing the inevitable truth. He was gone, her mate, her life partner, the father of her children. He was part of her and without him she was nothing.

Áine felt as though she were cut in half. She dragged herself around as though mortally wounded, and when she had accomplished the basic tasks of day-to-day living, she would lie down and hope not to wake up. She wondered how it was that she woke every morning and had not died. She used to pray for sleep, for death, for an end to the pain. Her children and their need for her kept her going on automatic pilot.

As time passed and there was no sign of a reconciliation or even the possibility of one, she fell into a desperate dullness which gradually slid into a full-blown depression. By December she had lost two stones in weight, she rarely slept, and never went out. Eating was a problem too; she survived on mashed bananas and milk, sometimes picking at the food she cooked her children.

By the time spring started its climb into summer, feeling the stir of new life, Áine began to shift. Her dreams changed from dark and looming to green and hopeful. In them, she was usually out of doors, often looking for someone whom she could never find, despite obscure clues left in mysterious places. But her reality never changed, as waking, the pain of her situation crashed down on her like a ton of bricks. Finally, propelled by some inner force and seeking to find relief, Áine came to therapy.

PART SIX

# HEALING LOVE WOUNDS
# AND
# THE JOURNEY
# TO WHOLENESS

# Chapter 10

## Healing Broken Hearts

Give sorrow words;
The grief that cannot speak
Whispers the o'er frought heart
And bids it break.

*Macbeth IV.111:* William Shakespeare

Heartbreak will catapult you into a great depth. It will move you, sear you and change you. Many people think that time is what heals a broken heart but, in fact, this is not true. Time may dull the pain, but we all know people who remain bitter and angry about their relationship break ups and divorces. No, time alone will not do it. Heartbreak, like love, demands more from us. To fully harness the healing power of love and heartbreak we have to be willing to fully engage with it. At a profound spiritual level, we are meant to have our hearts broken wide open, so that we can love more, so that we can know compassion, and experience unconditional love. As I said earlier, compassion is where our heart pain is meant to lead us.

To heal a broken heart, you have to go through a journey. There are various stages to this journey, and you will naturally progress through them in time. However, if you want to help yourself along the way, and harness the growth potential of the experience, you need to participate in the process with as much consciousness as possible. This means many things, for a start, not denying the hurt you feel, and not using various distraction techniques such as rushing into manic activity, or another relationship right away. In order to heal you must endure, suffer and express your feelings. You have to mourn. Remember that what you cannot feel, you do not heal; and healing always comes from within.

## Dark Night of the Soul

The death of a marriage or major love relationship can propel us into the dark night of the soul. When a relationship ends, it can precipitate feelings of profound depression, especially if one finds it hard to deal with the complex emotions that surface, such as anger, bitterness, betrayal, thoughts of revenge if a third party is involved, devastation, loss, rejection, abandonment and even shame. If you are the one that has been 'left', then you may find it even more difficult to handle the aftermath. Feelings of low self-esteem and insecurity will make you doubt yourself, and your self-confidence will take a tumble. You may wonder what you did, or did not do, to cause your partner to leave you.

If, like Áine in our last story, the break up of your marriage or relationship leaves you feeling profoundly depressed and without the will to live, it is likely that the abandonment you feel has touched your soul at its deepest level, and stirred up previous painful experiences that have not been resolved. When the wounds are very deep, the break-up will have touched on earlier experiences of rejection that have left a mark on your soul.

And if your partner has unconsciously filled a void in your life, then you may feel the emptiness left by his or her absence to be unbearable.

For many, the break up of a relationship catapults them into emotional darkness and pain. Sometimes the emotional pain becomes too much to bear, and you imagine you will never get out of it. Despair and deep depression may set in, as you struggle to try and make sense of what is happening to you. Alone, you will have to endure the dark night of the soul so beautifully immortalised by St John of the Cross in his book, *Dark Night of the Soul.*

Vision is limited in the dark, thus forcing you to face what lies beneath the surface, in the depths of your heart. You will be faced with a multitude of tangled feelings crashing around inside you. You may feel overwhelmed and unable to think straight, as you scramble to restore some kind of order to your tormented heart. You long for the forgetfulness of sleep, but even here, your pain follows you, as your dreams loosen dark figures from the depths of your unconscious. People and experiences from your past will tumble out of your already crowded psyche to further haunt you.

There is nothing to be done here but endure. The dark night of the soul must be suffered if there is to be a return to the light, and new life. The descent into the unconscious is like a death before a rebirth. There cannot be a rebirth, or true change, without such a death. Death and life come together, always.

We are no strangers to death. Psychologically, we suffer ego death frequently in the process of becoming conscious. We are faced with small and large ego deaths as a natural part of growing into greater maturity through different stages of life. In order to grow, we have to let go of what we were. Like a plant, we have to shed the dead leaves of our past to make room for new buds to sprout. If we do not shed what is no longer useful to our growth and progress, then we stifle and prevent further growth.

The experience of loss is always a catalyst for change and propels us out into the unknown. It forces us to face the fact that death is part of the natural cycle of life. Experiencing the dark night of the soul is part of our spiritual journey. Sometimes it is hard for us to accept this. Sadness, depression and emotional pain are difficult things to endure. In *Letters to a Young Poet*, Rilke writes:

> So you must not be frightened, dear Mr Kappus, if a sadness rises up before you larger than any you have ever seen; if a restiveness, like light and cloud-shadows, passes over your hands and over all you do. You must think that something is happening with you, that life has not forgotten you, that it holds you in its hand; it will not let you fall.[44]

Rilke's writing is filled with spiritual wisdom, and echoes the sentiments of lines from prayers and proverbs we hear commonly, such as 'May God hold you in the palm of his hand', or 'Lie back and the sea will hold you'; beautiful and comforting thoughts and sentiments, if we allow ourselves to feel them. In times of trouble it is hard to do this because a part of us has lost all trust. Emotional turmoil and psychic loss of faith usually mean we lose touch with our inner wisdom and our ability to trust in the bounty of the universe.

Also, since we have a great fear of falling into the unknown, we tend to hang on to what we know.

During a difficult period in my own life I consulted a colleague who is also a gifted and wise healer. She told me that, though I had progressed spiritually, I was like someone who had been told they could walk on water, but was still hanging on to the boat. I needed to let go; to lie back and let the sea hold me; to trust that everything I needed to move forwards in my life would be provided. I was finding it hard to 'let go and let God'. Fear and lack of trust was, in fact, holding me back, because at some level, I needed concrete proof that I was on the right path.

Sometimes we have to get out of our own way, and allow the cycle of life and death to happen. Experiencing heartbreak can help us do that.

## Letting Go: Dissolution

Death is a great leveller. The dark night is like death, in that everything we know is dissolved. Our castles are destroyed, and our troops are killed. The battle has been fought, and lost. Our dreams are smashed, and our hopes are dashed. And our old heart has to die, along with the relationship that is no more; we have to let go.

Often what we have to let go of is the thoughts, expectations and hopes we had about the relationship. As I wrote in an earlier chapter, Battlegrounds of the Heart, sometimes we hold onto a relationship, and ideas about out partner, that are no longer appropriate. Holding on to these sentiments will furthermore hamper our growth, and prevent us from moving on.

In the dark night everything is levelled. Like shards of splintered glass, our hopes and dreams lie broken and scattered. The old image we had of the relationship is shattered, and we do not know how to put the pieces together again. Our reality is no longer our reality, so that we are conflicted and confused about ourselves.

Isabel struggled with this, as her relationship with James was moving inevitably to its end.

> *Though I will at some level never stop loving him – my heart and spirit are completely broken. I feel totally in conflict with myself. The part of me that placed my trust and belief in him and in us, our union, our soul connection – I now doubt, and this is the hardest thing to bear. I feel demeaned, disempowered and abused. I feel I have made a very grave mistake and, right now, I regret the years I have known and loved him. I feel all my efforts, my blood, my tears and my heart, have been wasted on someone totally unworthy. I was stupid and blind, and I imagine that everyone out there is aware and laughing at my naivete, my*

> *stupidity, in falling for a man who never loved me, and who ill treated me.*

Isabel, who thought of James as the soul mate she would live out her life with, was forced to let go. The part of her that still loved him and believed in their relationship, fought with the reality that it was over. She had to let go of her dreams, and her wish to have things a certain way, and this caused her to turn against the loving part of her that had placed such hopes in their long-lasting relationship.

When our dreams are shattered and our hearts broken, we can turn against ourselves. When we do this, it adds confusion and inner conflict to our emotional turmoil. And this is the hardest thing to bear, but bear it we must. In the dark night, there is no choice anyway. When we arrive there, our dreams are already shattered, and our reality is upside down. We can but endure, and wait for day to arrive.

Below I have included a short checklist, which you can work with as you go through the journey to heal your heart. Each section (there are four, corresponding to different stages of the journey) contains a spiritual truth designed to help you maintain a sense of faith and spiritual purpose as you journey through the underworld of your soul. You can use this truth to meditate on and to move inwards to your centre. When you feel despair, hold these spiritual truths close to your heart. The checklist contains suggestions designed to help you work through the various stages of healing your heart. Remember though that each journey is unique, so that you may resonate with some of the suggestions and not others. Use the list as a guide, and make the journey your own, according to what feels right for you. Work at your own pace – you can always return to the reference points outlined below. What I have outlined is to be used as a reference guide for the soul work necessary to heal from within. Note your progress in your journal. Journaling is a way to dialogue with your soul – it's a valuable tool in healing. Painting or drawing can also be used in this way.

### Soul Work During Your Dark Night of the Soul
Spiritual Truth:
'Know that life has not forgotten you; that it holds you in its hand; it will not let you fall'

Rilke

- Hold on to spiritual and personal truths.
- Endure, suffer and accept.
- Understand you are going through a process and do not try to distract or force yourself out of it.
- Let go to where your soul pulls you, know your soul and your heart have a greater wisdom, and that you will come out of this in time.
- Let your feelings flow as fully as you can.
- Do inner work every day such as reflection, journal writing and dream recording.
- Listen to your inner voice.
- Nurture yourself and avoid extra stress.
- Give yourself space and plenty of time
- Avoid overburdening yourself with outer tasks.

### What Can Help During Your Dark Night:
Hold on to Spiritual truths.

- Remember that endings are part of life and there is a positive side to them, because an ending always brings a new beginning.
- Depression is a cry from the soul, alerting us to life changes we may need to make and to situations that are not good for us.
- Relationship break up can be the way the psyche frees

us from soul bonds that might be holding us back.

- Remember that Dark Nights of the Soul, if we allow ourselves to suffer them, will bring us to new life.
- Remind yourself of the cycles of life and the inevitability of death and rebirth (change).
- Spend time in nature if possible. Its constancy will calm you.
- Keep a journal and record your dreams.
- Spend time every day doing what you enjoy, i.e. listening to music, painting, watching films, walking, dancing, making music, writing, meditating, being with friends or family.

## Into the Desert

An encounter with the dark night of the soul will lead us to undertake a journey of self-discovery, but first we usually retreat into the desert, to a dry, barren place. Our broken heart is dry and barren because, like the desert, it does not contain water. Water in this sense symbolises emotions and the ability to feel. The feeling function is necessary for life, but when it is hurt it often retreats, so that for a while, we may live in an emotional wasteland. Broken hearts can often go numb for a time. That is okay too, and part of the process.

When we fall in love and it does not work out our ideal, along with our dream of love, is smashed. We retreat into the shadows of our disappointment. We may become hard and cynical, and decide to close the door on our hearts, if we have been hurt many times. Eventually, as I said earlier, we might become so cynical that we forget that we are spiritual beings of light; that healing is possible and love can happen again. When we are that hurt, we can imagine that love does not exist, and worse, that we do not need it; that it is for the foolish and for the hopeless romantic.

After the break up of a marriage or major relationship,

many of us retreat to the desert, to a place of no heart. In my personal life I have encountered this desert experience. Some years ago, while struggling with the break up of a relationship that meant a great deal to me, I retreated to a dry barren place inside myself. I shut down and walked around as though mortally wounded. I was operating on automatic, so that outwardly, apart from losing weight, everything appeared as normal. Like many people who are going through mental anguish and heart pain, I appeared calm. Inside though, a raging storm was gathering force. Writing was my only expression for the pain I felt.

The desert experience, however, often yields fruit. After some months of self-imposed exile, one evening, I wrote this poem; I called it 'Golden Boy'. This was my name for the love ideal embodied in the man I had loved, and lost. It also represented, I saw later, my soul at the time, my creative energy, which I had invested in him.

Borne on divine wings
The golden boy is swift in motion,
Passing this way and that
Hardly leaving a mark, so light is he.
Those fortunate enough to cross his path
Are sprinkled with the gift of joy
He brings on the wings of his desire.

But desire once born to mortals is fatal,
For it hurls us headlong into an endless search
Destined only to failure.
He, being unattached, can move on
And does not try to harness what is free.
I've met you golden boy,
We danced together for a while,
Your soul and mine held hands.
There was magic as we loved,

The kind lovers only dream of,
A million stars burst into song by night
And a warm golden sun followed us by day.

Then, as suddenly as you came,
You disappeared.
The stars dimmed their lights,
The sun went out of my life,
The magic gone,
I was left alone.

Empty after you left, I lived in a dark world,
With only memories to lighten the bruise in my heart
And the tear in my soul.
With bitter tears I called you back,
But you were gone, and only the wind answered.
I grew thin with pain,
And when, finally, I buried you on that still day
I had no life or hope
But a shell I carried wearily along.

I had loved him so much I had put everything into him, so that when I lost him, I imagined I had nothing. So many of us do this when we fall in love. We imagine we cannot live without the other person. In essence though, what we have lost is that part of ourselves we saw mirrored in the other, a lost fragment of our soul. Although we cannot see it then, what we are being challenged to do when a lover is gone is to find that lost part in ourselves.

I suffered, as anyone who has lost a lover does. Initially, I too closed the doors of my heart and dragged myself around as though mortally wounded. I turned inwards. I wrote, and my writing helped me. I returned to my soul home, and found peace in walking by the sea, and immersing myself in nature.

In the struggle to regain my sense of myself, and heal my heart of this love wound, I grew. I learned about my own ability to love. In a sense, I found my inner man, my own golden boy. I once read that nothing ever ends without something better beginning – and that when one door closes, another opens. I gained solace from that. Finally, some months later, I was able to write:

> Then one day,
> As I walked in the wet land of my tears,
> The pain in my chest grew too much
> for my soul to bear
> And I sat down on the damp earth to rest.
> Fearing death, I covered my heart with
> my hands
> And lowered my head, until it rested
> on the grass.
>
> After a while, I heard again the beating
> heart of nature,
> And my own,
> Then, I saw you rise from the earth,
> a small flame at first.
> Then your body of clay formed around
> the golden light
> And there you were, my golden boy.
> But a boy no more,
> For as I looked, you grew into the strong man
> I had mated with.
> You stepped across and lifted me up in
> the strong arms
> I had once known.
>
> In a timeless embrace,

The circle closed around us, and I knew,
I knew then, that it would never break again.

After this time of loss and grief, I found my golden boy again. What I had found was my inner lover, that part of me that my outer lover had represented. I made a deeper connection with myself. My outer lover was a man who radiated optimism and joy. Though inwardly wounded, he projected liveliness, good humour and optimism. When we were together, I thought of him as my sunshine. When we parted, and I was without him, I felt the sun had gone out of my life.

Gradually over time, and many tears later, I saw that symbolically he represented my creative energy, the part of me that was joyful, and liked to play. In that fallow period of loss, when I had truly mourned him, I reconnected with my own creative spark, my inner sunshine.

The spiritual challenge that this loss experience created for me at that time was to find and claim an aspect of my soul. It also represented an opening of my heart, and a call to unconditional love. Loving and losing this man was a life-changing experience, and one that I still regard as pivotal on my journey to understand and experience love.

## A Place of Essence

A period in the desert is part of the journey to heal a broken heart. The desert experience is a prelude to healing, and to growth. To be in the desert is to be uncrowded, unguarded, vulnerable and alone. Like the physical desert, it is a place of space, of bareness, and of essence. It is only in this place, or a place like it, away from distractions people, and the regular demands of our daily lives, that we can reconnect with our true essence. There we are naked and alone. There is no other. And if, as is common in relationship, we have been very taken up with our partners, here, in the space left by their absence, we have a chance to see ourselves, and in time to regain what we have lost.

After the break up of my relationship I went away and spent some time alone in the desert of southern Arizona, USA. It was a healing time for me. The vast space, the landscape with its endless level road and cloudless blue sky, held me somehow. In its bareness, it revealed to me the spirit of the world, the timeless essence of life. In the emptiness, I found only myself, and I reconnected in a powerful way with my own essence.

I was fascinated by the landscape, so different to my homeland. Its sparse sharp greenery, its exotic plants and the dry earth pulled me in, so that everyday, I would spend time walking and exploring my desert space. Desert creatures called me, so that every evening I would head out hoping to catch sight of the coyote as the sun edged towards the horizon, casting deep golden colours over the land. Knowing the temperature would drop dramatically after sunset, I went prepared for my journey, and was able to thus enjoy the sharp cold beauty of the night sky.

Night in the desert is wonderful. It is full of life, as desert creatures of earth and sky stir and awaken, after the heat of the day. Suddenly the vast, quiet space fills with life and sounds, under a clear navy and silver, sparkling sky. The moon in the desert is amazingly clear and powerful. It rose and shone brighter and larger there than I have ever seen.

The desert filled me with awe. It's majesty and starkness calmed me, and restored some kind of order to my chaotic, raw feelings and bruised heart. I felt I was seeing the world for the first time and, though I did not know it then, something beautiful was gently being restored to me. In my time in the desert, my heart began to heal and I regained my spirit. One evening I wrote a poem I called 'Coyote Song':

'Open the window,

Open the window,' said the man,
'You will see the coyote, and hear him sing.'

That evening, strolling through the desert bush,
Dry crackling earth beneath my feet,
And stillness all around me,
I did not see the coyote.
Instead,
A stabbing pain pulled me downward
To feel the sharp spines of a prickly tree
Embedded in my ankle, and shedding blood,
I cursed aloud.
I did not see the coyote, but
I thought of you,
And as usual, the knot in my heart swelled and
grew.

I did not hear the coyote sing,
But instead I heard your voice.
'Sing me a song,' you said.
So I sang the song of love,
Though I knew you were far away,
And deaf to the sound of my voice,
But I sang nonetheless.

After a while, the coyote did not come,
But you did,
The way you were a long time ago.
You opened your arms to me,
And I rested my head against your heart,
As I so often used to do.

Being in the physical desert alone allowed me to connect
with my heart, and experience my heartache. It bought me

back to myself, and showed me how strong and enduring my heart was. The beauty and constancy of nature relaxed me and allowed a crushed part of me to begin unfolding. In time, it helped me sing again, and eventually love again.

### Soul Work during your time in the Desert
Spiritual Truth:
We are all as one and our spirit is part of the spirit of the world.

- Hold on to personal and spiritual truths.
- Spend time alone so that you experience your aloneness.
- Reconnect with nature/the sea/mountains/ the desert.
- Keep a journal and record your dreams.
- Use your solitude to travel deeply into your own soul.
- Express your feelings and allow your heart pain to flow.
- Do something creative: if you like to write, write, to play the guitar, play the guitar, go hiking, walking and so on.
- Go inwards and discover your inner landscape.

### What Can Help During Your Desert Experience
Hold on to spiritual and personal truths.

- Remember that life always seeks to renew itself and that you will come through stronger.
- Know that this experience offers you an opportunity to get to know and appreciate yourself in a unique way.
- Without the emotional security of husband/wife

or partner, you have been given the opportunity to develop your own inner resources.

- Instead of loneliness you can begin to appreciate solitude so that your time alone is utilised to understand and heal your heart.
- Know that a new part of you is being gestated. You may find, for example, that you now have the space to develop a creative skill that has been latent.
- Trust that an inner wisdom is at work and will become clear in time.

Spend time in nature and avoid over rationalising. Also avoid, when possible, negative thinking, self-blame and seeing yourself as a victim. Such thoughts will not empower you. Spend time every day in contemplation and/or doing something that restores you. Get plenty of rest and savour your solitude rather than lamenting your loneliness.

## Separation and Aloneness

Some time in a desert, symbolic or otherwise, is part of the journey one has to take to heal a broken heart. The physical desert for me was a place of soul, and a place of essence. Away from the concerns of my daily life back home, and in the vastness of the desert space, I was stripped to my essence. The deep connection with nature forces one to stop, and restores a sense of life that is elemental. Life always goes on, and this experience showed me that healing happens naturally, when we give the heart space, and when we are willing to listen to our inner voice and trust that there is a deeper wisdom at work.

But first we have to leave what we know and be prepared to walk and wander alone, if necessary. A period of separation is often a vital part of the journey to healing a broken heart. If we have truly let go, then we face our own aloneness. With our previous frames of reference gone, and our life as we knew it disintegrated, we descend into an empty space with only ourselves for company.

After a while, we notice that something happens in the descent; a new space begins to open up, holding within it new possibilities, new life. But first we must turn to face ourselves, as we are, alone. To truly feel this, we often need to be physically, as well as emotionally, alone and apart from others for a time.

Separation, and coming to terms with one's aloneness, are an integral part of life. Most of us face aloneness at different times in our lives. From a psychological perspective, the experience of separation is generally necessary in order to truly individuate. Disengagement from the pack, from the family, from whatever group one is born into, is usually called for in order to grow into self-awareness.

Although separation is a normal part of growing up, many people struggle with it, because independence always comes at a price.

Separation and aloneness are very important when we are healing our hearts. Conscious, voluntary separation, however, is different to the separation that is imposed on us by circumstances beyond our control, such as the death of a loved one, or a relationship. Then, separation can become severance, and awakens in us feelings of rejection, and even betrayal. Abandonment by the group, family, or loved one, forces us into emotional and sometimes physical exile. This exile in turn propels us to search for, and to return home. The experience of being exiled pushes us forward, and is often a necessary part of healing the heart.

## The Ugly Ducking: Exile and the Healing Journey

On the journey to healing a broken heart we have to be prepared to be in exile for a while. Symbolically, we are in exile anyway, because when we are broken hearted, we are divided, and our search to return home to ourselves represents our healing journey. To be an exile is to be abandoned, apart from others, divided within and forced into a search for belonging. Exile is part of the journey to healing and wholeness, because when we are heartbroken, we have lost our connection with our essential selves. Reconnecting with our hearts is necessary in order to mend and heal what has become split.

Since the theme of exile is part of our healing journey after heartbreak, it is worth taking an excursion to further explore this idea. There are many stories written about the exiled or outcast, the most loved perhaps being The Ugly Duckling by Hans Christian Andersen. Jungian author Clarissa Pinkola Estes in her book, *Women who Run with the Wolves*, describes the tale of The Ugly Duckling as a psychological and spiritual root story. She writes:

> A root story is one that contains a truth so fundamental to human development that without integration of this fact further progression is shaky, and one cannot entirely prosper psychologically until this point is realised.[45]

What is the fundamental truth contained in The Ugly duckling? It is about our search for belonging. The theme of the exiled or outcast is archetypal and primeval, and often forms part of our spiritual journey. The outcast is compelled to find his way back home. The trials of his journey serve a spiritual purpose. When the outcast arrives home he finds he has, like the ugly duckling, grown up.

There are many different ways in which we can feel exiled or outcast. It sometimes happens that, like the ugly duckling, for example, we feel we are not spiritually part of our birth families. We feel different, or we are told we are different, and pressured to conform to values that deep down do not feel right to us. Because of our innate drive to adapt and conform, our parents' attempt to mould us and make us what they want us to be will develop in us a painful set of conflicting emotions. We want to be loved, but we feel rejected for who we are; we feel we cannot gain this love without compromising ourselves. Such a situation is very painful and wounding because, at base, our soul requires different things from us, and we find we cannot live our truth in our family. The pain of not being true to ourselves may eventually drive us out of the nest, like the ugly duckling.

Being the outsider in a family constellates within us the Orphan archetype. It is our Inner Orphan that impels us to find our true spiritual parents and family – a place where we can be ourselves, where our 'knowing' is accepted and acknowledged. The Orphan Child looks for his/her true home, where he/she will find nourishment and peace. Searching for, and finding where we belong is a crucial and central part of individuation.

The story of the ugly ducking is also about endurance and persistence. The ugly duckling wanders from pillar to post until he finds his true family and realises he is, in fact, a swan. Despite frequent lapses into despair, he wanders on, relentlessly seeking. He suffers in his exile; he is alone and lonely, but never wavers in his search because, deep down inside, he knows he will find where he belongs and he follows his nature. He is given a clue along the way and this is how it comes to him.

One day, when his loneliness is at its peak, and he swims in a cold pond, he hears the cry of creatures that fly overhead, and his heart leaps. Their cries resonate somewhere deep inside him. He looks up, and sees the most beautiful creatures he has ever seen, and they cry down at him. His heart rises and breaks at the same time, and he feels a desperate love for these great white birds that he cannot understand. After they leave he is even more bereft.[46]

The swan's cry of recognition is painful, because it is the

cry of belonging and the cry of loss at the same time. This part of the story always moves me, because this is the cry of the broken heart. Such pain touches the deepest part of us, and uncovers an essential spiritual yearning to return home.

The ugly duckling had seen his kind and his soul family had recognised him. But he was not yet ready to join his family. He had not yet recognised the swan in him, and he still had growing to do.

## Remembrance and Knowing: Finding Your truth

The story of the ugly duckling is a metaphor for finding one's truth. The central meaning of the exile is always about the search for true belonging. It is also about recognising one's difference, one's uniqueness, and finally coming to a place of belonging. Pinkola Estes explains how the search to belong is so basic in us as to be archetypal. Reminding us that early mothering and the sense of belonging activates in us innate wisdom, she writes:

> We all have a longing that we feel for our own kind, our wild kind. Something great and big in us longs to be connected again with this primeval mother, and the ugly ducking in us will go on, until we find it.

Reminding us too of the promise from the wild psyche to all of us, Este continues:

> Even though we have only heard or seen or dreamt a wondrous wild world that we belonged to once, even though we have not yet or only momentarily touched it, even though we do not identify ourselves as part of it, the memory of it is as a beacon that guides us toward what we belong to, and for the rest of our lives. In the ugly duckling a knowing yearning stirs when he sees the swans lift up into the sky, and

from that single event his remembrance of that vision sustains him.[47]

No matter how lost we are, we also have moments when a knowing comes in to warm us. However, during difficult times, these moments are seldom enough to keep us from feelings of despair. When our hearts are broken, we often lose faith, and our ability to be warmed by such moments pale. It is then that the constancy of nature can restore us to faith. It is the things of nature that are the most healing, because they are the deepest, and the simplest. That is why returning to my soul home by the sea never fails to lift me when I am upset. It takes only the simplest of things and moments for the magic to happen; the sight of a rainbow on a wave, a dewdrop on a leaf in the early morning, the night smell of peat. These wonderful things restore me to love and faith, and life. Estes tells us that 'continuance and endurance is a strange thing'; a second can feed you for a year.

It is thus for the lonely, lovesick heart. Somewhere along the way to healing a broken heart, we begin to remember and something starts to change. A gentle unfurling happens, as a precious part of us begins to be restored. We begin to see that our broken heart brings with it many gifts. We understand then that our broken heart has pushed us into an elemental search for belonging.

## Endurance and Soul Stamina

Nowadays we need to build soul stamina; we need to be able to endure hardship, and grow from it. It is no longer enough to simply be aware of soul and to be prepared to heal our wounds. We need to develop the capacity to endure. Stories can teach us. The story of The Ugly Duckling is also about persistence and endurance in the face of adversity. We can take lessons there; the Ugly Duckling's trials and hardship can help us in situations where we feel like giving up. His persistence and endurance pay off, and show us that we should never give up on finding where we truly belong. The Ugly Duckling is essentially about the Orphan Child, and can help us develop the faith we need that we will eventually be united with our own kind.

Orphan Children suffer a great deal, since they cannot find their true home. Like all un-mothered children, their instincts have not been sharpened and nurtured, so that they have to find their own way, not through guidance but rather, like the ugly duckling, through trial and error. They have to find their way alone.

You do not need to be actually orphaned to be an un-mothered child, to be an ugly duckling. Ugly ducklings can be born into rich families, poor families, and families from all parts of the world: all creeds, races, cultures and religions. If you feel you were not nurtured in your essential self, if you feel not part of your birth family because you are 'different', the ugly duckling in you will push you to find your truth.

You will do so or die. We all need to feel a sense of belonging. This sense is part of an inner wholeness necessary to the spiritual well being of every individual. Without it we are bereft. That is why we often need to recover lost parts of us that have been hurt as young children. When a child's natural instinctive and spiritual nature is suppressed or silenced, then a part of them closes down. It is the search for this lost part of the soul that often propels adult 'Orphans' into therapy.

The search for belonging continues throughout life until it is found.

A sense of belonging is essential to spiritual health. We know that when a person's individual soulfulness is acknowledged and accepted, it empowers that person. We all need to feel nurtured in our essential natures, and the search to find the right soil in which to grow is part of our journey to wholeness. Many of us are ugly ducklings, and our search for belonging is what propels us to endure the challenges involved in the journey to wholeness. Like the ugly duckling, we may go from house to house, and from lover to lover, seeking a sense of place, until one day, we hear the cries of our own kind, and we know we have arrived.

The story of The Ugly Duckling can help us take heart when, like him, we are cast out and forced into exile. Thrown back on our own resources, his lonely journey and eventual reconciliation with his true kind can help us develop the endurance and persistence necessary to complete our journey. We are all capable of embracing our 'swan' energy, and we will have moments like the ugly duckling, when we hear the cries of our own kind. Those moments are there to help us trust, and are signs held out by the universe to help us on our way.

Great myths and stories all contain the theme of loss or exile, and a return to wholeness. In the myth of Eros and Psyche, which we will look at in detail in the next chapter, the heartbroken Psyche too was helped many times during her ordeal, to complete her tasks. And although in her despair she tried several times to take her own life, her love for her husband, and her determination to be reunited with him, urged her on.

The lessons from both these stories can help us on our journey to heal our broken hearts.

## Mourning the Death of the Heart

Part of the journey to healing a broken heart involves grieving. The death of the heart must be mourned. Usually, after a period of shutting down, we begin to unfreeze, and it is only then that we are able to begin the process of mourning. However, true grieving is more difficult than it sounds because, again, it involves enduring – suffering the pain of loss.

It is well known that one of the greatest stumbling blocks to love is failure to deal with loss. It is very hard to heal if you are still holding on to an old hurt. If you have suffered the break up of a marriage or long-term relationship, then you may carry over this and other losses into your next relationship. If you have not adequately mourned a previous relationship, you are likely to see your current partner through the lenses of past experiences, thereby complicating how you relate.

Unresolved loss can have a very powerful influence on our lives and relationships. Many of us unwittingly carry around in our hearts the corpses of past relationships, together with thwarted expectations and unmet needs. Our hearts can be catacombs, incarcerating our former partners, and the memories that we retain of those partnerships. We confuse the present with the past and our new lover (if we have moved into a new relationship) assumes the mantle of his or her predecessors.

Mourning and letting go of the past also applies to negative or limiting belief systems. There is no doubt that our past does tend to inform us, so if we believe that we are unable to sustain healthy relationships, for example, then we will project these negative beliefs into the present and literally make it a reality. If we have not mourned a past relationship, we lose touch with the here and now as our future is mapped out by our fears.

Unhealthy self-esteem is responsible for most emotional difficulties in relationship, and without a good sense of self, we often sabotage our chances for love and happiness, as many of the characters in this book bear out.

If we have suffered loss in love in the past, then our fears of loving again will be very great. We will do almost anything to avoid the pain involved in betrayal and loss but, unconsciously, we will attract it to us through the power of negative thinking, unless we are willing to overcome our fears. If we have not mourned a previous lost love, then unshed tears can fill up our heart space, so that it becomes a block to loving. When we release the pain and grief associated with loss, the energy of love can flow freely again.

Sometimes, of course, since it is part of letting go, we find it hard to truly mourn and grieve what we have lost. Seeking relief, we might escape to the comfort of another relationship before we have truly mourned, and put the last one to bed.

Kevin did this. A middle-aged man, who found himself alone after his wife of twenty years left him, fell into another relationship within six months. But it soon became clear that he was numb and too anaesthetised to really feel. His new partner frequently told him she felt as though he were on drugs, not really there. Still shocked by the break up of his marriage, and inwardly hurting, Kevin was so split off from his feelings, he could not really relate emotionally. On automatic pilot, Kevin was withdrawn and uncommunicative, so that after some time, they split up. It was only then, in the emptiness of being alone, that Kevin was able to begin mourning his losses, and his marriage.

## What Might Have Been

Mourning losses is part of life, but since it is also part of nature to retreat from experiencing pain, we sometimes find it hard to grieve. We find it particularly hard when loss happens before time. Premature loss is something the psyche finds difficult to come to terms with, because there is the loss of what might have been. It is like winter happening during springtime, so that summer never gets to live. One feels cheated and betrayed.

The nearest symbolic equivalent that comes to my mind is of the loss of a child. Having lost two babies while they were still forming in my womb, I can resonate with the particular difficulties of grieving what might have been. The loss of a child, as a result of miscarriage or abortion, or shortly after birth is, I believe, one of the most painful things a woman can experience. It is an embodied loss by which I mean it is felt not only in the psyche and in the heart, but also deep within the body itself. In addition, the loss of a child is always the loss of unfulfilled life and this adds to its impact. To the trauma of loss is added the pain of losing 'what might have been', the loss of potential in all its manifestations.

Many broken relationships take on that quality of loss, since often one or other partner does not want the relationship to end. Though unhappy in his marriage, Kevin hated change, and did not want to be the one to end it. Staying in the comfort of his marriage was preferable to him than facing the world alone. For others, the ending comes much too soon. Still others are deeply in love with their partners, and do not want to be without them. If it has come to a timely end, and both partners are agreed on that, then the parting although painful, will not have the same impact as an unresolved ending.

### Soul Work during your Exile period
Spiritual Truth:
The wisdom of the heart knows no bounds;
Just as there are no limits to the soul, so deep is its mystery.

- Hold on to personal and spiritual truths.
- Begin letting go.
- Examine your feelings and begin disentangling and sorting them.
- Look at your patterns in relationships and your beliefs about yourself.
- Become aware of what story you might be living out of.
- Uncover your inner archetypes.
- Start analysing your patterns and sorting your emotions.
- Avoid negative thinking and self-blame.
- Keep a journal and record your dreams.
- Be methodical in your self-analysis; the aim is to become conscious.
- If necessary see a therapist to help you work through what you feel you cannot work through alone.

**What Can Help You During your Exile.**
Hold on to spiritual and personal truths.

- Know that if you work with the process, the emptiness left by your former partner will gradually be filled as you deepen your relationship with yourself.
- Stepping back will enable you to examine your-relationship patterns and free soul bonds that mighthave held you back.
- Know that healing the heart is essential to your emotional health and future relating.
- Turn your attention to nurturing your deeper self.
- Never let go of your goal – your search for belonging – for home.

In general, this is a time of inner work. When the rawness of the feelings decrease, it is possible to become conscious and aware of negative or limiting belief structures that might underpin your relationships. I call this time 'breaking stones' because it is only after the initial numbness and raw pain have subsided that we can begin to break the hardness that we have placed around ourselves as a protection. Awareness of your emotional patterns will in turn help you release and transform soul bonds and recover a sense of inner wholeness.

## Saying Goodbye

Saying goodbye is part of letting go. We cannot really move on without it. There is no one particular way to do this; everyone does it in his or her own way, but saying goodbye is a must if we want to move on.

Some years after losing my last child in pregnancy, I experienced the premature ending of a relationship. It was a brief love affair that ended abruptly, just as it was developing. To me, it felt like a terrible loss, quite similar to a miscarriage or an abortion. What was most difficult for me yet again was the loss of 'what might have been', the potential of a love just budding.

I suffered great pain. As a result of the inner work I was doing at the time, I know this loss dragged me back to my lost babies, and beyond. In the depths of despair, and in the struggle to heal that loss, I wrote a poem entitled 'Benton'. It expresses the pain of premature loss. I include it here because, for many people, a relationship ends before time, and it can be hard to heal that loss. It can also be difficult to hold on to love when a relationship ends and not throw 'the baby out with the bath water'.

> Benton lies buried in the soft womb
> that created him.
> We rowed across,
> My guide and I,
> To the little island that would be his
> final resting place.
> As we tenderly placed his little body in the bed
> that had been prepared for him,
> You came to join us.
> Together we watched as the tiny grave
> was filled.
> Standing side by side, we placed two daisies
> on his grave
> And said I love you.
>
> Then you disappeared,
> My tall blonde lover,
> My quiet man.
> You left as quietly as you had arrived.
> The little boy we buried that evening

Had blonde curly hair
And my brown eyes.

On the way across,
A bright golden light rose up from
the tiny body
I held in my lap.
It rose and rose, and now shines down
from the stars.
But it is also in the Olearia bush by the
gable of my home,
It is wherever I call it into being.

Goodbye my Benton,
Goodbye my quiet man.

In this poem I created an ideal. I did not kill off my lover in a fit of rage and pain, as I might have done. I let him live in the airy realms of my dreams and my imagination, so that I could speak to him whenever I wanted to. Although I did not realise it then, I had preserved him in my heart as someone I could find in the future. In the poem, I buried the child that symbolised our relationship, but I immortalised the love ideal. This meant that though I mourned the death of the heart, I kept love alive. I did not shut down. This was my way of healing my soul wound, and it enabled me to move forward in my life, and to dare to eventually love again.

Whatever way we seek to express our grief we must do so, in order to heal the heart and to move on. The method I chose was writing; or rather, it was writing that chose me! Something in me knew that this love had not been completed, and it took time for me to heal the loss of what might have been. Expressing what was in my soul was very much part of the healing process. My lover was immortalised in my poetry.

In my writing, I gave birth to the creative spark in me that had been ignited by our love affair.

It is always important to express the feelings involved in loss. People express their feelings in many different ways. Some will resolve their feelings of loss alone. Others will seek out another person to confide in. Writing, painting, working with one's dreams, drawing or simply working in the garden or walking in nature, all these methods work. The most important thing is to follow the dictates of the soul, and to listen to its voice.

### Soul Work: Saying Goodbye and Returning Home
Spiritual truth:
The path to spiritual consciousness is through
the heart and love is divine power.[48]
When we return to ourselves we find that love is within.

- Hold on to personal and spiritual truths.
- Say goodbye.
- Write a letter to yourself/to your ex partner with the intention of taking your spirit back from the past and forgiving them and yourself.
- Have a closing ritual.
- Reclaim your inner feminine and your ability to love by practicing forgiveness and compassion.
- Open your heart to yourself and all things.
- Recover your inner king and be empowered through your heart by understanding the spiritual lessons involved in your wounds.
- Live in appreciation and gratitude.
- Establish a spiritual practice.
- Come home to yourself.
- Live in the now and think love.

**What Can Help You During This Time**
Hold on to spiritual and personal truths.

- Know that your 'broken heart' is a conduit to greater spiritual maturity.
- Healing happens through acts of forgiveness.
- A heart wound will lead you to open your heart and feel compassion for God, others, the earth and yourself.
- Know that every experience of loss and suffering, as well as stretching our souls, can bring us closer to others.

Initiate a daily spiritual practice and try to stick to it. The discipline will pull you back when you begin to waver or get too involved in your emotional pain. Overall, positive instead of negative thinking and attitude will pull you through it along with friends and loved ones, walks in nature, doing what you enjoy most and quality time alone.

## Returning to Wholeness

When we have moved through the various stages involved in healing a broken heart, we are almost at the end of the journey. This journey takes time. Mourning is a process, and it cannot be rushed. The body heals in its own time, and so does the soul. The important thing is to dare to go to that place of hurt in the first place, instead of clamming up and hoping that the pain will disappear. Time eases the pain of hurt. But no amount of time will heal the heart, if one does not open it. And this, by necessity, will hurt.

Healing a broken heart involves recovering our inner feminine natures, because the feminine in us is what feels. Reclaiming our inner feminine means having the willingness to suffer our heart wounds. To dare to be lovers in a time of broken heart is all that is necessary to keep the heart open. The heart that loves is always young. It may be a sad and battle-scarred heart that guides us to healing, but it is also a wise heart. Having experienced life with its ups and downs, pains and joys, we can move forward, armed with the wisdom that only an empowered heart can give us.

## Eros and Psyche: A Story of Love and Healing[49]

Once there was a king and a queen with three lovely daughters. The youngest daughter, Psyche, was so beautiful that she was revered throughout the land, and her father's subjects reached out to touch her as she passed. However, no suitors dared to cross her doorstep, so highly was she worshiped. Psyche was deeply lonely.

Her beauty became legendary far and wide and it was not long before it reached the ears of Aphrodite, the epitome of all beauty, the goddess of love. Tales of the young princess enraged the jealous goddess and she made plans to dispose of her. Aphrodite arranged for Psyche's father to present Psyche as a sacrifice, in order to prevent his kingdom being devoured by a monster, and this he grudgingly did, placing her on a mountaintop, and bidding her a tearful farewell.

Eros, the errant son of Aphrodite, was sent to murder Psyche but he too was entranced by her gentle ways and beauty, and implored Zephyr, the West Wind, to lift her down from the hillside and place her in a lush and verdant valley. When Psyche opened her eyes she found herself in front of a sumptuous palace unlike any she had ever seen before. Here her every need was catered for. When she thought of food, delicious food was laid at her disposal, and though she saw or spoke to no one, she felt a quiet and calm presence that soothed her. When she grew tired a soft bed was presented and she slipped dreamlessly into sleep.

Psyche woke in the night. A presence had stirred her but she felt no fear. A warm and calm presence pervaded the room and she closed her eyes, sinking into its musky perfume. She was joined and embraced by a body so inviting, she gave herself at once, filled by a sense of joy that overwhelmed her. 'Who are you?' she whispered but a finger was laid gently to her lips. She said no more, spending the night in tender love. When she awoke, her bed was empty.

And so the days passed, with Psyche growing ever more peaceful and happy. She had clothes and jewels, which miraculously appeared, and her every comfort was seen to. Her happiness would have been complete but for her loneliness, for apart from the moonlight visits from her phantom husband, she was entirely alone. She had tried to learn more about this man who every night held her in a passionate embrace, but he had told her that his identity must remain secret or their alliance could be no more. She agreed to his wishes because she loved him and because he filled her with a sense of belonging that she had never before experienced.

One day, her peaceful idyll was interrupted by the cries of her two sisters. Concerned about her disappearance, they had spent many weeks looking for her and now stood just beyond the bend of the valley. Shrieking with delight, Psyche raced up the mountain and drew them back into her new home. As she toured her sisters around her exquisite palace she failed to notice their growing silence, their sullen looks. They were green with envy and they teased their sister about her ghostly lover. 'No,' she protested, 'he was/is real'. She felt him, explored him each night and held him warm in her arms.

But her sisters teased and taunted her until Psyche agreed to seek out his identity. That night, when he came to her again, she broke her word for the first time and leaned across him to light the oil lamp. As she moved, a drop of the hot liquid fell onto the skin of her lover, waking him, but not before she had seen the most beautiful of the gods, Eros. Eros was her lover but, burnt and bewildered, he rose from their bed and disappeared from her forever.

Psyche's torment was so deep that she tried to take her own life. Eros, still deeply in love with his wife, but now invisible to her, saved her on each occasion, caring for her as she travelled across the kingdom in search of him. He longed to touch her, but the wrath of his mother was more than he could bear. He longed to speak to her, but could only use the trees, the winds and the creatures of the forest to deliver his words.

Searching far and wide, Psyche came, by and by, to the home of Aphrodite. Poisoned by her jealousy, Aphrodite resolved to dispose of the young princess, caring only that Psyche was more beautiful than she, and that Psyche had eluded her careful plot to send her to her death. She set the princess impossible tasks, determined to punish her further.

Her first task was to sort through a pile of grain and Aphrodite led her to a large shed, full of various grains. Here lay oats, black beans, millet, lentils, vetch and poppy seeds, wheat and rye, mixed together in an overwhelming pile. Psyche was to sort through this pile before she could be free. Psyche crouched down and began gingerly picking at the pile. Tears welled in her eyes and she began to feel despair in her heart as she surveyed her impossible task. As the first glistening tear fell, a tiny voice woke her from her sorrow. An ant, enchanted by the lovely princess, had moved to her side. He could help, he said, and so it was that thousands of ants marched to the pile and sorted within a short time.

The next task Aphrodite assigned to her was to pluck the golden wool from a flock of bloodthirsty solar rams. As Psyche stood by the edge of their paddock, she heard the quiet song of the reeds in the wind. As she listened, their words became clear. She was not to pluck the wool from their backs and she was to wait till they dispersed for the night. There, on the gorse bushes that lined their field, was the wool that had been brushed from their sides each time they passed. She crept over and filled her basket. Gleefully she returned to Aphrodite, basket held high, but her mistress was not happy and demanded more tasks so that Psyche's hopes of freedom vanished.

The goddess sent her out again, this time to fetch water from the stream that flowed to the Styx, the river of the Underworld. As she neared its banks, Psyche grew frightened. The stream itself cut through a deep gorge, and all her efforts to reach its waters failed. Furthermore she saw that the river was guarded by dragons whose fiery breath boiled the seething waters, making it impossible for her to approach. She sank down in despair, her empty bottle by her side. Suddenly it was snatched up, clutched by Zeus' great eagle who effortlessly dodged the dragons, filled her flask with water and returned it to her. He had been told of Psyche's plight by the winds and, enchanted by her loveliness, had vowed to help her.

Aphrodite was ill pleased by this success and set Psyche a fourth and final task. She was to journey to the Underworld and beg Persephone for some of her beauty, which should be returned to Aphrodite. Once again, aware of the impossibility of yet another task, Psyche tried to take her own life. Deep in desolation, and frustrated by the seemingly impossible tasks set before her, she longed for her husband, Eros. Yet again, she was plucked from death by Eros and through him was helped to realise her next task.

Psyche was to follow the path nearby, which would take her to the Underworld. She was to take with her several things – barley cakes and honey cakes for Cerberus, the three-headed dog who guarded the entrance to the Underworld and two coins to pay Charon, the ferryman. She was to ignore the messages of her own kind heart and refuse help to anyone who sought her assistance along the way.

Psyche set off. As she travelled, she was met by various hapless travellers who called out for her help but, remembering her instructions, she passed them by. At every turn lay another trap set by Aphrodite, who was determined for Psyche to remain trapped in the Underworld. But Psyche, fuelled by her love for Eros to whom she longed to return, was also determined. She made her way through the various pitfalls that were presented to her and at last stood before Persephone, where she asked for some of her beauty. Persephone presented her with a box.

As she returned once more to the land of the living, struck by curiosity, she opened the box. It seemed empty. But as she struggled to close it, she felt an overwhelming sleep begin to take over, drawing from her her final breath. Death clung to the princess but the ever-vigilant Eros flew down and brushed the sleep of death from her eyes, placing it back in the box.

Psyche, revived and glowing with new life, returned to Aphrodite and handed back the deadly box. She waited in anticipation; surely the goddess was finished with her now?

Aphrodite was enraged but wise enough to know that Psyche was not going to succumb to her plots so she set her free. Psyche set off once more in search of her lover, Eros. Eros himself, deeply disillusioned by his mother's antics, flew to Olympus to consult with Zeus, who was renowned for his wisdom and sense of justice. Zeus examined the goodness of Psyche, her dedication and her exquisite charms. He agreed to allow her to marry Eros, thus making her immortal. In return Eros was to reconcile with his mother.

And so it was that Psyche became a daughter of Aphrodite and entered a union with Eros, the god of love. She returned once again to her palace in the valley, to a happiness that was enriched by the goodness in her heart and which was, as a result of her tribulations, now complete.

Chapter 11

# Healing from Within

Go deeper than love, for the soul has greater depths,
Love is like the grass, but the heart is deep wild rock
Molten, yet dense and permanent.
Go down to your deep old heart, and lose sight
of yourself.
And lose sight of me, the me whom our
turbulently loved.
Let us lose sight of ourselves, and break the mirrors.
For the fierce curve of our lives is moving again
to the depths
Out of sight, in the deep living heart.

*Know Thyself:* D.H. Lawrence

Healing from within means travelling into the profound terrain of our souls. It means exploring the older wisdom in our 'deep living hearts', and surrendering to something far greater than the narrow focus of our ego-driven minds. To truly touch this place within we must 'lose sight' of ourselves, and move beyond, to the tide of life that stirs in the 'depths, out of sight, in the deep living heart'.

Healing from within means that we do not blame others for what they did, or did not do, to make us unhappy. True healing involves taking responsibility for the choices we make and the relationships we have. When we lose love, we empower ourselves through a journey of healing which includes honest self-examination and evaluation. And since we have learned that love can bring us back to ourselves and reveal our souls in a way not possible otherwise, our journey to healing after heartbreak will result in a stronger, more beautiful and resilient soul, and an open heart.

The Greek myth of Eros and Psyche symbolically expresses some of the challenges involved in the journey to healing after the loss of love. It is, in this sense, a metaphor for psychological growth through love. Although it is about a woman, it is applicable to both men and women since it is about love lost and found, and outlines certain inner tasks that need to be accomplished before healing and reunion with love can happen. Men will identify Psyche as their lost anima, and her tasks as psychological work they, and women, need to do, to re-engage in healthy relationships, and find love again.

Psyche's four tasks, presented to her by the jealous Aphrodite, have important symbolic meanings. Each one represents capabilities that women need to develop in order to grow psychologically. Each time Psyche masters a task, she acquires a capability she did not have before. In Jungian psychology the acquiring of certain capabilities refers to the development of the animus in woman. As we saw earlier, the animus represents the masculine energy or the inner man in a woman. Having a well-developed animus helps women to be more assertive and grounded, and less at the mercy of their emotions, so they can make more empowering choices about their lives and relationships.

Developing her animus helps a woman potentially become more whole, as long as she remains conscious and does not overdevelop masculine qualities at the expense of her feminine self. Aphrodite is the goddess of love, creativity and sexuality. Symbolically, these gods and goddesses represent aspects of ourselves so that we tend to identify with certain ones and not others. An Aphrodite woman is usually a beautiful woman for whom physical beauty, love and sex are important, and women who identify with Aphrodite will be very aware of their sexual charms. When a woman is strongly identified with the Aphrodite qualities within her, she will often put everything into her love relationships, and has a tendency to lose herself in others. Love, and her search for it, will often make her put her relationships first, and she will react instinctively to others.

Many people are involved in relationships with partners they feel treat them badly, minimize, and in some cases, abuse them. The more their lover hurts them, the more they are propelled to seek their love, convincing themselves, despite evidence to the contrary, that he or she does love them. Such men and women will subordinate everything in their lives for the 'crumbs' of attention they might occasionally get from their lovers. These people (often women) are typically tormented by the relationship, and very ambivalent. She knows she deserves better, but she is still pulled by the possibility or the need to win his love. To feel better, of course, she would have to give up the destructive relationship, but it has an addictive hold on her.

To free herself, she will need to develop certain abilities, which will help her leave a destructive relationship and move on. Psyche's tasks represent in symbolic form, the various stages of becoming conscious. By becoming conscious of your patterns in love and relationships you will be aware of the power to change things, and to make choices. Once we are consciously aware of what our tendencies and attachment patterns are, we have the power to make empowering choices; we have a chance to sort out our priorities, and to act on them. Psyche's tasks represent a symbolic journey on a developmental path that women can follow.

For men, the task is the same. If a man does not have strong boundaries and is overly developed in his feminine, then he will fear the hold love (and his lover) has over him. He will have to develop and use his masculine attributes so as to find a balance, where he can hold his own, and yet be open and keep his heart open. In my experience, a lot of men are afraid of love, because of the dependency needs it stirs up in them. Brought up to be strong and resilient in the face of their emotions, the thought of being emotionally dependent on their wives or partners can fill them with dread. What if she leaves? How will they cope with the tearing pain inside them and still manage to carry on their outer lives and responsibilities?

## Task one. Sorting the Seeds

Aphrodite leads Psyche into a room and shows her an enormous pile of mixed seeds, telling her she must sort each kind of seed into its own pile. The task seems impossible but for a host of ants who come to her aid, placing each sort, grain by grain, in its own mound. This represents the sorting a woman has to do when she is confronted with a crucial decision involving her emotions. She has to sort through her conflicted, confusing and jumbled emotions that may be hampering her seeing straight, and making an empowering decision. A woman in love, as a man, can lose all perspective. When we are overwhelmed by our emotions we lose perspective, we lose the ability to think straight, and therefore to make a clear decision.

Usually we are told to wait until the heat of a situation has abated before making a decision about anything. Sometimes we are told to count to ten before responding in an argument. Whatever we do, we need to wait and go inwards rather than reacting instinctively, as most lovers do. No rational decision can be made in the heat and turmoil of emotions.

Sorting the seeds is thus an inward task, requiring that a woman look honestly within, sift through her feelings, values and motives, and separate what is important from unimportant.[50] When we learn to stay with a conflicting and unsettling situation until clarity emerges, we have learnt to trust our 'ants', our inner voice. Ants represent our small inner intuitive voices that are there underneath the layers of ego conditioning and cultural belief systems. The ants represent our inner voice, and listening and trusting our intuition is vital in this process.

Again, intuition is not something men are taught to trust. *In Reclaiming Father*, I wrote about how hard it is sometimes for a man to reach his heart in our western society. It is a sign of weakness to show emotional hurt and pain. Sex is often divorced from love, and the man cannot reach his heart for he has amputated it in the mistaken belief that this makes him more of a man. Guy Corneau, Jungian analyst and author of *Absent Father, Lost Sons*, expresses it thus:

> It is not that men have no sensitivity; it is rather that they are forbidden to express it if they want to be considered men by other men. In this sense, becoming a man requires cutting oneself off successfully from both the heart and body. In fact one is all the more a man if he manages this amputation without crying or complaining.[51]

## Task two. Acquiring Some Golden Fleece

Psyche's second task is to acquire golden fleece from the fierce sun rams. These are huge, aggressive, horned beasts, constantly at war with each other. If Psyche were to go amongst them, and try to take their wool, she would be crushed or trampled to death. Once again, though the task appears impossible, she listens to the counsel of the reeds, who tell her to wait until sundown, when the rams will have dispersed. Then she can safely pick from the branches of the brambles the wool/ golden fleece left by the rams in passing.

Symbolically, golden fleece represents power, which a woman needs to acquire without being possessed or destroyed by it. Power, typically associated with an animus position, can be a tricky and difficult issue for women. Women who consciously seek self-empowerment may have to tread a fine line between being seen as 'animus ridden' and unfeminine, or appear weak and vulnerable to potential manipulation or abuse. Women who are naturally loving can have a hard time dealing with power, and are often open to being controlled by their lovers. When a sensitive woman, who loves easily, has to go out into the competitive world where others battle aggressively for power and position, she can easily be hurt and disillusioned if she does not recognise the dangers. Similarly, an attractive and sexually alluring woman needs to recognise how others may be envious and jealous of her, and may try and undermine her.

Collecting the golden fleece is a difficult task, if you are open and loving by nature. A man or a woman, who is naturally trusting, can also be naïve, and thus court danger. If a woman who is open by nature enters the outer world and becomes hurt and disillusioned by other's attitudes towards her, she may become cynical, and lose her caring and trusting self. This loss of faith is symbolic of being trampled on by the ferocious rams. The sun represents solar energy, a quality associated with the masculine. Being trampled and crushed by solar rams is symbolic of being crushed by an overly-patriarchal masculine power. The lesson of this task is that such a woman must approach power, like Psyche does, by waiting, observing and taking an indirect route. This way she can acquire the power she needs to stand up for her own needs and integrity.

Men will learn from this that they must curtail their aggression and need for control in such a way that they are instead assertive. A healthy masculinity has nothing to do with 'power over' anything or anyone. It is about being strong, and yet capable of vulnerability. To be too identified with solar energy will mean squashing the feminine rather than protecting it. It means identification with 'patriarchy' – a system of control. The dangers involved in tackling the rams head on indicates the necessity to avoid acting rashly and impulsively in a way one might regret later.

Jungian writer Jean Shinoda Bolen suggests that 'acquiring the golden fleece without destroying Psyche is a metaphor for the task of gaining power and remaining a compassionate person'.[52] Learning to assert yourself can be the major task of many women who are natural lovers, and who tend to project their animus onto their partners. They need to learn to develop the qualities of discrimination, judgement and assertion themselves, so that they are equipped to hold their own in relationship.

## Task three. Filling the Crystal Flask

Psyche then has to collect water from a special river, forbidden to mortals. It is guarded by fierce dragons and impossible to get to. This stream flows from the highest peak to the lowest depths of the Underworld. Metaphorically, this spring symbolises the circular flow of life, into which Psyche must dip to fill her flask. Once again, help comes by way of the eagle that swoops down from the sky, circumvents the fierce dragons, and fills her flask. The eagle represents the ability to see the bigger picture, to have a broader perspective, something which a woman like Psyche finds hard, because she is so overwhelmingly personally involved that she cannot see 'the forest for the trees'.

It is especially important for a woman who loves easily to get an emotional distance on her relationship, in order to see her overall patterns, and what she is playing out. Having taken a step back and gained an emotional distance, she can become clear on what her priorities and values are. She is then in a better position to assimilate her experiences, and shape her life.

For a man, the task is the same, since when we are overwhelmed with emotions, we cannot see clearly. An ability to stand back and see the bigger picture is very important, so as to gain a sense of perspective. Typically associated with an animus quality, eagle eyes are necessary if we are to ride the storm of our emotions, and emerge clear and focused.

## Task four. Learning To Say No

For her fourth and final task, Psyche has to descend into the Underworld and confront Persephone. She must receive some beauty potion from her and return it to Aphrodite. A descend into the Underworld is a metaphor for death – ego death – and it is a journey one seldom returns from without having fundamentally changed. On the way, Psyche is told she will meet people who will ask for her help, but she must ignore these pleas, and harden her heart to compassion.

Women like Psyche, who love too easily, and are so responsive to the needs of others, often at the expense of their own needs, have to practice saying no. Saying no is harder than it seems. The task Psyche accomplishes when she says no three times is to exercise the power of choice. Again, many women allow themselves to be imposed on and diverted from their own tasks or what is best for them, until they learn to say no. Until a woman can say no to her particular susceptibility, whether it is to be perpetually in the caring role, or the attraction of an erotically charged relationship, she cannot determine her own course.

Men also need to be able to say no to their needs and desires sometimes. When a man is able to distinguish between what his ego desires and what his soul needs, he can make decisions based on a more wholesome view of his life. Men whose mothers have had a strong and enduring influence on them can sometimes find it hard to say no to having their more unconscious childish needs met. Such men need to be willing to accept the responsibility involved in growing up and understand that you cannot have your cake and eat it. Men can also be held hostage by their anima, and need to learn to say no.

Through the four tasks, Psyche evolves. She develops capabilities and strengths as her courage and determination are tested. Yet, despite all she acquires, she maintains her basic nature and priorities. She appreciates a love relationship, and she never ceases or wavers in her search for her love, Eros. She values a love relationship, risks everything for it, and wins. After her ordeal, her love is returned to her.

Women who are identified with the qualities of Aphrodite, and who tend to put everything into their love relationships, can identify with Psyche. Such women tend to lose sight of themselves in relationships because at bottom, they are dependent on their lovers for confirmation of their worth.

Claire, a strong, articulate woman, recalled many occasions when she allowed Bill, her partner, to hurt her – when she endured verbal barrages attacking her personality, her mental abilities, and her essential nature. Instead of taking him on and defending herself, she would become like putty, and end up weeping and begging him to see how gentle and loving she really was. Once she told me that instead of being indignant at his attacks on her she had ended up apologising for herself. When I asked her what made her deny and minimize herself like this, she replied that at some deep level, she had felt flawed and ashamed. She recalled this later with great pain, since she saw how deeply she had demeaned herself in such encounters. At some deep level, she had tuned into her partner's lack of confidence in himself as a man, his envy and jealousy of her strength and, protecting him, had humiliated herself.

Many of our problems emanate from a basic sense of lack of worth. Self-esteem is a precious commodity, essential to healthy living and healthy relationships. However, since life often forces us into situations where the steadiness of our self-esteem is challenged, we will frequently be presented with opportunities to heal an unsure sense of self. As we have seen again and again with the characters in this book, a loss of self can happen when we are lonely, and our search for love blinds us to the reality of our situation. Afterwards, when we have a chance to think, to stand aside and to disengage from our emotions even a little, we are able to see what has happened, and to recover some of the ground we may have lost.

The myth of Psyche and Eros can be used to help such men and women grow. It is easy to lose yourself and your boundaries when you love, because love loosens the boundaries of the soul, and opens our hearts. Usually our inner wounded child will be awakened, and we will project many aspects of our souls onto our lovers. We will act as mirrors to each other, and see in each other what most needs healing in the other. That is why love relationships are a challenge, and offer us great opportunities to grow. Ultimately, our soul contract and unfinished stories propel us into our love relationships, so that we may learn the lessons we need to learn.

In essence, Psyche's trials represent the journey to the inner marriage.

In terms of healing love wounds, the myth of Eros and Psyche is about love lost and found, and reading it can help us work with our heartache. The psychological interpretation I have included serves as a road map to help us heal our hearts and move back to loving again.

## Healing from Within: A Workbook

Throughout the chapters in this book we have learned how our soul contracts, archetypal and family patterns, early lives and relationship experiences, all influence the way we live, and the way we love. We have learned that our earliest relationships form a template for future relationships, and that inner forces and archetypes, such as the anima and the animus, are always at work in our relationships. We have learned the fundamental part that self-esteem plays in how we view ourselves, and others, and how we relate. We have also learned that we live out of stories – belief systems – that we carry around with us and that form the basis out of which we live.

The truth is, however, that although these factors all influence us, they need not determine how we live our lives. No matter how hurt or damaged we are, or think we are, we always have a choice. Do we choose to be crippled by our past, or empowered by it? The fundamental basis of healing from within is having the willingness to look inside and examine your patterns – look at your story. The goal of this work is to become more conscious – to move towards healing inner fractures as well as outer fragmentation. The ultimate result is individuation and the inner marriage.

I have outlined a simple checklist and workbook that provides a framework for healing, and for understanding how our early experiences often diminish our capacity to live from our essential selves. Identifying and engaging your inner figures and archetypal patterns will enable you to gain insight into your self-protective mechanisms and destructive patterns, which often push love away. It will enable you to relate with more consciousness.

Look at how you are relating. Begin by identifying your inner archetypes, because these figures will be at play in your relationship. A more detailed description of these archetypes, which I described as architects of love, forms part of the chapter, Inner Landscapes. Refer back to this chapter to help you work with the following:

## 1. Identify Your Inner Archetypes

First you need to try to become familiar with your own archetypes, your inner figures. Engage with your inner Orphan Child, for example, and ask yourself honestly if your feelings of abandonment and rejection within your relationship emanate from your childhood. Review your childhood memories and become aware as to whether your painful experiences arise from the sense that your family never accepted you.

If you identify with the Wounded Child, engage with him

or her, allow yourself to fully feel and experience your feelings, and practice compassion and forgiveness so that you can move on. You may be using your wounds as a way of being, and as a way to control others. Some people identify with their childhood wounds to the extent that the wounds become confirmations of identity. This identity then provides a safety net to truly relating, and keeps a person locked in their wounds, unable to move on.

A man I knew, who had been sexually abused as a child, always introduced himself as such. He was not John or Peter but a sexual abuse survivor. His whole life revolved around the abuse survivors group he was a member of. When I suggested he was much more than that, he was annoyed and insulted. He felt I did not understand him. He was taking refuge in his wounds. It took him a long time to grow into the idea that he was more than his wounds, and to admit what he had invested in being wounded. When he allowed this thought in, he began to see himself as a healthy man with a wounded Inner Child, capable of moving on.

Repeat this exercise with your Inner Victim, Inner Saboteur and Inner Prostitute. Refer back to the chapter Inner Landscapes where each archetype is described in detail. It is important to engage with honesty, and to question the origin of your feelings. Review your childhood and your history and ask yourself the same questions with each inner archetype.

Bring back to mind childhood experiences where you might have felt shamed or humiliated, for example, and ask yourself do your current feelings emanate from there. Ask yourself where you might be playing victim, and whether your sense of powerlessness comes from your childhood. If you have a tendency to sell yourself short in return for love and security, review your early life and see if your fear of abandonment comes from a feeling of not being loved as a child.

Healing from within is not a short process. Reviewing is

not enough – you will have to engage with and feel your feelings. You will have to work very hard sometimes to practice love and compassion, and to honour your feelings rather than being impatient with them. It is important, no, vital, that you engage these inner figures with love and compassion. These wounded energies are there in us to help us learn to overcome obstacles on our spiritual path. It does not help to berate or dismiss these archetypes within us simply because we consider them inconvenient or shameful.

Cassie had great trouble forgiving herself for having given her love and abandoned herself to a man that later abused and left her. She considered it shameful that she allowed herself to love him and to stay in a situation that was unhealthy and abusive. Abandoned as a child, Cassie had a strong inner Prostitute who gave herself easily to any man that promised her emotional and financial security. Unable to assert herself, and leave a relationship that in later years demeaned her almost on a daily basis, she lost faith in herself and her self-esteem plummeted. She grew to hate the part of her that stayed.

When we began this process, she had hardened her heart against herself. Later, as we worked together at uncovering and engaging her inner archetypes, she gradually softened, and opened her heart to the pain and suffering she had endured. She learned to respect her loving heart and the openness of her spirit. One day, she was finally able to hold and thank her old hurt self for bringing her to this point in her life. She appreciated the wisdom of her inner Prostitute that had propelled her to seek love and had finally brought her to a place of trust and faith.

## 2. Identify your Patterns

We are compelled to repeat patterns. As we have seen, our early life experiences and our first relationship with our parents are all influences on how we go on to life our lives, and how we relate. Our first relationships, and the parental one in particular, essentially create 'attachment' patterns that we are compelled to recreate in later relationships. Intimate love relationships are where these patterns are played out.

We learn about intimacy from our very first bond. Sometimes this bonding has not happened, thus leaving an emotional scar on the soul so that we develop a mother or a father hunger. We may search for that bonding, that first love in every subsequent lover we meet, but we will never find it whilst we continue to project it outwardly. When we have such a narcissistic wound, we may become self-absorbed as a way of dealing with the pain and hurt of not being loved for ourselves.

Other times there has been ambivalence or uncertainty in our bonding and early relationship with our mother/father, so that we develop ambivalent and/or insecure attachment patterns.

We may have a pattern of emotional push and pull, for instance. This will often happen when we have had inconsistent and unpredictable parenting. The push and pull kind of energy is common if we grow up in homes where a parent suffers from alcoholism or other addiction. Addictive personalities are, at base, chaotic. The child may be picked up and hugged to pieces, and then be abandoned for long periods of time. He or she never knows what to expect. This child may build up the ambivalent and insecure attachment pattern which translates as 'come here/go away'!

In a relationship this dynamic will resemble an emotional see-saw. She craves love and draws him in and then, when he gets too close, she pushes him away because she feels suffocated; or he might do the pulling because he needs her love and then, when she gets too close, he pulls away. The more one pulls the more the other feels trapped. It is like a dance. Each is trying to find the in-between secure place just as the relationship needs to find the balance between vulnerability and togetherness.

Sometimes, when we start exploring our inner patterns in relatonships, we find we have to go further back than our own childhoods. We have to go to our father's or mother's history. We are influenced at a deeper level, as we saw earlier, by our archetypal, family and cultural heritage; and further back and deeper still, by our soul contract and any spiritual lessons we have agreed to and are destined to struggle with and learn.

At the familial level, we may carry certain family patterns we are unconscious of but that nonetheless influence us. I wrote about this in *Reclaiming Father*, when we looked at the influence of the father on the psyche. As I have already said, it is the fate of all children to carry and in some cases live out their parents' unlived lives. This is a very subtle and complex process because it is what is unconscious in the parent that is passed on. As Jungian analyst M.L. Von Franz puts it:

> When parents fail to live out their inner wholeness and fail to realise substantial components of themselves, the weight of these parts falls onto the children in the form of a projection and endangers them. The children find themselves driven by a dark compulsion to live out everything the parents have repressed.[53]

And so we live the stories of our family over and over again. We all know of cases where there have been several generations of the same pattern, such as unmarried mothers, fugitive fathers, suicides, mental illness, alcoholism, depression and so on. These archetypal patterns are like any others; they continue until we become conscious of them and integrate them. They are like ghosts that need to be set free and who continue to haunt us until we attend to them.

A family may be carrying a long line of very wounded women who were abandoned and betrayed in love, for instance. If you find that you are having a hard time finding love, or that you have had several failed and painful love affairs, then you may be the one chosen to heal this family pattern. It would be helpful then to look at your mother and her sisters, and your female lineage for similar patterns.

Or a family may have an extended line of depressed men or absent fathers. If some of these difficulties are present in your relationship, ask yourself whether you may be repeating some pattern you have inherited or picked up from your own father, grandfather or male lineage.

At a spiritual level, repeating patterns is about learning lessons. If a lesson has not yet been learned, the pattern continues. Our sacred contract and our archetypal energies will draw certain people and experiences to us so that we may learn these lessons. When we have overcome the obstacles to growth and learned from our experiences, we complete spiritual tasks of empowerment that were originally laid down for us.

It is helpful to remember that, at a spiritual level, we are always provided with everything we need in order to fulfil our sacred contract. It is up to us to meet the challenges we are offered on our soul's journey so that we may progress spiritually.

Look into your life and your relationships and see where you might be repeating patterns. If you have had more than one relationship, and especially if your relationships have failed, ask yourself what patterns you were repeating. If you find that you attract and are compelled to the same type of man or woman over and over again, then you are repeating a pattern.

Are you choosing a man who cannot give you what you want, for example? Or a woman from whom you cannot get the love and affection you are craving? Or do you repeatedly run away from commitment and love?

If the answer is yes, then perhaps you are recreating a wound from your childhood or seeking to heal a family pattern. If you felt unloved and uncared for, if you sought endlessly to get your father or your mother to love you and failed, then you will unconsciously be seeking this in every lover you take, and every intimate relationship you have.

As I said earlier, our bonding experience has a huge affect on how we learn about love and intimacy. If there has been a disturbance in the very early mother-baby bonding, there will be difficulties with intimacy. Such an early experience means we have no healthy template to refer to, with the result that we will have to learn to be intimate. We have to learn to trust and learn that it is OK to open ourselves up to the other. When we are hurt as children a part of us closes down to protect ourselves. Getting involved in a relationship means this hurt will be uncovered, and this can scare many people. Ultimately, our childhood wounds have to be suffered so that eventually we can be healed and we can become healthy again.

Uncovering your patterns and the underlying story and belief system that you are living out of is not enough. It is not the end of the story. The question always remains the same. What will you do with your pain, your memory of childhood trauma, the scars that are left on your soul? Will you allow it to control you and use it to manipulate others? Will you drag it around you and use your wound as a crutch, a refuge or worse, an excuse to disengage from life and relationship? Or will you suffer it, learn from it and move on, armed with the wisdom imparted by it?

If you live it, you will learn the lesson and restore some of the missing parts your soul needs to become whole.

## 3. Identify Your Story

As we saw in the chapter Stories We Live By, we all live out of a particular story or drama. And every love affair dramatises a myth or story. At the heart of every story, as at the heart of every love affair, is a vision of totality, of wholeness. Review your life patterns in relationships and ask yourself what story you might be living out of. If you have or had a favourite fairy story or myth then you will already have a clue what or whom you are living out. Generally you will find that you will be living out aspects of a character you identified with, or felt emotionally connected to.

The Little Mermaid, for example, is a story of the impossibility of love. There is too high a price to be paid to gain the love of a man and so love fails. At a psychological level, The Little Mermaid, as well as Rapunzel, are stories of the struggle to emerge from the devouring mother complex. By winning the prince or finding love, then these women are able to break free from the mother and find their own voice and places in the world. The princes, in this instance, symbolise the inner man, the animus. In women our animus is our creativity and our ability to stand on our own. He is also our counterpart, our other half. All women need to activate their inner masculine so that they can stand in the world with their integrity and self-respect intact.

Once you have identified your story then you can begin to see how you (and your partner) might be living out of it. You will generally project other characters in the story onto your lovers. Is your lover the prince you cannot have unless you, like the Little Mermaid, surrender your voice? Or are you the prince who braves the ramparts and climbs the tower to rescue your princess? Or perhaps your love, like the Little Tin Soldier, is out of reach? Is your lover the mother witch who refuses to let you go and keeps you cooped up in a cage so only she can have you? Or perhaps your lover is Beauty, whom you fear will forsake you, and whose true love you need to break the spell of the Beast inside you.

When we are living out of our stories a part of us is unavailable. Our stories make us opaque, because we are living out of a belief system. This means that by identifying with our stories we lose our essential selves. We live as the Little Mermaid for so long, for example, that we begin to believe we can never find love; that in order to be loved we have to surrender our most precious possession. Our stories become belief systems that are damaging to our body and souls, and impede our growth.

The stories become structures we depend on to live. If you believe, as Ben did as the little Tin Soldier, that your anima, your feminine, your love is out of reach, then you will be fearful of full commitment to a lover. You will not trust yourself to love, you have only one leg, and you are damaged. You cannot reach your heart. To love at a distance is something you know and are comfortable with. But full-on intimacy is threatening. If you can identify with this pattern, then when a relationship moves onto the next stage and a long-term commitment is involved, you panic and may leave.

Whilst we are living out of specific belief systems we are not present to our essential selves. Our hearts are not really available to the transcendent power of love because they are employed by the story. The part of us that needs to move on and grow cannot because the greater part believes we are the Ugly Duckling, the Little Mermaid, Cinderella, Prince Charming and so on.

Living out of stories we relate to others as part of this belief system, and do not see them for who they really are. We need to free ourselves from these stories and begin to live out of our essential selves. By emptying ourselves of our stories, then we create free space in our hearts for love. We can then see and appreciate our partners for who they are rather than for what we want them to be.

Healing from within involves delving into your heart and learning what story you might be living out. It is unlikely that you will be able to let go of your story all at once, although there are some rare creatures that achieve awakening or enlightenment in a single flash of light. Mostly, awareness comes gradually, like grace. Typically, people need to build soul stamina so that they can have the courage to move on from what they know. We build soul stamina through having the willingness to endure, and to be able to live with questions and with paradox.

# Chapter 12

## Return to Wholeness

The time will come when, with elation,
You will greet yourself arriving at your own door,
In your own mirror,
And each will smile at the other's welcome,
And say, sit here, eat.
You will love again the stranger who was your self.
Give wine, give bread, give back your heart to itself,
To the stranger who has loved you
All your life, whom you ignored for another,
Who knows you by heart.
Take down the love letters from the bookshelf,
The photographs, the desperate notes,
Peel your image from the mirror.
Sit. Feast on your life.

*Love after love:* Derek Walcott

When we go on a deep soul journey into our interior, we rarely return without being fundamentally changed. Most of us go through dark periods in our lives, and the journey to heal a broken heart is one such journey. When we return from our encounter with the dark night, we return with gifts. The gifts, too numerous to be counted, include a renewed sense of strength and self belief – a new you. Like Psyche in the myth, after we have completed our journey, we are reunited with our lost love, our inner lover – we return to ourselves in a mystical union. Our prize is the inner marriage – the union within. This inner union is essential to our spiritual well being, and may also lead us to an outer marriage, to love again. However, connecting with our inner lover is an essential stage to healing our heart and loving again.

Working through and healing heartbreak can bring you to a place of inner wholeness and spiritual purpose. You learn that love does indeed lie within and that whilst you are connected with this essential truth, you will never be alone. Knowing this helps you understand that projecting love outside yourself only brings disappointment. When you understand that your broken heart has helped you connect with your inner lover, and that your love relationships are part of your spiritual journey, it both heals and frees you. You no longer look to and blame others for your unhappiness because, ultimately, it is the projection of love 'out there' that makes us unhappy. In time, you even become grateful to your former partners and soul mates who brought you to experience this healing and soulful inner journey.

## The Lover Within

Who is the lover within that is awakened? Derek Walcott tells us in his beautiful poem 'you will love again the stranger who was your self'. Often we become strangers to ourselves when we put all our energies into loving and needing the person we feel we cannot live without. We bankrupt ourselves in a desperate effort to gain someone's love, not realising that it can often be at our own expense. All our energies are focused outwardly as we try to bring about and control situations according to the dictates of our ego desires. Projecting and then expecting another to fulfil our deepest needs is always a recipe for disaster. Often we do not see this until it is too late.

Walcott tells us in 'Love after Love' that 'you will love again the one you have deserted in favour of the other'. Sometimes we have to take the leap of faith that parting from a lover means just that. It will mean we return to appreciating and loving ourselves. No matter how clichéed loving yourself sounds, it is an essential truth without which we cannot expect to love another person.

In my own life, I have more than once had to suffer the pain of parting from a lover, not because there was no longer any love between us but because in some deep place we both knew that we needed to grow alone. When one has not healed the wounded lover within, it is very hard to love another outside. Sometimes, often even, we just need to heal a little before we can truly accept the love of another person and be capable of loving in return.

Love has a great power to heal; and, as we know, love relationships frequently offer the opportunity to heal childhood wounds. However, this process is far from smooth, as we have seen. We frequently love from a wounded place so that we expect our lover to heal us, thus placing a huge burden on our relationships. Additionally, since we are generally fragmented and see love as outside of us, at some unconscious level, a battle begins in our hearts and we are torn between loving ourselves and loving the other. As we saw earlier, loving another person can stir up all kinds of unresolved issues in our lives and open the scars of our past. Unless we strive to remain conscious, our partners will carry all our projections, and our relating will be tainted by our childhood and past experiences. Sometimes, being in relationship can be an avoidance of relating truly to our deepest selves. This is particularly so when we are using our partners to fill a great void inside us.

Experiencing heartbreak can help us heal this inner void so that we feel more whole and less needy for outer recognition and affirmation. Retreating to the desert, symbolically or otherwise, alone, we have a chance to find our own hearts and to fill that void for ourselves so that one day we will 'love again the stranger who was your self'. Like the popular heroine Shirley Valentine, a contemporary middle-aged woman who leaves her marriage and embarks on a holiday alone, we fall in love with ourselves. In this sense, our love affair is with ourselves. The inner lover you awaken is you – your heart, your soul and your true self.

## Recognising and Recovering your Essential Self

Certain life experiences can bring you to a depth in yourself where you connect with your soul purpose. Being in an emotional desert after heartbreak can also reveal your essence and even help you recover your soul purpose. The period of aloneness can propel you into a self-awareness not possible had you remained enmeshed in your relationship. In the space left by your partner, you will find yourself, providing, of course, that you do not fill the space with other things. Fear of aloneness, for example, can push us to fill spaces left vacant by our former partners with other 'material things', a new relationship, manic activity, over work and so on. However, if we continue to fill the spaces, we may never uncover or even allow a vital part of us to be revealed.

Isabel's struggle to regain her sense of herself after her relationship break up tells its own story. She felt empty and alone, but gradually with time, endurance and inner work, she recovered her essential self.

Isabel struggled to recover her inner king. Without James, though nursing yet again a wounded heart, she grew. Despite the pain she felt, over time she became stronger. She became more creative. In the space left vacant by James, she discovered herself. Though losing James pulled at her heart, her suffering honed her, forming her in a unique way. It was as though her love and loss gave her wings. Her soul soared with the wings of her love. She attended to her own work with the attention she had previously given to James. She wrote, and in her writing she gave birth to a part of herself she had not even known existed.[54]

## Being Oneself

Although relationships give us an opportunity to be with ourselves and with another simultaneously, sometimes we are not completely ourselves in relationships. When we relate, we have to constantly juggle our own truths, feelings and beliefs with those of our partner. Learning to negotiate the complexities and layers of a relationship, and being open and loving whilst remaining conscious, is very difficult. Our partner's inner processes will often rub against ours as our respective inner archetypes and emotional history come alive. We can find ourselves compromising ourselves because of fears of abandonment, or trying to control our partners because of our insecurities.

The journey to healing involves exploring the opportunity to be truly oneself. Again, being true to oneself is not something we can take for granted because it often takes a leap of faith for us to feel we can be accepted as we are. Unless we have an unshakeable self-esteem, most of us fear we are not enough – we will not be accepted for who we are, in our essential selves. Because of this, we usually compromise our integrity to a greater or lesser extent, in relationship to others. To be true to yourself in a situation is always a relief and, at a profound level, very healing.

I remember one such occasion in my own life. I had just told my partner of the time that I could no longer be in the relationship the way he wanted me to. After months of hanging on in a situation where I almost daily compromised myself, I finally told him I had to leave him. It was extremely painful for me because I loved him very much and wanted, above all, to be with him in a committed partnership. But he was an archetypal Puer, a man who did not want such a commitment, so we parted.

I remember the terrible pain I felt and the anguish that would crash down on top of me every morning as I woke to the reality of being apart from the man I loved. But I also remember another part of me that felt whole and good for having spoken my truth and for remaining true to myself. I had told him everything, my desire for a closer commitment, my love for him, and my inability to continue a relationship that was, in the end, causing me more heartache than if I were outside of it and true to myself. There was a great relief in being so honest.

When we honour our integrity we feel good, because we are in tune with our essence. I knew at a deep level that my soul required more from me in relationship, and that I was ready for something deeper and more nourishing. I also knew he was not ready for such a commitment.

But my heart was torn at the thought of being without him.

Remaining true to ourselves means also bearing the pain of the consequences, and accepting responsibility for the choices we make. I knew that there was a likelihood I would lose him, but I was prepared to pay the price if it meant being true to myself. It took me a long time to get to the stage where I could risk losing him – but when it came to it, my heart pushed me to speak a greater truth.

This is the sacrifice we pay for truth. I did lose him for a while but, in fact, this parting and honouring of each other's truths brought him back to me a short time later. In the space created by my departure, my lover realised he missed me, and that he too wanted something more real and enduring. The honouring of our respective selves meant we were able to carve out something that worked for both of us for a time.

## Returning Home
The journey we undertake to mend our hearts after a relationship dies will take us to where we can meet ourselves. As I wrote earlier, vulnerability and heart pain take us to where a deeper

intelligence comes through. It is a place of soul where, like the lonely Ugly Duckling, we are more open to receiving the call; the call of belonging that our soul recognises. Receiving and answering the call, we return home to ourselves.

Recognising our own kind, as in the story of the Ugly Duckling, is symbolic of coming home to oneself. It means to come to know and appreciate our hearts and our spiritual natures. In the desert of Arizona, after my relationship ended, I connected again with my heart, and I learned about its ability to love and endure heartache. I came to know about my emotional depth and the strength this depth gave me. I also learned that I have the capacity to endure and that I can survive incredibly painful experiences. As a wounded healer, I understood I could help others heal their heart wounds. Most of all, suffering heartbreak enabled me to develop soul stamina and to experience compassion.

Emotional struggle does help us grow. Endurance and the ability to suffer always add extra layers onto our soul. That is because painful experiences represent challenges and spiritual tasks of empowerment. Endurance, persistence in overcoming the challenges involved on the way to recovering our inner voice and the soft part of us that loves, helps us grow.

## Unconditional Love

The call to love unconditionally is an integral part of an evolving consciousness whose time has come. Answering the call demands we embrace our humanity, our wounds and our vulnerability. It is very hard to love unconditionally but suffering heart break in this sense is a conduit to unconditional love because in truly enduring a heart wound, our heart is opened. Heartbreak is then a sacred initiation connecting you with all of humanity. A love wound can take you straight to the divine and to discover your essential self. But it can also lead you to compassion and to unconditional love.

When we are truly in tune with our ability to discover and love others, and ourselves, we are on a spiritual path. The love we think of as being outside ourselves is only found within and when we have returned home, we find it. Myss reminds us that 'the only path toward spiritual consciousness is through the heart. The truth is not negotiable, no matter what spiritual tradition one chooses as a means to know the divine.'[55]

There is no doubt that love, acceptance and endurance transform consciousness. On an individual level, enduring heart break opens you to the pain of others so that you have the opportunity to practice compassion and help your fellow travellers on their spiritual journey. As the great mystic Saint Theresa of Avila writes:

> If you want to make progress on the path and ascend to the places you have longed for, the important thing is not to think much but to love much, and so to do what best awakens you to love. If you fall sometimes, do not lose heart. Keep striving to walk your path with integrity.[56]

In losing love, you will have found it.

# Love Lost and Found

*Part One: The Battlefield*

Zarah lay exhausted on the bloody battlefield. It was quiet now. Though the field still reverberated with the sounds of death and slaughter, its stillness calmed her beating heart. She lay where she had fallen, by the silver river now swollen with the blood of slain lovers. There were so many lovers, so many broken hearts, her own included.

Zarah's heart had become a battlefield. Longings mingled with the pain of loss, dreams were splintered and dragged into corners where sunlight for a moment brought them alive, and round corners the ever encroaching crash of mangled feelings advanced with a deadly, dark calm. But, as ever, her aching need and the parts of her as yet unborn, cried out to be recognised and so wearily, she had dragged herself here, to the desert of love. It was a long way, but here hopeful souls and bruised hearts came to learn the secrets of love. They came in packs, they came in pairs and they came, like Zarah, alone.

It had been a long journey and a rough night, and many times she had felt like turning back. But the small ember of memory lodged deep inside her urged her on. It won't be too long now, keep to your light, follow where your bruised heart and torn soul lead you, she told herself when her courage failed. In the darkest moments, the tender memory of love returned to her and she clung on to its exquisite scent. The ember inside her burned, and she quickened her step, eager to reach her destination.

Then the battle had been fought and lost. For entering the desert of love Zarah saw nothing but angry, bitter, broken hearts, many armed, thrashing and beating everything in sight. Blinded by pain and their mindless search for love, they destroyed it. The desert had become a battlefield.

How was it, she wondered, that the search for love had turned into a battleground? How was it that love became blotched with dark tangled feelings and lovers became to each other not joy but a source of guilt and pain?

Shaking the damp earth from her head and sitting up, Zarah looked around and saw him. He was kneeling by the foot of a large statue surrounded on two sides by barren scrub bush. She saw that he was tall and though his clothes were worn and bloodstained, nonetheless he had a noble look. His battle-weary head held something higher, greater than the degradation he had wrought upon himself. He seemed to be speaking to someone and held his head at an angle, his bloodied sword still by his side. Realising he had not seen her and believed himself alone, Zarah stood up and quietly came closer.

Raul turned and gazed at the woman approaching him on the battlefield of love. Who and what was this? Fighting like a warrior and now believing himself triumphant over love, he could not believe what he saw. Surely he had won over every other broken heart? Standing alone, exhausted and battle weary, he had slain and conquered. As she came closer, he saw that though worn and exhausted, she held herself with pride. And he saw that though small in stature, there was courage in her stride. Through her tear-stained face he perceived her beauty. She looked forlorn, as though the memory of a thousand losses had driven love to an ideal, a dream buried deep inside her.

Looking at her, something stirred in his own broken and battered heart.

Zarah looked at Raul, and a memory passed momentarily over her face and settled in her chest. She wondered if he had felt the pangs, the surgings and the shattered dreams. She wondered if he felt at all. She did not know.

He began to speak, but try as she might she could not understand his words. Did he speak another language? Was he a foreigner? There were many who travelled here to the desert of love so he could be a stranger from distant parts. She wanted to touch him but wondered if he would feel it, or if he would pull back from her. And since he still held his sword, she wondered would he draw it against her. Recognising a fellow warrior, she wanted to touch his hand and put her head against his chest to hear his beating heart. If she heard that then she would know he was alive and, like her, a pulsing heart in search of love. But he seemed distant, a stranger and yet he was here.

Raul looked at the woman a long time. He could not understand what she seemed to be saying. She was small yet strong and he was not sure. His own heart was beating yes, but to a muted tune. Tired after his battle to win love, he was weary and also wary and cautious.

Zarah wondered about him. What would he say if she told him she needed love, the kind you hold at night close to your heart. The strong love of a man who will hold you tight so that you can rest against the hardness of him. What would he do if he knew that holding the memory of a thousand lost embraces, Zarah wanted the tender gestures and whispers of love, his fingers on her cheek, the pressure of his hand on her back. Weary of battling, she wanted to rest, and she knew that love lay nestled in the place where opposites meet.

Zarah longed for the full embrace of this tall stranger. Would he be too weary to reach for her? Would he hold back and wait for her to come to him? Would he draw his sword and push her away? Would he open his arms to hold her? Should she go to him at all?

Zarah thought all this and mulled it over in her heart.

## Part Two: The Desert Of Love

Zarah drew back. Despite the passionate embrace of the night before, the stranger had somehow indicated he was not open to receiving her. Still hostile after his battle, he had little to offer in the way of engagement, or love. Yet she had felt compelled to follow his gesture of opening, no matter how small. She sensed the conflicted nature of his need, for she had housed it herself some time ago. She had felt its texture and scent but knew it had changed as she had grown. She knew too that she could never know the true nature of a man's heart but could only receive it and allow herself to be enfolded in it.

Zarah looked at the stranger one more time before turning her face to the sun and walking ahead. Her heart a battlefield once more, she covered her face with her desert scarf and resolutely marched onwards. But her step was weary and her heart leaden again with the weight of untold losses freshly opened by her encounter with the stranger. As she walked, she chided herself; why had she opened her heart so soon and given her body to this man, a warrior of the desert? – a stranger whose eyes spoke to her, and whose body enveloped her in a timeless and desperate embrace.

Remembering the mutuality of their need and the fierceness with which they had loved, Zarah knew that if she had that time again, she would do exactly the same.

As she walked she began pondering on the nature of love. Who could say that there was no love in this encounter? In the desert of love everyone was seeking the same thing, elusive though it appeared to be. Every being is created in love and the memory of love lies deep inside. It awakens in encounters with others in whom we perceive the same energies. Is love an energy, she wondered? It is certainly a force.

In her encounters, Zarah had met many variations of that powerful force that is love. Sometimes, the best times, it is shared between two people equally, though in its expression it varies in intensity and comes and goes between the lovers, like waves of the sea. Other times, if one partner is fearful of the heart, then the other, seeking to heal her lover, takes it on alone. In this type of encounter, the great force of healing gets activated. He or she will seek to heal the loved one. And if one is not careful, one risks losing all for the sake of 'love'. For, thought Zarah, such a love is surely conditional and dependent on the other person being and behaving a particular way. Is this, she wondered, what is meant by a co-dependent relationship?

Zarah cared not what it was called. She knew that she loved, that she rarely regretted her encounters, and that she would continue to love as long as she had breath in her body. She also knew that with each encounter she was closer, closer to finding her soul mate, her true love, and her life partner. If she thought about it, the men she had loved all had different qualities but held one essential force, their desire for her. So she divided them into two, those who desired her body, and those who desired her soul.

In essence, fearful of loving, and aware of her distain once desire was fulfilled, those who desired her body soon melted away. Zarah found such experiences empty and meaningless, and had long abandoned such entanglements. Those who desired her soul proved more problematic, for they were the ones who held her, often against her will, and certainly her better judgement. Couching their need to 'possess' her in the language of love and sex, they controlled her through her fears. When you fear any number of things, being left alone or not being loved, you will do almost anything to avoid such a situation. So, you sell your soul.

Zarah remembered that many years ago, when she had visited the gypsy woman at the fair, she had drawn a card. Seeking answers and to know her destiny, she had questioned the gypsy woman who in turn had responded by asking her to pick a card. She held out a colourful, age-worn tarot deck. Zarah looked at the cards and hesitated, for she could sense a thousand stories and battles lost and won. kings, queens, knights, fools and lovers all jostled in a frenzied battle to be recognised. Yet one card beckoned, and she pulled it from the pack. Turning it over she read 'The Prostitute'. On it was a picture of a beautiful woman wearing layers of colourful desert scarves and exotic jewellery. Despite her finery she was sad and lost, and looked out at Zarah with sorrowful eyes. What could this mean? Zarah had wondered.

The answer had come gradually and profoundly over many years. Each year and each lover gave her a clue. The years of life and love had given Zarah shape. And each lover and her experience of loving had added depth to her soul and flesh to her heart.

She learned that in the eyes of her lovers, she was many things. Each one saw and placed in her his own brand of dreams, his bundle of complicated feelings, memories, thoughts and desires. To one she was his teacher, a wise woman and mother rolled into one; to another she was his muse, responsible for his creative acts; to yet another his jailor, responsible for holding him back; to one she had been his temptress and an object for his self-hatred. Sometimes she was a princess, awakening in her lover his need to recognise his inner majesty; to many she was mother, wife and daughter. Sometimes she was a sister but not often, for desire does not lie well there. Lately, she had begun to find that her lovers sought in her also a companion. She liked that. It made her feel more real, more accepted for who she was, rather than for what others wanted her to be.

There had not been as many lovers as one would imagine. But each was significant and had a part to play in shaping who she was now. Each time she loved and lost, Zarah found that she grew. Though loss would bring hurt and pain, in the emptiness left by her lovers she discovered herself. In time parts of herself returned to her like lost fragments of her soul, so that she became more whole. In each experience she found a different part of herself.

Despite the pain she felt, over time she became stronger. She became more peaceful and in a strange way, more creative. In the space left vacant by her lovers, she discovered herself. Though losing a love pulled at her heart, her suffering honed her, forming her in a unique way. It was as though her love and loss gave her wings. Her soul soared with the wings of her love. In a strange yet ordinary way, she attended to herself with the attention she had previously given to her lovers. For Zarah, like a true desert woman, gave herself up to love. She abandoned herself each time to her lovers, and then wondered why without them she was lost.

Lately though, that too had changed. With time and experience, and as her heart became stronger and her soul more whole, she abandoned herself less.

This last experience, for instance. Lying with the stranger, she had not lost herself. Though she had loved him and maybe loved him still, she had not abandoned herself to him. She had given herself willingly in love, but had held back her soul. There had not been time for anything more wholesome to develop.

He was still a mystery to her, however, and this gave him added interest. It made it hard to leave, because a part of her wanted to solve the mystery, to seek it out and resolve it in some way. She sensed his difference, and this drew her to him even though she also sensed his sharpness, for even in their short encounter, Zarah felt the stranger's hurt. It rose from him like a thousand arrows ready and poised for battle. She felt the anger in his heart and retreated from it, placing a gentle protection around her own.

Zarah was pleased that her encounter with the stranger had not damaged her. Some time ago she would have perceived his pulling back as a rejection that would have plunged her into self-doubting despair. She would have wondered what she did or did not do to deserve his dismissal of her. In essence though, the stranger had not dismissed her, but really simply indicated his frailty, and his fear of love. He feared engagement because he did not trust himself, he had said. When she had asked him what he meant, he told her that he had lost too much already and needed to conserve his energy for himself. This puzzled Zarah because she knew that he desired her, and that their desire was mutual. She also knew that he feared his heart would open its wounds again if he were to allow himself to love her. With the intuition of a woman, she knew too without words, that his heart still housed many lost lovers, and that perhaps there was simply no room for her there. And even too that wounded, he had rarely, if ever, allowed himself to love, since his heart was largely taken up with fear.

Zarah thought about all this, and was surprised how much had passed between her and the stranger. Without words, for they did not speak the same language, they had communicated. Their communication had been deep and meaningful, unlike many other such encounters. Perhaps when one meets after a battle in the desert then this is the only communication possible. In a short time she had learned many things from the stranger. She had learned about the power of passion to heal, and she had learned about the frailty of the human heart. Unwittingly, she had also learned about her own strength, for she knew that though she was a woman and small in stature, she was stronger than the man she had lain with and loved. She learned that love can be given and taken without hope and without the burden of expectation. Without taking the weight of her lover's pain, Zarah learned she could love and not be tainted or lost in that love. She could walk free, leaving him to his own devices.

The stranger had at times been tender. This surprised Zarah because it contrasted with the roughness of his manner and the anger he held in his heart. It was as though at times the loving child peeked through, seeking love and approval. At those times, Zarah's heart was caught and squeezed. She knew something of the lost child, and innocence was something she had had a difficult relationship with. She was only just beginning to retrieve her lost innocence and bask in the joy of her Inner Child. Possessed of a natural vitality, Zarah had never really learned to hold back her life force and so, when she saw the stranger stifle his Inner Child and essential vitality, though not surprised, it saddened her. She wondered what had made him so full of hate that he could not see his beauty, and enjoy his playfulness. He seemed to be ashamed of something.

Last year at the same fair where she had encountered the gypsy woman so many years ago, Zarah had met a wise old man who was said to have magical powers. He had told her that in order to live and love well, it was necessary to empty yourself constantly of your story, your life story. That way, by telling and retelling your life experiences, you would clear yourself and make room for love, new love. For love to flourish, it needed an open welcoming space uncluttered by old lost and painful loves, old partners and their stories.

This impressed her. She felt the truth of what the wise old man had told her, and had made a habit every night before going to bed of telling her story to herself, and then releasing it. In this way, gradually over time, she felt lighter, and yet paradoxically more filled with love and the capacity to give and receive love. Emptying her heart of her old stories and her old loves gave her a new, open heart.

Zarah doubted that the stranger had heard of this method of release because he seemed crowded, filled with lived and unlived stories; and his heart had no space. Though tall and slender, he had seemed bigger than he was. This feeling had pushed Zarah away because she sensed that if you probed you would get hurt by one of the pointed arrows he carried inside his wounded heart. She would love to have told him about the wise man's counsel, and somehow shown the stranger how to lighten his load. But perhaps he was not ready yet to be happy, or to love.

The approaching night found Zarah in a pensive mood as she hurried along to the desert camp.

# Endnotes

**Chapter 1**
1   Jung, CG., *Collected Works 8.*

**Chapter 2**
2   Rilke, R.M., *Letters to a Young Poet*, p. 74.
3   Ibid., p.98.
4   Ibid., p.21.
5   Eliot, T.S., East Coker – *4 Quartets.*
6   Eliot, T.S., *4 Quartets.*
7   Rilke, R.M., *Letters to a Young Poet*, p. 35

**Chapter 3**
8   St John of the Cross, *Dark Night*, in *Ten Poems to Change your Life*, ed. Housden, R.
9   Swartz-Salant, N., *The Mystery of Human Relationship-Alchemy and the Transformation of the Self*, pp. 15, 16.
10  Ibid., p. 18
11  Mauger, B., *Songs from the Womb – Healing the Wounded Mother.*
12  Swartz-Salant, *The Mystery of Human Realtionship*, p. 161.
13  Carotenuto, A., *Eros and Pathos – Shades of Love and Suffering*, p. 7.
14  Ibid., p. 16.

**Chapter 4**
15  Bly, R & Woodman, M., *The Maiden King*, p.177.
16  Ibid.,
17  Dickinson, E., *Collected Poems*, p. 246.
18  Jung, CG., *The Psychology of the Transference*, p. 34.
19  Carotenudo, A., *Eros and Pathos*, p. 10.
20  Mauger, B., *Reclaiming Father*, p. 6.

## Chapter 5

21 Mauger, B., *Songs from the Womb – Healing the Wounded Mother.*
   Mauger, B., *Reclaiming Father – The Search for Wholeness in Men, Women and Children.*
22 Myss, C., *Sacred Contracts,* p. 47.
23 Koltuv, B., *Solomon & Sheba,* p. 64.
24 Myss, C., *Sacred Contracts,* p. 59.
25 C.G. Jung, *Collected Works 4,* para 728.
26 Mauger, B., *Reclaiming Father*
27 Myss, C., *Sacred Contracts,* p. 6.
28 ibid., p. 17.
29 Mauger, B., *Songs from the Womb.*
30 Myss, C., *Anatomy of the Spirit,* p. 103.

## Chapter 6

31 Mauger, B., *Songs from the Womb,* p. 156.
32 Winnicott, DW, *The Maturational Process and the Facilitating Environment.*
33 For consistency purposes I have in this instance referred to the child as 'he'.
34 Mauger, B., *Reclaiming Father,* p. 71.
35 Ibid., p. 35.
36 Jung, E., *Anima and Animus,* p. 6.
37 Jung, E., *Anima and Animus,* p. 28.
38 Jung, E., *Anima and Animus,* p. 10.

## Chapter 7

39 M. Deane, referenced in *Changing Fathers* ed. Mc Keown, K. (1998) p. 53.

## Chapter 8

40 Myss, C., *Sacred Contracts,* p. 372.
41 Bly, R., *The Maiden King,* p. 22.

**Chapter 9**

42   Pinkola Estes, C. *Women who Run with the Wolves,*
     p. 141.
43   Mauger, B., *Reclaiming Father,* p. 202.

**Chapter 10**

44   Rilke, R.M., *Letters to a Young Poet,* p. 70.
45   Pinkola Estes, C., *Women Who Run with the Wolves,*
     p. 167.
46   Ibid., p. 171.
47   Ibid., p. 189.
48   Myss, C., *Anatomy of the Spirit,* p. 217.
49   Version taken from *Greek Myths & Legends* by
     Sullivan, K.E.(1998) Brockhampton Press.

**Chapter 11**

50   Shinoda-Bolen, J., *Goddesses in Everywoman,* p. 259.
51   G. Corneau, *Absent Fathers, Lost Sons* Shambhala,
     (1991) p. 24.
52   Shinoda-Bolen, J., *Goddesses in Everywoman,* p. 260.
53   M.L. Von Franz, *Projection and Recollection in
     Jungian Psychology,* Open Court, 1980.
54   Mauger, B., *Reclaiming Father,* p. 205.
55   Myss, C., *Anatomy of the Spirit,* p. 217.
56   Teresa of Avila., *The Interior Castle.*

# Bibliography

Barks, Coleman, ed., *Rumi: The Book of Love: Poems of Ecstacy and Longing*, Harper Collins, 2005

Barnstone Willis, ed., *The Poems of St. John of the Cross*, New Direction Books, 1972

Berry, P., Ed., *Mothers, Fathers*, Spring publications, 1991

Carotenudo, A., *Eros and Pathos – Shades of Love and Suffering*, Inner City Books, 1989

Bettelheim, B., *The Uses of Enchantment – The Meaning and Importance of Fairy Tales*, Peregrin Books, 1979

Bly, R. & Woodman, M., *The Maiden King – The Reunion of Masculine and Feminine*, Henry Holt Books, 1998

Corneau, G., *Absent Fathers, Lost Sons*, Shambhala, 1991

Cooper, D., *A Little Light on the Spiritual Laws*, Piatkus Books, 2000

Desteian, J., *Coming Together – Coming Apart – The Union of Opposites in Love Relationships*, Sigo Press, 1989

Dethlefsen, T., *The Healing Power of Illness*, Element Books, 1990

Dickinson, E., *Collected Poems*, Courage Books, 1999

Dieckmann, H., *Twice-told Tales – The Psychological Use of Fairy Tales*, Chiron, 1986

Elliot, T.S., *Selected Poems*, Faber & Faber, 1954

Holmes, J., *John Bowlby and Attachment Theory*, Routledge, 1993

Housden, R., *Ten Poems to Change Your Life*, Harmony Books, 2001

Illich, I., *Limits to Medicine*, Penguin, 1988

John of the Cross, *Dark Night of the Soul*, Dover Publications, 2003

Johnson, R., *The Fisher King and the Handless Maiden*, Harper Collins, 1993

Jung C.G., *Collected Works*, ed. Fordham et al., Routledge 1953-78 and Bollingen Series XX, Princeton University Press, 1961-78

- *Memories, Dreams, Reflections*, Fontana Press, 1961 Jung, E., *Anima and Animus*, Spring Publications, 1987

Krishnamurti, J., *The First and Last Freedom*, Harper & Row, 1975

Krishnamurti, J., *Think on these Things*, Harper & Row, 1970

Lawrence, D.H., *Selected Poems*, Penguin, 1972

Leonard, L., *On the Way to the Wedding – Transforming the Love Relationship*, Shambhala, 1986

Leonard, L., *Witness to the Fire – Creativity and the Veil of Addiction*, Shambhala, 1990

Mauger, B., *Songs from the Womb – Healing the Wounded Mother*, The Collins Press, 1998

Mauger B., *Reclaiming Father – The Search for Wholeness in Men, Women and Children*, Soul Connections, 2004

Mitchell, S., ed., *The Enlightened Heart – An Anthology of Sacred Poetry*, Harper & Row, 1989

Mood, J.L., *Rilke on Love and other Difficulties*, WW Norton, 1975

Moore, T., *Soul Mates*, Element Books, 1994

Moore, T., *Care of the Soul*, Harper Collins, 1992

Moss, Richard, *The Black Butterfly: An Invitation to Radical Aliveness*, Celestial Arts, Berkeley, California, 1986.

Myss, C., *Sacred Contracts – Awakening your Divine Potential*, Harmony Books, 2001

Myss, C., *Anatomy of the Spirit*, Bantam Books, 1996

Myss, C., *Entering the Castle – An Inner Path to God and Your Soul*, Simon & Schuster, 2007

Oliver, M., *New & Selected Poems*, Beacon Press, 1992

Olivier, C., *Jocasta's Children*, Routledge, 1992

Rilke, R.M., *Letters to a Young Poet*, WWNorton, 1954

Rilke, R.M., *Sonnets to Orpheus*, trans. MacIntyre, Univ California Press, 1960

Rilke, R.M., *Duino Elegies*, WWNorton, 1992

Koltuv, B., *Solomon & Sheba – Inner Marriage an Individuation*, Nicolas-Hayes, 1993

Pinkola-Estes, C., *Women Who Run with the Wolves*, Rider Books, 1992

Shinoda-Bolen, J., *Goddesses in Everywoman, Harper & Row*, 1984

Shinoda Bolen, J., *Crossing to Avalon*, Harper Collins, 1994

Stevens, A., *On Jung*, Routledge, 1990

St. John of the Cross, *Dark Nights of the Soul*, Piatkus, 2004

Swartz-Salant N., *The Mystery of Human Relationship*, Routledge, 1998

Teresa of Avila, trans. M. Starr, *The Interior Castle*, Riverhead Books, 2003

Von Franz, M.L., *Interpretation of Fairy Tales*, Element Books, 1970

Wilde, O., *The Fairy Stories of Oscar Wilde*, Gollancz, 1985

Wilde O., *The Works of Oscar Wilde*, Collins, 1967

Wilmer, H. ed., *Mother, Father*, Chiron Publications, 1990

Winnicott D.W., *Through Pediatrics to Psychoanalysis*, Hogarth Press 1965

- *The Maturational Process & the Facilitating Environment*, Hogarth Press, 1987

- *Human Nature*, Free Association Books, 1988